DATE DUE

ILh Dec. 29		
JAN - 7 1980		
AUG - 3 1983		
SEP 1 0 1983 B R		
SEP 2 0 1983		
SEP 1 0 1984		
NOV 7 1984		
OCT 3 0 1984 B R		
OCT 3 1 1984		
JAN 2 1985		
JAN - 4 1985 B R		
JAN - 6 1985		
JUL - 1 1986		
MAR 2 0 1992		

38-297

Handbook
of
Real Estate Mathematics

Handbook
of
Real Estate Mathematics

Leonard Kleeman

Prentice-Hall, Inc.   Englewood Cliffs, New Jersey

Prentice-Hall International, Inc. *London*
Prentice-Hall of Australia, Pty. Ltd., *Sydney*
Prentice-Hall of Canada, Ltd., *Toronto*
Prentice-Hall of India Private Ltd., *New Delhi*
Prentice-Hall of Japan, Inc. *Tokyo*
Prentice-Hall of Southeast Asia Pte. Ltd., *Singapore*
Whitehall Books, Ltd., *Wellington, New Zealand*

© 1978 by
Prentice-Hall, Inc.
Englewood Cliffs, New Jersey

Library of Congress Cataloging in Publication Data

Kleeman, Leonard
  Handbook of real estate mathematics.

  Includes index.
  1. Business mathematics--Real estate business.
I. Title.
HF5716.R4K57   513'.93'024333   77-17368
ISBN 0-13-380717-7

Printed in the United States of America

To Fran, my wife,
For her love, patience, wisdom, and encouragement

What This Book Can Do for You

This book presents in a simplified and concise manner the complete application of mathematics to the real estate business. The simplified format will help alleviate the fear of mathematics for some of you and substantially increase the recall of those who, through disuse, may have forgotten certain mathematical procedures.

Even those professionals with a good background in business mathematics will find the book valuable. You will be able to increase your technical ability because the book encompasses elements of real estate mathematics not normally covered in ordinary business mathematics. These elements include the mathematics of appraising, estimating, investing, construction and leasing as well as others. The inclusion of these mathematical concepts within a single book creates a complete real estate reference manual and handbook. With the help of this book, real estate problems can be solved swiftly and effortlessly. All you have to do is turn to the appropriate section, review the clear, concise instructions, then follow the formula or step-by-step instructions. You can follow the fully worked-out examples to be sure your grasp of the concepts and procedures is complete.

The continued growth and increased competitiveness of the real estate business requires that the professional have a more thorough understanding of aspects of the business not ordinarily encountered in routine conduct of the business. The successful professional must also remain a bit more sophisticated and knowledgeable than his competitors. In order to completely understand these aspects, the mathematical processes involved must be thoroughly understood.

An understanding of "net yield" and "capitalization," for example, is necessary in order to intelligently discuss the purchase of an apartment house with a prospective buyer. If you can analyze an "operating statement," you have a decided edge over the broker or salesman whose knowledge is strictly limited to residential purchases. Even the professional who limits his practice to the residential field has an edge when he can utilize his knowledge of the mathematical concepts of interest, mortgages, secondary financing, construction, and rehabilitation costs. The real estate broker or salesman cannot compete today without knowing how to quickly and accurately compute interest, figure prorations, or calculate the cubic content of a building.

This is one of the first books devoted exclusively to the mathematics of the *entire* real estate business. It is important to note that the book is not intended as a mathematics book or a study of mathematics. It is also not intended for use as an arithmetic refresher or examination preparation guide. There are no practice problems to solve and no discussions of methods to use in order to pass an examination. It is a *real estate book* telling what mathematics to use and how to apply mathematical concepts and procedures to certain aspects of real estate.

The book is written so that it can be used by *everyone* in the real estate business, either as a reference manual or handbook. The professional can refer to it for any particular problem that might arise in the course of the business day, whether in the office or in the field.

The first six chapters of the book deal with the mathematical concepts of interest, discount, amortization, commissions, profit and loss, and proration. These are the basic applications of mathematics to the real estate business. Although most professionals will perhaps have a familiarity with these concepts, a review of each should be done in order to prepare for the more complex subjects in the ensuing chapters. For instance, a comprehensive review of the chapters on interest should be made before undertaking the chapter on mortgages and financing. These first chapters are not only important for review, but each contains new shortcuts and new simplified approaches to each subject. You will find these chapters easy to use for reference purposes.

Measurement and mensuration, as treated in Chapters 7, 8, and 9, are vital subjects. Without measurement and description of land and structures, there would be no real estate business. Some geometry is dealt with in these chapters. However, it is assumed that there is no prior knowledge of geometry on the part of the reader and any necessary geometric formulations are explained fully in simplified terms.

As is the case throughout the book, the mathematical applications to real estate *only* are emphasized. Therefore, these chapters deal mainly with real estate measurements or spatial relationships pertinent to real estate.

The last chapters in the book deal with the utilization and combination of all the preceding mathematical concepts with the more formal and complex aspects of the business. Individual chapters are included covering mortgages and financing, depreciation, leases, appraisals and valuation, building and remodeling, and investments in real estate. Because of the voluminous publications available on these subjects, and the diversity and complexities of each, a complete discussion of each is impractical and unwarranted. Some familiarity with the subject must be assumed. This assumption, therefore, allows an in-depth discussion of only the mathematical applications and aspects of each subject.

The discussion of appraising, for instance, is limited to the mathematical applications necessary in the formulation of a proper appraisal and the utilization of mathematics in each phase of appraisal and valuation. Of course, understanding of the mathematical concepts leads to a better and fuller understanding of the entire subject. The real estate broker or salesman who is not an appraiser will gain a more thorough understanding of appraising terminology and procedures by reviewing this chapter and utilizing it for future reference.

The appendix contains a concentrated and simple review of arithmetic calculations. Some will find this very useful as a refresher and it will, perhaps, re-teach fundamentals never clearly understood. A section on the metric system has also been included in the appendix so that the value of the book as a reference work will not be lost at some future date. You will be familiar *now* with the coming changes. The appendix also contains a variety of essential and useful tables and facts that can be easily referred to at any time.

The book will serve as a handy and complete reference. With this book you will be able to enhance your professional status with a thorough understanding of the mathematics of real estate.

Leonard Kleeman

TABLE OF CONTENTS

1

How to Compute Simple Interest

Interest is money paid for the use of money. It is one of the most widely used applications of mathematics in the real estate profession. In the following chapters you will find the use of interest and its various equations appearing many times. All mortgage financing, amortization, bank loans, investments, appraisals, and valuations involve interest, interest tables, or certain interest factors.

The amount of money on which the interest is paid is called the *principal. Simple interest* is interest paid *only* on the principal owed. Real estate brokerage and sales would normally be concerned only with simple interest except in the case of mortgage payments which are determined by use of compound interest tables.

Compound interest is interest paid on accrued interest as well as the principal. More advanced real estate subjects such as appraising and valuation would be concerned with compound interest. These applications include rates of capitalization, investment yields and property income analysis, annuity approaches, sinking funds, etc.

The *Rate of Interest* is the percentage rate of the principal paid in interest for one year. It is extremely important to remember that the rate is on the basis of one year. The most common error in figuring interest is confusion with the rate of interest for one year and *time. Time* is the period for which interest is paid and may be expressed in years, months, or days.

17

In all interest problems we are involved with the three variables defined above, namely: *principal, rate,* and *time.*

SIMPLIFICATION OF
SIMPLE INTEREST

Simple interest is found by multiplying the *principal*, the *rate*, and the *time*, thus:

**Principal (in dollars) $\times$ Rate (per cent per year) $\times$ Time (in years)
= Interest (in dollars)**

For simplicity, we express this in the formula:

$$I = P \times R \times T$$

Using mathematical notation, we can eliminate the multiplication signs and we now read:

$$I = PRT$$

This is the standard formula for computing SIMPLE INTEREST. Although different letters may be substituted sometimes for each of the variables or factors, the basic formula remains the same. Later we will be using different letters or symbols in the formula in order to conform with certain standard tables. However, at present you will find it easier to use the above and, once mastered, will have no trouble with substitution.

How to Find Interest for One Year or
Multiples of a Year

To find interest for one year it is only necessary to multiply principal by rate as the other variable, time, will be one year. We know that anything multiplied by one remains the same. For multiples of a year, we use the number of years for time (T) and complete the formula.

Example:

Find the interest on $800. for 1 year at 6%.

Solution:

$$I = PRT$$
$$I = \$800 \times .06 \,(\times \; 1)$$
$$I = \$48.00$$

Example:

Find the interest on $920.50 for 5 years at 6%.

Solution:

$$I = PRT$$
$$I = \$920.50 \times .06 \times 5$$
$$I = \$55.23 \times 5$$
$$I = \$276.15$$

Finding Maturity Value

The maturity value, which we shall call *amount,* is the sum of the principal and the interest. Repayment of the amount would cancel the debt. We indicate amount by the letter S, which can be remembered by thinking of it as the *S*um of principal and interest. Hence,

$$S = P + I$$

However, we know that I = PRT, so if we substitute for I in the amount formula, we arrive at:

$$S = P + PRT$$

With this formula we can solve for amount conveniently without using two separate formulas.

Example:

A man borrows $500 for 3 years at 6%. How much does he repay at the end of the 3 years?

Solution:

$$S = P + PRT$$
$$S = \$500 + \$500 \times .06 \times 3$$
$$S = \$500 + \$90$$
$$S = \$590.$$

How to Find Interest for Part of a Year

Although time may be expressed in years, months, or days, its application in the formula *must* be in terms of years. Therefore, if we want to find interest for part of a year, we must convert that part to a fractional part of a year (or decimal equivalent) before applying it to the formula. For simplicity and convenience, we will use a year of 360 days and 12 months of 30 days each. This is called *ordinary time.*

If we want to find interest for 90 days we can convert it to days per year which would be 90/360 reduced to ¼ or decimally to .25. Or, we can convert it to months per year using 3/12 which also reduces to ¼ or .25. We can also use months and days as a fraction as long as we are consistent in use of the divisor (360 for days and 12 for months).

Example:

Convert 1 month and 15 days to a fractional part of a year.

Solution:

$$
\begin{array}{l}
1 \text{ month} = 30 \text{ days} \\
\underline{+ 15 \text{ days}} \\
45 \text{ days, therefore, } \dfrac{45}{360} = \dfrac{1}{8} \text{ or } .12\tfrac{1}{2}
\end{array}
$$

Example:

Find the interest on $525 for 90 days at 5%.

Solution:

90 days = 3 months = 3/12 of a year = ¼ or .25

$$I = \$525 \times .05 \times .25$$
$$I = \$26.25 \times .25$$
$$I = \$6.562 = \$6.56 \text{ (rounded off)}$$

Example:

Find the interest on $950 for 3 years and 2 months at 6%.

Solution:

2 months = 1/6 of a year; + 3 years = 3-1/6 = 19/6

$$I = \$950 \times .06 \times 19/6$$
$$I = \$57 \times 19/6 = \$1,083/6$$
$$I = \$180.50$$

Sometimes we are given months and days that are not easily converted to fractions or decimals. In this event it is simpler to find the yearly interest and then find the monthly by dividing the yearly by 12. We can find the daily interest by dividing the monthly by 30 or the yearly interest by 360.

Example:

Find the interest on $800 at 7% for 3 months and 8 days.

Solution:

Yearly interest = $800 × .07 = $56.00 (I = PRT)
Monthly interest = $56. divided by 12 = $4.666
Daily interest = $4.666 divided by 30 = $.155
Therefore:

3 months × $4.666 = $13.998 (total interest for 3 months)
                                                        +
8 days × $.155   = + 1.24 (total interest for 8 days)
                                 $15.238 = $15.24

METHODS OF COMPUTING TIME

In addition to its usage in interest problems, time is a very important facet of many real estate transactions. It is therefore necessary in normal real estate practice to be able to properly compute time whether it be for a calculation of interest or finding the number of days elapsed from one date to another for other purposes. Two measurements of time used for determining the number of days are called *Ordinary Time* and *Exact Time*.

When time is expressed in years or months, it does not matter whether the year is considered containing 360 days or 365 days. The interest problem as such will be worked with multiples or fractions of the number one (for years). However, when time is given in days, one of the following methods *must* be used.

Ordinary Time

In ordinary time it is assumed that the year has 360 days and that each of the 12 months has 30 days. Most real estate loans and other long term loans in which periodic payments are made on both principal and interest use ordinary time. The 360 day year is sometimes called the "business year" or "statutory year." (These will be discussed in Chapter 6.)

Because we are finding the *difference* in days between two dates, our computation for time will be a subtraction problem. The problem is set up with the earlier date (from) as the subtrahend and the later date (to) as the minuend. Years (if necessary), months, and days are used in separate columns similar to tens, hundreds and thousands digits. Subtraction is then performed and borrowing from the left is used if necessary. In borrowing, months are converted to 30 days in the day column and years are converted to 12 months in the months column.

Example:

Find the ordinary time from May 15 to August 27.

Solution:

August 27 = 8 months   27 days   (minuend)
May 15   = 5 months   15 days   (subtrahend)
            3 months   12 days   (difference)
3 months = 90 days; 90 days + 12 days = 102 days.
Answer: 102 days

Example:

Find the ordinary time from May 15 to August 6.

Solution:

Months	Days			
8	6	=	7	36
-5	-15	=	-5	-15
			2	21

(Borrow 1 month, add 30 days to the 6 days)

2 months = 60 days; 60 + 21 = 81 days

Example:

Find the time from May 16, 1975 to March 30, 1976.

Solution:

Years	Months	Days		Years	Months	Days
1976	3	30	=	1975	15	30
-1975	5	16	=	-1975	5	16
					10	14

10 months = 300 days; 300 + 14 = 314 days
Because 5 months cannot be subtracted from 3 months, 1 year
(12 months) is borrowed from 1976 changing it to 1975 and
the borrowed 12 months is added to the 3 months making it
15 months and thus forming a subtractable problem.

No matter what method is used for counting days, you will note
that the FIRST day is *not* counted but the LAST day *is* counted.
Thus the time from May 16 to May 17 is one day. The time from
May 16 to May 18 is 2 days, etc. By using the above subtraction
method this is automatically done (17 – 16 = 1). If one of the dates
is 31 (October 31) it must be changed to 30. If both dates are 31 it
is not necessary to make the change.

Exact Time

Exact time is the *actual* number of days using the 365 day year
(366 days for a leap year). Although exact time is not commonly
used in normal real estate transactions in most states, it is a very necessary element of interest to understand. In order to figure exact
time it is essential to know how many days in each month. Memoriz-
ing the old rhyme of months would be helpful:

> *Thirty days hath September,*
> *April, June, and November;*
> *All the rest have thirty-one,*
> *Excepting February alone,*
> *Which hath but twenty-eight, in fine,*
> *Till leap year gives it twenty-nine.*

Because of the variation of days in some months, the same
method of computation that was used in ordinary time cannot be
used with exact time. The easiest method is to list the months and
the number of days in each. Then, by addition, the total number of
days is found.

Example:

Find the exact time from July 15 to October 25.

Solution:

July	16 days	(31–15)
August	31 days	
September	30 days	
October	25 days	
Exact time =	102 days	

Note that for the first month we subtract the initial date from the number of days in the month. This will give us the correct number of days remaining in that month without having to count.

While exact time is not used in real estate loans or installment loans, it is generally used in most other loans and in discounting. However, because these other loans rarely extend over time periods of a few months, it is usually not necessary to calculate exact time for periods in excess of 120 to 180 days.

Exact time can also be computed from tables. Table I, is such a table. To use this table, select the day-number of each date, subtract the day-number of the first date from the second date and this difference will be the exact time between the two dates.

For instance, the exact time from April 12 to July 15 is 196 – 102 = 94 days. For periods that extend over the year end, simply add 365 to the second date before subtracting. If a leap year, add 1 day to the second date if the time period includes February 29.

THE MEANINGS OF ORDINARY
AND EXACT INTEREST

As shown previously, when finding interest for part of a year we convert time in our equation to a fraction. For ordinary time we used the number of days as the numerator and 360 days as the divisor. However, we know now that there are two methods of determining time, ordinary and exact. It therefore becomes obvious that there must also be two methods of determining interest. One where the base or year is 360 days and the other where the base or year is 365 days.

For example, given 60 days as time, whether ordinary or exact, we can solve for interest using 60/360 or 60/365. For convenience, we have used 60/360 thereby finding *ordinary interest*. If we use 365

TABLE FOR DETERMINING EXACT NUMBER OF DAYS

Month

Day of Month	J	F	M	A	M	J	J	A	S	O	N	D
1	1	32	60	91	121	152	182	213	244	274	305	335
2	2	33	61	92	122	153	183	214	245	275	306	336
3	3	34	62	93	123	154	184	215	246	276	307	337
4	4	35	63	94	124	155	185	216	247	277	308	338
5	5	36	64	95	125	156	186	217	248	278	309	339
6	6	37	65	96	126	157	187	218	249	279	310	340
7	7	38	66	97	127	158	188	219	250	280	311	341
8	8	39	67	98	128	159	189	220	251	281	312	342
9	9	40	68	99	129	160	190	221	252	282	313	343
10	10	41	69	100	130	161	191	222	253	283	314	344
11	11	42	70	101	131	162	192	223	254	284	315	345
12	12	43	71	102	132	163	193	224	255	285	316	346
13	13	44	72	103	133	164	194	225	256	286	317	347
14	14	45	73	104	134	165	195	226	257	287	318	348
15	15	46	74	105	135	166	196	227	258	288	319	349
16	16	47	75	106	136	167	197	228	259	289	320	350
17	17	48	76	107	137	168	198	229	260	290	321	351
18	18	49	77	108	138	169	199	230	261	291	322	352
19	19	50	78	109	139	170	200	231	262	292	323	353
20	20	51	79	110	140	171	201	232	263	293	324	354
21	21	52	80	111	141	172	202	233	264	294	325	355
22	22	53	81	112	142	173	203	234	265	295	326	356
23	23	54	82	113	143	174	204	235	266	296	327	357
24	24	55	83	114	144	175	205	236	267	297	328	358
25	25	56	84	115	145	176	206	237	268	298	329	359
26	26	57	85	116	146	177	207	238	269	299	330	360
27	27	58	86	117	147	178	208	239	270	300	331	361
28	28	59	87	118	148	179	209	240	271	301	332	362
29	29		88	119	149	180	210	241	272	302	333	363
30	30		89	120	150	181	211	242	273	303	334	364
31	31		90		151		212	243		304		365

(If a leap year, add 1 day to the terminal date if the time period includes February 29.)

TABLE I

days as the divisor (base) we are finding *exact interest.* Letting d equal time in days, we can see that

$$d/360 = \text{ordinary interest}$$
$$\text{and,}$$
$$d/365 = \text{exact interest}$$

We also know that d can be expressed in ordinary time or exact time. As a result, there are four possible combinations with which to work. Using the period of time as April 30 to June 30, these combinations are:

1. Ordinary simple interest at ordinary time:

$$\frac{60}{360} = \begin{array}{l}\text{ordinary time from April 30 to June 30} \\ \text{year expressed as 360 days}\end{array}$$

2. Ordinary simple interest at exact time:

$$\frac{61}{360} = \begin{array}{l}\text{the exact time from April 30 to June 30} \\ \text{year expressed as 360 days}\end{array}$$

3. Exact simple interest at ordinary time:

$$\frac{60}{365} = \begin{array}{l}\text{ordinary time from April 30 to June 30} \\ \text{year expressed as 365 days}\end{array}$$

4. Exact simple interest at exact time:

$$\frac{61}{365} = \begin{array}{l}\text{the exact time from April 30 to June 30} \\ \text{year expressed as 365 days}\end{array}$$

The use of each of the foregoing is usually dictated by custom. As mentioned in the section on ordinary time, real estate mortgages, installment loans, some personal notes and certain bonds use ordinary simple interest at ordinary time.

The largest amount of interest for the creditor is developed by using ordinary simple interest at exact time. Commercial banks usually use this method and it is therefore known as the *Bankers' Rule.*

Exact simple interest at ordinary time is rarely, if ever, used. It is mentioned only to show the possibility of such a combination.

The last combination, exact simple interest at exact time, is also known as *Accurate Interest* for obvious reasons. It is used for calculations by the government and Federal Reserve Banks in certain cases of interest and discounts. Although the terms *accurate interest* and *exact interest* are sometimes used synonymously, accurate interest only exists when exact simple interest is used with exact time.

THE 60 DAY, 6% METHOD OF
COMPUTING ORDINARY INTEREST

When the rate of interest is 6%, use is often made of the 60 day, 6% method. This is a handy and easy method to use when computing ordinary simple interest without tables. It can be used with times other than 60 days and can also be used for rates other than 6%. The method, however, is only used with ordinary simple interest. Of course, you will rarely be involved with exact interest.

With interest 6% and time 60 days, our formula shows:

$$I = P \times .06 \times 60/360$$

Reducing the fraction, we arrive at:

$$I = P \times .06 \times 1/6$$

and by further cancellation,

$$I = P \times .01$$

We can therefore conclude that *to find the interest for 60 days, at 6%, we simply multiply the principal by .01.* To multiply any number by .01 we only have to move the decimal to the left by two places. For instance:

$$\$245.36 \times .01 = \$2.4536$$
$$\$4,500. \times .01 = \$45.00$$

The above rule is easy to remember because if the yearly rate is 6% then the rate for two months (60 days) is 1% (or .01). This leads to another shortcut because if the rate for two months is 1%, then the rate for one month or 30 days is ½% (or .005). Therefore, *to find the interest for 30 days at 6% we multiply the principal by .005.* (This is the same as dividing by two and moving the decimal place two places to the left.) Or, to find the interest for 30 days, first find the interest for 60 days and then divide by two.

Example:

Find the ordinary simple interest on $650 for 90 days at 6%.

Solution:

90 days = 60 days + 30 days

Interest for $650 for 60 days at 6% = $6.50
+ Interest for $650 for 30 days at 6% =   3.25
Therefore, interest for 90 days   = $9.75

How to Find Times Other Than 60 Days

As you can see, once we have found the interest for 60 days at 6%, we can easily find the interest for other times at 6% by reducing or increasing the interest for 60 days in proportion to the time desired. Thus, if the interest for 60 days at 6% is $24.00, then:

The interest for 120 days is $48.00 (2 times 60 days; 2 × 24)
The interest for 30 days is   12.00 (½ of 60 days, ½ of 24)
The interest for 20 days is   8.00 (1/3 of 60 days, etc.)
The interest for 15 days is   6.00 (¼ of 60 days, . . .)
The interest for 10 days is   4.00 (1/6 of 60 days. . . .)

Because 6 days is 1/10 of 60 days and therefore 1/10 of the interest we can say that *to find the interest for 6 days at 6% we multiply the principal by .001.* (1/10 of .01) If we divide this answer by 6 we will find the interest for one day. (To multiply by .001, move the decimal place three places to the left.)

Using this method we can find the interest at 6% for *any* number of days. If the number of days is not an aliquot part of 60 days, it is necessary to break up the number of days into aliquot parts. Therefore, to find the interest for 39 days we must break the 39 days into 30, 6, and 3 days, all being aliquot parts of 60 days. We then find the interest for each part and the total is the required interest.

Example:

Find the interest on $890 for 57 days at 6%.

Solution:

57 days = 30 days + 20 days + 6 days + 1 day

Interest for 60 days at 6% = $8.90
Then,
Interest for 30 days = $4.45   (½ of 60 day interest)
+ Interest for 20 days = 2.966   (1/3 of. . . .)
+ Interest for 6 days =   .89   (1/10 of. . . .)
+ Interest for 1 day =   .148   (1/6 of 6 days interest)
Total Interest   = $8.454 = $8.45

How to Find Rates Other Than 6%

Now that you are familiar with use of the 60 day 6% method for finding interest for any period of time we can apply this same method for finding interest at any given rate of interest. This has become increasingly important now that rates other than 6% are in common usage.

Using the same rules, we find the interest at 6% then use the corresponding fractional part (or decimal equivalent) of the interest at 6% to find the interest at the given rate. For instance, to find interest at 4% we know that 4% is 2/3 of 6%. We then find interest at 6% and 2/3 of that answer will be the interest at 4%. Or, it might be easier for some to break it down on a 1% basis. If we divide the 6% interest by 6 we find the interest for 1%. We can then multiply this answer by the needed rate of interest.

Example:

Find the interest on $950 for 90 days at 5%.

Solution:

90 days = 60 days + 30 days

$$\begin{array}{ll} & \text{Interest on }\$950\text{ for 60 days at 6\%} = \quad\$9.50 \\ + & \text{Interest on }\$950\text{ for 30 days at 6\%} = \quad\underline{4.75} \\ = & \text{Interest on }\$950\text{ for 90 days at 6\%} = \$14.25 \end{array}$$

Then,

$14.25 divided by 6 = $2.375 = Interest at 1%

And,

$2.375 X 5 = $11.875 = $11.88 = Interest at 5%.

You can readily see in the above that we actually have taken 5/6 of the interest at 6% to find the interest at 5%. We have thus used the fractional part that 5% is of 6%.

We have now explored the various methods for finding simple interest. It is up to you to decide which method is easier for you to use. Normally when years and months are involved as time it is easier to use the standard formula I = PRT. When you are working with days only it might be easier to use the 60 day 6% method.

FINDING INDIRECT CASES
OF INTEREST

There are certain situations wherein we must find one of the variables in our Interest formula other than interest. In solving for other variables we use the mathematical system of equations. (See Appendix I, Basic Arithmetic Calculations.) In this manner we can derive new formulas for such unknowns using our standard interest formula, $I = PRT$.

Derivation of Essential Formulas

Finding Rate of Interest

To find rate of interest, we use our standard formula and solve for "R." We can rearrange our formula first or we can substitute our numbers and then solve for the unknown. However, in order to formulate new equations for continued usage, we will use the former method.

To solve for R in the equation $I = PRT$, we see that we must *divide* each side of the equation by PT, thus,

I/PT = PRT/PT and, by cancellation,
I/PT = R, thereby formulating an equation for rate of interest as
$$R = I/PT.$$

Example:

In two years, a principal of $5,000 earns $800 in interest. What is the rate of interest?

Solution:

Formula for rate of interest is $R = I/PT$

$R = $800/$5,000 \times 2 = $800/$10,000 = 8/100$
$R = .08$ or, rate of interest of 8%

Finding Principal

Using the above procedure and solving for P, we find we must divide through by RT, thereby;

I/RT = PRT/RT, and by cancellation,
I/RT = P and our equation for principal becomes
P = I/RT

Example:

How much money will you have to lend to get $24 interest at 6%, if you lend it for 6 months?

Solution:

P = I/RT
P = $24/.06 X ½   (time is ½ year)
P = $24/.03
P = $800.

Finding Time

If we again use the same procedures of substitution and cancellation, we find that the equation for finding time is:

T = I/PR

Example:

How long will it take $800 to yield $128 in interest at a rate of 8%?

Solution:

T = I/PR
T = $128/$800 X .08
T = $128/$64
T = 2 years

By now you should readily see a pattern in the above equations. If you understand the pattern it will never be necessary to memorize the various formulas other than the original standard formula for interest I = PRT. The rule for this pattern can be quoted as: *To find any one variable other than interest, divide the interest by the product of the remaining two variables.*

2

The Applications of Discount

MEANINGS OF BANK DISCOUNT

Interest charges can be collected *in advance* by deducting them from the amount of a financial obligation prior to its maturity date. This process of interest payment is called *discounting* and the amount thus deducted is called *Bank Discount*.

Although usually associated with short-term loans and notes, bank discount is used in all types of transactions involving commercial paper and not necessarily limited to use by commercial banks. For instance, in order to increase the yield on the interest of a mortgage, the lender could *discount* the loan. The discount rate thus used is referred to in real estate as *points*. The discount is collected before the maturity date of the mortgage and is actually an interest payment *in advance* and in excess of the interest rate of the mortgage itself.

Points are frequently used in construction loans to increase yield to the lender. In order to get a construction loan to build a house, the builder might have to pay a point (1%), or more, in addition to the monthly interest charge on the outstanding balance of the loan.

Discounts are also used to increase yield in the sale, transfer, or reassignment of mortgages. Additionally, bank discount would determine what price to pay for a mortgage if it is to yield a certain return on the investment at maturity. More details involving applications of bank discount to mortgages are discussed in Chapter 10.

The nature and meaning of bank discount itself should be thoroughly understood by all persons involved in the real estate profession as it is a necessary element in the mathematics of real estate.

For continuity in our discussions on bank discounts we will refer to the commercial paper or financial obligations involved as "notes," understanding, of course, that the mathematics involved could be applied to any financial instrument.

Terminology of Bank Discount

As mentioned previously, the interest payment deducted from the loan or note, in advance, is called Bank Discount. It is
> (1) the interest on the *maturity value*
> (2) for the actual number of days
> (3) from the *date of discount* to the due date
> (4) at the *rate of discount* charged.

The number of days (exact time) from the date of discount to the due date is called the *Term of Discount* (or Discount Period). The *Discount Date* is the date the note is actually discounted, whether it is the date the original note was made or any day prior to its due date. The due date of the note is its *Maturity Date*. The remainder left when the discount has been deducted is called the *Net Proceeds*.

How to Find Discounts and Proceeds

Bank discount is interest, so we can utilize the simple interest formulas from the preceding chapter by substituting terms. In the formula I = PRT, we can substitute Discount (D) for Interest (I), and Maturity Value (M) for Principal (P).

Although interest rate and discount rate are both percentage rates, they are not interchangeable in the formula. The reason for this will be seen later in this chapter. We will continue to use R for interest rate and will use *d* for discount rate.

Time (in years) and Term of discount (in years) are similar and we therefore retain the T for either one in the formula. As with simple interest, we must always express T on the basis of a year. If we are finding discount for part of a year we use 360 days (ordinary interest) as the denominator and actual number of days (exact time) as the numerator. This ratio of exact time to ordinary interest was discussed previously and called the Bankers' Rule.

The interest formula then, in terms of bank discount, becomes

Discount = Maturity Value × Discount Rate × Term, or
$$D = MdT$$

Example:

What is the discount on a 60 day note for $500 if the discount rate is 6%?

Solution:

$$D = Mdt$$
$$D = \$500 \times .06 \times 60/360$$
$$D = \$30 \times 1/6$$
$$D = \$5.00$$

Example:

A $400 note is discounted for 90 days at 5%. What is the discount?

Solution:

$$D = Mdt$$
$$D = \$400 \times .05 \times 90/360$$
$$D = \$20 \times 1/4$$
$$D = \$5.00$$

Because Net Proceeds (P) is the remainder after the discount has been deducted, we can easily see that

Proceeds = Maturity Value minus Discount, or
$$P = M - D$$

In the first example above, if the maturity value (M) is $500 and the discount (D) is $5, then

$$P = M - D$$
$$P = \$500 - \$5$$
$$P = \$495.$$

Using the same formula in the second example, it can be reasoned that if the maturity value is $400 and the discount is $5, then the net proceeds are $395.

By combining the formula for discount and the formula for proceeds we can arrive at an easy-to-use formula for finding proceeds without finding the discount. If D = MdT, and P = M – D, then by replacing D in the proceeds formula we have

$$P = M - MdT$$

and, by factoring the right hand member of the equation, we have the resulting formula for proceeds,

$$P = M (1 - dT)$$

This formula can now be used as a one-step formula for finding proceeds without knowing the bank discount. Using the same information from the preceeding examples we can re-work the problems to find the net proceeds.

Example:

What are the net proceeds of a 60 day note for $500 if the discount rate is 6%?

Solution:

P = M (1 – dT)
P = $500 (1 – .06 X 1/6)   Note: T = 60/360 = 1/6
P = $500 (1 – .01)
P = $500 (.99)
P = $495.

Example:

What are the net proceeds of a 90 day note for $400 if the discount rate is 5%?

Solution:

P = M (1 – dT)
P = $400 (1 – .05 X 1/4)
P = $400 (1 – .0125)
P = $400 (.9875)
P = $395.

It should be noted that in all the foregoing examples the discount date is the same as the date of the note and therefore, the term of discount is the same as the number of days for which the note is written.

Discount, however, can be taken any time prior to the maturity date. It is then necessary to determine the actual number of days in the term of discount.

How to Find Maturity Date

The maturity date must be known in order to properly ascertain the term of discount. When the time is designated in months, only months are used in determining maturity date. A three month note dated July 6 will have a maturity date of October 6, and a two month note dated April 20 will have a maturity date of June 20.

Notes that are dated on the last day of a month will mature on the last day of the maturity month regardless of whether it has 30, 31, 28, or 29 days. Maturity dates that fall on Sundays or legal holidays are advanced to the next business day.

If the time of the note is stated as days, then the actual number of days must be counted. (See Chapter 1, page 25 and Table I)

Example:

Find the maturity date of a 90 day note dated April 4.

Solution:

April   26 days   (30 days in April – 4 days)
May   31 days
June   30 days
         87 days total
90 – 87 = 3 days left for July, so the maturity date becomes July 3.

Note that in the above example, if the note were a 3 month note instead of a 90 day note, the maturity date would be July 4. Because July 4 is a legal holiday, the maturity date would become July 5.

Example:

Find the maturity date of a 90 day note dated August 30.

Solution:

August	1 day	(31 – 30)
September	30 days	
October	31 days	

62 days,   90 – 62 = 28

Maturity date = November 28

How to Find the Term of Discount

Once the maturity date is known, finding the term of discount is simply a matter of determining the exact number of days from the date of discount to the maturity date. For simplicity, use should be made of Table I for finding maturity date and term of discount. If tables are not available, term of discount is found by using the same process as was used for finding maturity date.

Example:

A three month note dated March 3 is discounted on April 14. What is the term of discount?

Solution:

Maturity date is June 3.   (March 3 + 3 months = June 3)

April	16 days	(30 – 14)
May	31 days	
June	3 days	

50 days = term of discount

Example:

A 60 day note dated July 12 is discounted on August 6. What is the term of discount?

Solution:

Using Table I,

July 12 = day #193, 193 + 60 = 253
Day #253 is September 10 = maturity date.

August 6 is day #218 and September 10 is day #253.
The difference is (253 – 218 = 35) 35 days which
is term of discount.

NON-INTEREST AND INTEREST-BEARING DISCOUNTS

Maturity Value

The maturity value is determined by whether the note is non-interest bearing (NIB) or interest-bearing. The maturity value of a NIB note is the same as its *face value* because no interest or charges are added to it at maturity.

To find the bank discount on a NIB note, we simply substitute in our formula, $D = MdT$, using the face value as M (Maturity value).

Example:

A non-interest bearing, 60 day note for $2,500 dated September 4, is discounted on September 20 at 5% discount. What is the bank discount?

Solution:

1. Find maturity date. From Table I, September 4 is day #247. Add 60 days and find day #307, which is November 3, maturity date.

2. Find term of discount. The difference between September 20 (day #263) and November 3 (day #307) is (307 – 263 = 44) 44 days for term of discount.

3. Find bank discount.

$$D = MdT$$
$$D = \$2,500 \times .05 \times 44/360$$
$$D = \$2,500 \times .05 \times .1222$$
$$D = \$15.277 \text{ or } \$15.28 = \text{bank discount}$$

How to Find Maturity Value on an Interest-Bearing Note

The interest earned on an interest-bearing note must be added to its face value to determine its maturity value. This is the same as interest added to the principal to find *amount* (Chapter 1) and we can therefore use the same formula,

$$S = P(1 + RT).$$

By substituting maturity value M for S, and face value F for principal P, we have

$$M = F(1 + RT).$$

Example:

Find the maturity value of a $3,000, 90 day, 6% interest-bearing note dated April 12.

Solution:

$$M = F(1 + RT)$$
$$M = \$3,000(1 + .06 \times 90/360)$$
$$M = \$3,000(1 + .06 \times 1/4)$$
$$M = \$3,000(1 + .015)$$
$$M = \$3,000(1.015)$$
$$M = \$3,045.$$

Note: **Any** of the short-cuts for finding 6% interest on the $3,000 for 90 days could also have been used. The interest thus found and *added* to the face value would be the maturity value. If there is any doubt, or, if the problem is complicated, it is best to use the above formula.

Finding Discounts and Proceeds on Interest-Bearing Notes

Once the maturity value of an interest-bearing note has been found, we can find the discount or proceeds by substituting in our formulas

$$D = MdT, \quad \text{and/or}$$
$$P = M(1 - dT).$$

Example:

A $4,000, 90 day, 8% interest-bearing note dated April 12,

1977, is discounted on May 27. The discount rate is 7%. Find the bank discount.

Solution:

1. Find maturity date. From Table I, April 12 is day #102. Add 90 days (102 + 90 = 192) and we find that July 11 is day #192. Therefore maturity date is July 11.

2. Find term of discount. Again from Table I, discount date of May 27 is day #147 and maturity date of July 11 is day #192. The difference (192 – 147 = 45) of 45 days is the term of discount.

3. Find maturity value. Using the formula

M = F(1 + RT), and substituting, we find
M = $4,000(1 + .08 × 90/360)
M = $4,000(1 + .08 × .25)
M = $4,000(1.02)
M = $4,080. = maturity value.

4. Find bank discount. Use the formula D = MdT and substitute the values we have found for maturity value ($4,080) and term of discount (45 days). Use the given discount rate (7%).

D = MdT = $4,080 × .07 × 45/360
D = $4,080 × .07 × .125
D = $4,080 × .00875
D = $35.70 = bank discount

To find the net proceeds we use the formula P = M – D, and find

P = $4,080. – $35.70
P = $4,044.30.

If in the above example we had been asked to find net proceeds initially rather than bank discount, we would have used the formula

P = M(1 – dT).

Then, by substituting our values we would find net proceeds by using *one* formula instead of finding bank discount and subtracting it from the maturity value in order to find the net proceeds.

P = M(1 – dT)
P = $4,080(1 – .07 × .125)
P = $4,080(1 – .00875)
P = $4,080(.99125)
P = $4,044.30 = net proceeds

Direct Solution to Net Proceeds

We can simplify the finding of net proceeds further by deriving one formula for finding proceeds of an interest-bearing note *without* finding maturity value first. From the formula for maturity value,

$$M = F(1 + RT),$$

we use the right hand member, $F(1 + RT)$, as a substitute for M in the proceeds formula

$$P = M(1 - dT),$$

and arrive at

$$P = F(1 + RT) (1 - dT)$$

Now we can solve directly for net proceeds knowing *only* the face value, rates of discount and interest, and the time elements involved in each.

Thus, to find proceeds in the foregoing example, once we have found the term of discount (45 days), we substitute our values into our new formula

$P = F(1 + RT) (1 - dT)$, and have
$P = \$4,000(1 + .08 \times 90/360) (1 - .07 \times 45/360)$
$P = \$4,000(1 + .02) (1 - .00875)$
$P = \$4,000(1.02) (.99125)$
$P = \$4,000(1.011075)$
$P = \$4,044.30 =$ net proceeds

By using the above formula to find net proceeds, we eliminated steps 3 and 4 and use of the other formulas for proceeds. The above should be used only when it is not necessary to find the bank discount or maturity value but is necessary to find net proceeds.

THE MEANINGS OF TRUE
DISCOUNT AND PRESENT VALUE

True Discount is the discount made from the face value of an obligation payable at some future date in order to determine the *present value* of the obligation. In other words, it is the difference between the present value and future value of an obligation.

It differs from bank discount in that bank discount is interest taken on a full maturity value and paid in advance, whereas true discount is actually a part of the maturity value. When bank discount is taken it is also taken on the true discount as part of the maturity or face value. Bank discount will therefore always be greater than true discount.

Present Value can be defined as that sum which when invested at a given rate of interest will produce a required future value at a given future time. The term "present worth" is sometimes used instead of present value. Both terms have the same meaning.

The concept of present value will be used constantly throughout this book. It is an extremely important element in appraising, mortgage computations, and real estate investments.

How to Find Present Value

Because true discount is the same as interest, and present value is the same as principal, we can use our simple interest formulas in solving present value problems. By substitution, let true discount = interest (I), present value = principal (P), rate of true discount = interest rate (R), and term of true discount = time, in years, (T). Maturity value, as noted earlier in the chapter, will be designated by M instead of S (amount). Although we will be working with discount, we use R for rate of true discount and retain the use of *d* exclusively for bank discount.

When solving for present value, we find that our standard formula for principal, P = I/PRT, is not suitable because we will normally not know the true discount, I. We must therefore derive a formula for finding P, given R, T, and maturity value, M. The formula for finding maturity value, M = P(1 + RT), satisfies this requirement. By solving for P we arrive at the formula for finding present value,

$$P = \frac{M}{(1 + RT)}$$

Once we have found present value we know that

True Discount = Maturity Value - Present Value or, in formula terms,

$$I = M - P$$

Applying these two formulas we can easily solve for present value and true discount.

Example:

What are the present value and true discount of $3,000 for 90 days at 6%?

Solution:

(1) $P = \dfrac{M}{1 + RT}$

$P = \dfrac{\$3,000}{1 + .06 \times .25}$

$P = \dfrac{\$3,000}{1.015} = \$2,955.665$

$P = \$2,955.67 =$ present value

(2) $I = M - P$

$I = \$3,000.00 - \$2,955.67$

$I = \$44.33 =$ true discount

For a better understanding of present value we can reword the above example and demonstrate more exactly the meaning of present value.

Example:

What *principal* must be invested at 6% simple interest to produce $3,000. in 90 days?

Solution:

We use the same formula, values, and computations in this example as we did in the previous example. It is obvious that the principal to be invested is the same as the present value in the previous example, $2,955.67, and the income, or yield, on this investment will be equal to $44.33, the true discount.

In solving for present value, the note or obligation involved can be NIB or interest-bearing because maturity value, M, would be either face value in the case of a NIB note or amount (face plus interest) in the case of an interest-bearing note.

Example:

Find the present value and true discoun on May 24 of a

$5,000, 6% interest-bearing 90 day note dated March 15, at a true discount rate of 8%.

Solution:

1. Find maturity value: Use the same formula for maturity value as in bank discount.

$$M = F(1 + RT) = \$5,000(1 + .06 \times 90/360)$$
$$M = \$5,000(1 + .015) = \$5,000(1.015)$$
$$M = \$5,075. = \text{maturity value}$$

2. Find maturity date: From Table I, March 15 = day #74, 74 + 90 = 164, day #164 = June 13 = maturity date.
3. Find term of discount: From Table I, May 24 to June 13 = 164 − 144 = 20 days = term of discount.
4. Find present value:

$$P = \frac{M}{1 + RT}$$
$$P = \frac{\$5,075}{1 + .08 \times 20/360}$$
$$P = \frac{\$5,075}{1 + .0044}$$
$$P = \frac{\$5,075}{1.0044}$$
$$P = \$5,052.77 = \text{present value}$$

5. Find the true discount:

$$I = M - P = \$5,075.00 - \$5,052.77$$
$$I = \$22.23 = \text{true discount}$$

It might be helpful here to note that the formula for present value can be stated, "To find present value, divide the maturity value by the amount of $1 for the given rate (true discount rate) at the given time (term of true discount)." An examination of the formula we have used will show the simplicity of this statement.

PARTIAL PAYMENTS

Partial payments are sometimes allowed to be made on a financial obligation prior to the maturity date. In such cases, the computation of amount due at maturity would necessarily change because of the effect of calculating the interest on the partial payment. NIB obligations cause no problem because the payment is merely deducted from the face value to find the amount due at maturity.

On interest-bearing obligations, the interest on the partial payment can be calculated in different ways. There are, however, two common methods in use today for computing the interest and finding the balance due at settlement. These two methods are termed The United States Rule and The Merchants' Rule.

The United States Rule

The United States Rule, so named because of its use in government accounting and the affirming of its legality by the U.S. Supreme Court, is used mostly for long term payment periods (over 1 year). The fundamental principles of the rule are:

1. A partial payment must first be applied to the accrued interest.
2. After the accrued interest has been paid, the balance, if any, of the partial payment is applied to the principal.
3. Interest must not be charged on interest.

Should any payment be insufficient to pay the accrued interest due at the time of the payment, then the payment is held and not applied until the next payment is made. Each time a payment is made a new face value is determined on which to compute the interest due.

The procedure then, under the United States Rule, is as follows:

1. Add the interest from the date of the note to the date on which a payment is made to the face.
2. Deduct the first payment. The remainder then becomes the new face.
3. To the new face add the interest from the date of the first payment to the date of the second payment.
4. Deduct the second payment.
5. Continue the process until the date of settlement.

Example:

A note for $10,000 with interest at 8% dated March 17, 1976, has the following endorsements of payments made: June 5, 1976, $2,000 and September 20, 1976, $1,500. Using the United States Rule, find the balance due on the note at maturity.

Solution:

Date of maturity is March 17, 1977.

Face Value of note 3/17/76	$10,000.00
Interest on $10,000, 3/17 to 6/5 (80) days)	+177.78
Amount due on 6/5/76	10,177.78
Partial payment on 6/5/76	-2,000.00
New face of note 6/5/76	8,177.78
Interest on face, 6/5 to 9/20/76 (107 days)	+194.45
Amount due on 9/20/76	8,372.23
Partial payment on 9/20/76	-1,500.00
New face of note 9/20/76	6,872.23
Interest on face, 9/20/76 to 3/17/77 (178 days)	+271.83
Amount Due at Maturity	$7,144.06

The Merchants' Rule

The Merchants' Rule, although rarely used in real estate transactions, is used sometimes when partial payments are made on an interest-bearing note which runs for less than a year. The principles applicable to the Merchants' Rule and the procedures to follow are:

1. The face value of the note draws interest from the date of the note to the settlement date (usually maturity date).
2. Interest is computed on each partial payment from the date of payment to the settlement date.
3. On the final settlement date, the amount of the payments made and interest accrued is deducted from the amount due on the note.

To show the difference in interest costs for the two rules, we will use the same note, dates, and values as the preceding example, but will use the Merchants' Rule to determine the balance due at maturity.

Example:

Same as the preceding example. Use the Merchants' Rule to find the balance due at maturity.

Solution:

Date of maturity is March 17, 1977.

Face value of note 3/17/76	$10,000.00
Interest for 1 year at 8%	+800.00
Maturity value of note on 3/17/77	$10,800.00
Partial payment 6/5/76	$ 2,000.00
Interest on payment 6/5/76 to 3/17/77 (285 days)	+126.67
Value of payment 6/5/76	$ 2,126.67
Partial payment 9/20/76	$ 1,500.00
Interest on payment 9/20/76 to 3/17/77 (178 days)	+59.33
Value of payment 9/20/76	$ 1,559.33
Total value of payments	$ 3,686.00
Maturity value 3/17/77	$10,800.00
Less value of payments	–3,686.00
Amount Due at Maturity	$ 7,114.00

REGULATION Z AND CREDIT SALES OF REAL ESTATE

The Federal Truth in Lending Act, or Regulation Z, became law on July 1, 1969. The purpose of the Act "is to assure that every customer who has need for consumer credit is given meaningful information with respect to the cost of that credit which, in most cases, must be expressed in the dollar amount of finance charge, and as an annual percentage rate computed on the unpaid balance of the amount financed."

Although the regulation does not cover all types of credit it does include most consumer credit (up to $25,000) and includes *all real estate transactions.*

It is not within the scope of this book to present the various requirements or details of Regulation Z except in the manner in which it does affect real estate mathematics.

The thrust of the regulation, as can be gathered from the foregoing quotation, is that *full disclosure* of the total and actual costs of financing must be made to the consumer.

Because financing is involved in most real estate sales, we find ourselves confronted with a disclosure term called Annual Percentage Rate (APR). In addition to finding APR, we should know how to find the True Discount Rate of bank discount.

True Discount Rate of Bank Discount

When the face of a discounted note is repaid, the difference between the face and the proceeds is interest income. To determine this interest rate we use the simple interest formula $R = I/P$, where R is the interest rate *and* true discount rate, and I is the Interest. P is proceeds which is the same as the principal earning interest. In other words, the True Discount Rate of a bank discount is the ratio of the interest to the proceeds.

Example:

A $1,000 note is discounted for 1 year at 10% bank discount. What is the true discount rate?

Solution:

1. Find the proceeds:

$$P = M(1 - dT)$$
$$P = \$1,000(1 - .10 \times 1)$$
$$P = \$1,000(.90)$$
$$P = \$900.$$

2. Find the interest:

$$I = F - P$$
$$I = \$1,000 - \$900$$
$$I = \$100$$

3. Find the true discount rate:

$$R = I/P$$
$$R = \$100/\$900$$
$$R = 1/9 = .1111$$
$$R = 11.11\% = \text{true discount rate}$$

Annual Percentage Rates and Discounts

The APR is the true or effective annual interest rate "determined in accordance with the actuarial method of computation with an accuracy at least to the nearest quarter of 1 percent ..." (.0025). It is determined by application of the United States Rule when applied to partial payments.

Our discussion of APR here is limited to its use and comparisons to bank discount and true discount rate. Because of the complexity in the mathematical calculation of APR and the ready availability of APR Tables, we will not attempt any detailed computations of APR. The use of the APR in conjunction with mortgages and settlement disclosures will be discussed in Chapter 10.

Discounts are computed on a 360 day year. The APR is the

ratio of discount to proceeds computed on a 365 day year. For purposes of comparing discount rates and APR we will use the formula

$$APR = \frac{Discount/Proceeds}{Term\ of\ Discount} \times 365,\ or$$

$$APR = \frac{D/P}{T} \times 365$$

Example:

A $1,000 note is discounted at 10% for 1 year. What are the bank discount, true discount, and APR?

Solution:

1. Find bank discount:

$$D = MdT$$
$$D = \$1,000 \times .10 \times 1$$
$$D = \$100. = bank\ discount$$

2. Find proceeds:

$$P = M - D$$
$$P = \$1000 - \$100$$
$$P = \$900. = proceeds$$

3. Find true discount rate.

$$R = I/P$$
$$R = \$100/\$900 = 1/9 = .1111$$
$$R = 11.11\% = true\ discount\ rate$$

4. Find the APR.

$$APR = \frac{\$100/\$900}{360} \times 365$$

$$APR = \frac{.1111}{360} \times 365$$

$$APR = .0003086 \times 365 = .1126$$
$$APR = 11.26\%$$

Thus, by computation we find that the APR at a 10% discount rate for 360 days is 11.26% and the true discount rate is 11.11%. The disclosure form in accordance with Regulation Z would show the APR of 11.26%.

3

Understanding Compound Interest, Annuities, Sinking Funds, and Amortization

**DEFINITION AND EXPLANATION
OF COMPOUND INTEREST**

Compound Interest is the interest on the total of the principal and the accrued interest. For each time period, the interest is added to the principal to form a new principal. Each succeeding time period has a new principal on which to compute the interest.

The interval between the time periods is called the *conversion period.* These periods may be monthly, quarterly, semi-annual, or annual. For computation purposes, the conversion period is usually taken as an exact part of a year. Monthly mortgage payments that include an interest payment have a conversion period of one month.

The time interval between the date of the original investment and the date of repayment is called the *term.* Therefore, a 20 year monthly payment mortgage has a *conversion period* of one month and a *term* of 20 years.

The *sum* of the principal and the total interest is called the *compound amount.* This sum is also referred to as *maturity value,* or *accumulated value.* The initial sum that is invested, or the principal, is also called *present value* (see Chapter 2). If we use the terminology of present value for the amount invested, we can likewise use the expression *future value* for the compound amount at the end of any given term. These expressions are used frequently in mortgages, appraising, valuation, and real estate investment analysis. They have the same connotations and use in compound interest.

Conversion Periods

The compound interest rate is usually given as an annual rate unless stated otherwise. It must be changed to the interest rate per conversion period for computation purposes. The annual interest rate is called the *nominal interest rate* and when it is changed fractionally to the conversion period it is called the *periodic interest rate.*

For computing interest on interest, we can use the standard simple interest formula $I = PRT$ to find compound interest. The symbol i is used instead of RT; i being the annual rate divided by the conversion periods per year.

Example:

How much interest is earned on $1,000 if it is invested for 2 years at 8% interest compounded semi-annually?

Solution:

The conversion period is semi-annual so the interest must be computed every 6 months. The periodic interest rate i is 4% (8% divided by 2 conversion periods).

$$\text{First Period:} \quad I = Pi$$
$$I = \$1,000 \times .04$$
$$I = \$40.$$

For the second period, the interest of $40 must be *added* to the principal to arrive at the *new principal* for computation.

$$\$1,000 + \$40 = \$1,040 = P$$
$$\text{Second Period:} \quad I = \$1,040 \times .04$$
$$I = \$41.60$$

and, adding this to the principal, we arrive at the new principal for the end of the second period (first year) as $1,040 + $41.60 = $1,081.60.

$$\text{Third Period:} \quad I = \$1,081.60 \times .04$$
$$I = \$43.264 \text{ and, by adding,}$$
$$P = \$1,124.864$$

Fourth Period: I = $1,124.864 × .04
                 I = $44.995 and
                 P = $1,169.859 rounded to $1,169.86

Interest for the 2 years totals $169.86 ($1,169.86 - $1,000)

The compound interest for the 2 years in the above example is $9.86 more than simple interest would have been. Because interest is computed on interest, compound interest always results in a higher yield on an investment.

The above method of determining compound interest or compound amount is relatively easy to compute because only four conversion periods were required. However, as the number of conversion periods increases, the computations become more tedious and complicated. It therefore becomes necessary to derive or establish certain formulas in order to simplify the computations.

Interest Rate Per Conversion Period

As shown in the previous example, the interest rate per conversion period is found by dividing the nominal rate by the number of conversion periods per year. Using the standard notation of

**i = periodic rate or interest rate per conversion
      period (decimally),
j = the nominal or annual interest rate,
m = number of conversion periods per year,**

we derived the formula for *i* as

$$i = j/m$$

Example:

What is the periodic rate if the annual interest rate is 9% and it is compounded monthly?

Solution:

j = .09
m = 12 (12 conversion periods per year)
Therefore, i = j/m = .09/12 = .0075

Compound Amount Formula

For simplicity, traditional standard notations or symbols, with only slight variations, are used for compound interest formulas and tables throughout the banking and finance world.

The fundamental standard formula (or General Interest Equation) for simple interest as developed in Chapter 1, is transformed for compound interest into

$$S = P(1 + i)^n$$

where:

   S = compound amount, maturity value, or accumulated value.
      (The S is used because it designates the *Sum*.)
   P = the original principal, or the present value of S,
   i = the interest rate per period, or periodic interest rate,
   n = the total number of conversion periods in the term or,
      the number of years multiplied by the number of conversion periods per year.

The formula finds the compound amount S on the principal P for n periods at the rate i. It is used for finding compound amount when P, i, and n are known. It can also be used, by manipulation, to find any of its quantities when the other 3 are known.

As in simple interest, compound interest is found as the difference between the maturity value (compound amount) and principal, or

$$I = S - P$$

Example:

What will the compound amount be on $1,000 invested at 6%, compounded semi-annually, for a term of 2 years? What will the total interest be?

Solution:

$$i = j/m = .06/2 = .03$$
$$n = \text{periods} \times \text{years} = 2 \times 2 = 4$$
$$S = P(1 + i)^n = 1000(1 + .03)^4$$
$$S = 1000(1.03)\ (1.03)\ (1.03)\ (1.03)$$
$$S = 1000(1.1255088)$$
$$S = \$1,125.508 \text{ or rounded to } \$1,125.51$$
$$I = S - P = \$1,125.51 - \$1,000.00 = \$125.51$$

Although the above formulas simplify the computations of compound interest, they do become increasingly difficult as the period n becomes larger. Because n is an exponent in the formula, many computations are needed for the solution as n increases.

If, in the above example, the interest were compounded monthly and the term were 5 years, n would be 60 and (1.03) would have to be computed to the 60th power of $(1.03)^{60}$. This can be done mathematically with logarithms or by binomial expansion. To avoid the intricacies of these methods, tables have been constructed that eliminate the necessity for difficult computations at various rates of compound interest.

Compound Interest Tables

The compound interest tables and annuity tables (discussed later in this chapter) have been combined and standardized because of their constant use in financial mathematics. The tables are called "Compound Interest and Annuity Tables" and consist of six columns, each being one of the compound interest (or annuity) functions. Each table presented in this chapter is used as a *column* in the combined tables.

We have included the most frequently used tables in the Appendix. Because the tables are readily available in most real estate and mortgage company offices, our discussion in this chapter will be limited to the construction and usage of such tables rather than difficult computations from the various formulas. Proper usage of the tables or columns requires an understanding of the formulas and notations used in them.

Accumulation Factor and
Compound Interest Tables

In the formula $S = P(1 + i)^n$, the factor $(1 + i)^n$ is used to accumulate P and is therefore called the *accumulation factor*. Finding compound amount or the accumulated value is simply a matter of multiplying the principal by the accumulation factor.

The standard compound interest table is constructed for the *Amount of $1* by using a principal of $1 in the formula. In so doing, the S is traditionally changed to s and the formula becomes $s = 1 (1 + i)^n$ and, because $1 \times (1 + i)^n = (1 + i)^n$, we have the equation for Amount of $1 resulting in

$$s = (1 + i)^n$$

By using various values of i in conjunction with the number of periods n, the table gives the accumulation factor, or $(1 + i)^n$, for the *Amount of 1*. Multiplying this factor by the principal gives us the compound amount or S. Compound interest tables give the accumulation factor and are generally labeled "$(1 + i)^n$", "Compound Amount of 1," "Amount of 1 at Compound Interest," or just "Amount of 1." The accumulation factor is the fundamental building block of all compound interest, annuity, and amortization tables.

In the standardized tables of compound interest, the *Amount of 1* is the first column. Table II consists of excerpts of the combined first columns from the Compound Interest and Annuity Tables for 2%, 3%, and 4%.

For illustrative purposes, we can use this table to solve the preceding example on page 54. We found that $i = .03$ and $n = 4$. In the tables, find $n = 4$ and locate the accumulation factor under the column for $i = .03$ that corresponds to $n = 4$. The table gives an accumulation factor of 1.25509. Multiply this by the principal amount of $1,000. The answer (rounded-off) is the same as our preceding answer, $1,125.51.

Example:

What is the compound amount on an investment of $1,500 at 8% interest in 5 years compounded quarterly?

Solution:

$$i = j/m = .08/4 = .02$$
$$n = 5 \times 4 = 20$$

Find the 2% column and move down to the factor adjacent to $n = 20$. The accumulation factor is 1.485947. Multiply this by the principal of $1,500:

$1,500 \times 1.485947 = $2,228.92 and,
Compound Amount = $2,228.92.

By formula,

$$S = P(1 + i)^n$$
$$S = 1500(1 + .02)^{20}$$
$$S = 1500(1.485947) = \$2,228.92$$

AMOUNT OF $1 AT COMPOUND INTEREST. $s = (1 + i)^n$

n	2%	3%	4%
1	1.020 000	1.030 000	1.040 000
2	1.040 400	1.060 900	1.081 600
3	1.061 208	1.092 727	1.124 864
4	1.082 432	1.125 509	1.169 859
5	1.104 080	1.159 274	1.216 653
6	1.126 162	1.194 052	1.265 319
7	1.148 686	1.229 874	1.315 932
8	1.171 659	1.266 770	1.368 569
9	1.195 093	1.304 773	1.423 312
10	1.218 994	1.343 916	1.480 244
11	1.243 374	1.384 234	1.539 454
12	1.268 241	1.425 761	1.601 032
13	1.293 607	1.468 534	1.665 074
14	1.319 479	1.512 590	1.731 676
15	1.345 869	1.557 967	1.800 944
16	1.372 786	1.604 706	1.872 981
17	1.400 241	1.652 878	1.947 901
18	1.428 246	1.702 433	2.025 817
19	1.456 811	1.753 506	2.106 849
20	1.485 947	1.806 111	2.191 123

TABLE II

How to Find Present Value

Present value is the principal needed *now* in order to accumulate a given sum of money at some future date. It is what $1 to be paid in the future at compound interest is worth today.

The difference between the present value and the compound amount is the interest that is earned on the principal. If the earned interest is subtracted from the compound amount, the result is the principal or present value. The amount subtracted is referred to as the *compound discount* (true discount at compound interest) and should not be confused with bank discount. Although the discount of a compound amount does result in the present value, we will only be concerned here with finding present value.

As mentioned previously, the P in the formula $S = P(1 + i)^n$

represents principal or present value. By solving the equation for P, we arrive at the formula for finding P. It becomes

$$P = S/(1 + i)^n$$

The formula in this form can be used by finding the value of the accumulation factor $(1 + i)^n$ from Table II and dividing it into the value for S.

Example:

If the compound interest rate is 6% compounded semi-annually how much must be invested now in order to accumulate $10,000 in 5 years?

Solution:

$$i = .06/2 = .03$$
$$n = 2 \times 5 = 10$$
$$P = S/(1 + i)^n = \$10,000/(1.03)^{10}$$
Find $(1.03)^{10}$ from Table II (under column 3% to n = 10)
$$(1.03)^{10} = 1.343916, \text{ then,}$$
$$P = \$10,000/1.343916$$
$$P = \$7,440.94$$

The above example required a computation in long division (10,000 divided by 1.343916). Because multiplication is easier than division, we can rearrange the formula to

$$P = S\, \frac{1}{(1 + i)^n}$$

and, because $1/(1 + i)^n$ is the *reciprocal* of $(1 + i)^n$, we can construct a table of reciprocal values of $(1 + i)^n$. In effect, the table would list the values of 1 divided by each value of $(1 + i)^n$. (In mathematical notation, $1/(1 + i)^n$ is the same as $(1 + i)^{-n}$, and, to avoid the fraction, our formula can be stated as $P = S(1 + i)^{-n}$.) The solution of the formula then, involves only the multiplication of compound amount S by the reciprocal of the accumulation factor.

The present value of 1 is sometimes designated by the symbol v so that $v^n = 1/(1 + i)^n = (1 + i)^{-n}$. The Present Value of 1 is always the reciprocal of the Amount of 1, so when $P = 1$, $v = 1/s$.

In the Compound Interest and Annuity Tables, the present value of 1 is the fourth column. The columns are arranged so that the first three columns are *future values* and the last three are *present values*. The symbol v^n is used to designate present value of 1. "Present *worth* of 1" is commonly used and is synonomous. Column 4 and Column 1 are reciprocals of each other.

Table III consists of excerpts of the combined fourth columns from the Compound Interest and Annuity Tables for 2%, 3%, and 4%.

PRESENT VALUE OF $1 AT COMPOUND INTEREST.

$$v^n = 1/(1 + i)^n$$

n	2%	3%	4%
1	.980 392	.970 874	.961 539
2	.961 169	.942 600	.924 556
3	.942 322	.915 142	.888 996
4	.923 845	.888 487	.854 804
5	.905 731	.862 609	.821 927
6	.887 971	.837 484	.790 315
7	.870 560	.813 092	.759 918
8	.853 490	.789 409	.730 690
9	.836 755	.766 417	.702 587
10	.820 348	.744 094	.675 564
11	.804 263	.722 421	.649 581
12	.788 493	.701 380	.624 597
13	.773 033	.680 951	.600 574
14	.757 875	.661 118	.577 475
15	.743 015	.641 862	.555 265
16	.728 446	.623 167	.533 908
17	.714 163	.605 016	.513 373
18	.700 159	.587 395	.493 628
19	.686 431	.570 286	.474 642
20	.672 971	.553 676	.456 387

TABLE III

Example:

Same as the previous example above.

Solution:

$$P = S(1 + i)^{-n}$$
$$P = \$10,000(1.03)^{-10}$$

From Table III, $(1.03)^{-10} = .744094$ so,

$$P = \$10,000(.744094)$$
$$P = \$7,440.94$$

Nominal and Effective Interest Rates

As mentioned previously, the compound interest rate is usually given as an annual rate. Because it is a *named* rate, it is called the *nominal interest rate*. The nominal interest rate, however, will differ from the actual earnings rate depending upon how many times per year it is compounded. The rate that is actually earned in one year is called the *effective interest rate*. When the nominal rate is compounded annually, it will be the same rate as the effective rate.

For instance, using the compound amount formula, \$10,000 of principal invested at 6% nominal interest rate, compounded *annually*, will accumulate to \$10,600.00. The interest earned will be \$600 at an *effective interest rate* of 6%, the same as the nominal interest rate. However, if we invest the \$10,000 at 6% interest *compounded quarterly*, it accumulates to \$10,613.64, and the interest earned will be \$613.64, which is an *effective interest rate* of 6.14%.

If we designate effective interest rate as e, then \$1 at rate e for 1 year will amount to $1 + e$. The accumulated value for \$1 at the nominal interest rate for 1 year compounded m times per year will be $(1 + i)^m$, where m is the number of conversion periods for the year. These values will be equal so that

$$1 + e = (1 + i)^m$$

Because $n = m \times$ years, and in this formula, the term is always *one* year, $n = m \times 1$, and n therefore equals m. If $n = m$, then $(1 + i)^m = (1 + i)^n$, and $(1 + i)^m$ can be found in Table II by substituting the exponent m for the exponent n.

From the foregoing equation $1 + e = (1 + i)^m$, we can find the effective interest rate for any given nominal rate converted m times a year.

Example:

What is the effective interest rate if the nominal rate is 8% and it is compounded quarterly?

Solution:

$$i = .08/4 = .02$$
$$m = 4$$
$$1 + e = (1 + i)^m$$
$$1 + e = (1 + .02)^4 = (1.02)^4$$
$$1 + e = 1.08243 \quad \text{(From Table II)}$$
$$e = 1.08243 - 1$$
$$e = .08243 = 8.24\%$$

If two interest rates, either nominal or effective, result in the same compound amount for one year, they are called *equivalent rates*.

THE USE OF ANNUITIES IN REAL ESTATE

An annuity is a sequence of equal payments made at equal intervals of time. Mortgage payments and rental payments on a lease are forms of annuities. Calculation of the present value of an annuity is used in various methods of appraising real estate. Capitalization of income as a method of appraisal or as a consideration of real estate investment involves annuity computations. Although the term *annuity* creates some bewilderment for many real estate personnel, it is not a difficult concept to grasp if the basic annuity terminology is understood.

Annuity Terminology

The interval between payments on an annuity is called the *payment period* or *rent period.* The amount paid at the beginning *or* end of each payment period is called the *periodic rent, periodic payment,* or, more simply, the *rent.* The use of the term *rent* in annuities includes any periodic payment made on an annuity including a lease, mortgage, installment purchase, pension, etc. The *rent* is the *value* of each periodic payment.

If the payments are made at the *end* of each payment period, the annuity is called an *ordinary annuity*. If the payments are made at the *beginning* of each payment period, the annuity is called an *annuity due*.

The *term* of an annuity is the time from the beginning of the first payment period to the end of the last payment period. When the term of the annuity is fixed, or established by definite time limitations, the annuity is called an *annuity certain*. When the term of the annuity is of an indefinite duration, or dependent upon some uncertain event, such as death of an individual, the annuity is known as a *contingent annuity*. A life insurance policy is a contingent annuity.

The interval between consecutive conversions of interest is called the *conversion period* or *interest period*. When the conversion period and the payment coincide, the annuity is called a *simple annuity*. If those periods differ, the annuity is called a *general annuity*.

In real estate, we are primarily concerned with the *simple annuity certain*. A 30 year residential mortgage amortized monthly is an *annuity certain* with a *term* of 30 years. The conversion and payment periods of one month coincide so it is a *simple annuity*. It is also an *ordinary annuity* because residential mortgage loans are paid in arrears at the end of each payment period.

Formulas and Symbols

Because annuities involve the same definitions as compound interest, many of the same symbols are used in the formulas for annuities as were used in the preceding section on compound interest.

i = the interest rate per period determined by j/m.

n = the total number of payment periods in the term, determined by the number of years in the term multiplied by the number of periods per year.

S = accumulated value or, in annuities, the value of the annuity at the end of its term, also referred to simply as *amount*.

The accumulation factor $(1 + i)^n$ is also used in the annuity formulas. Using all of the foregoing, for instance, the formula for finding amount *S*, or the *sum* of an ordinary annuity, is derived as

$$S = R \frac{(1 + 1)^n - 1}{i}$$

where R is the periodic rent payment.

The formula was derived using geometric progressions, and is not necessary to show here. The availability of various tables also precludes the necessity of actually computing with the formula. Computations would involve the use of logarithms.

Tables, as mentioned previously, cannot be used properly without reference to, or an understanding of, the formulas. In constructing annuity tables, the same procedures are followed as in compound interest.

How To Find the Amount of an Annuity

Table IV represents values of the *amount* (or accumulated value) of ordinary annuities of $1 per period for certain values of n and various rates i. For simplification, the formula

$$\frac{(1 + i)^n - 1}{i}$$

is abbreviated to the symbol

$$s\,\overline{_{n|}}\,i$$

which is read as "*s* angle *n* at rate *i*" and means the value or amount of an annuity of n payments of $1 each if interest is compounded at the periodic rate i. It is also called the *annuity value factor of $1*.

Table IV is compiled from *column 2* of the Compound Interest and Annuity Tables. It differs from column 1 in that the *amount of 1* here is *deposited periodically* with a deposit of 1 at *each period*. The compounding is therefore not only on the initial lump sum, but on each subsequent deposit at each period.

To find the amount of an annuity we use the above formula and find the value of $s\overline{_{n|}}_i$ from Table IV. The factor across from n and under the column for i will be the value of $s\overline{_{n|}}_i$.

Example:

A periodic payment of $300 is made semi-annually into a fund for 8 years. Interest is 6% compounded semi-annually. What is the amount of the fund at the end of its term?

Solution:

R is the *rent* of $300, i is the periodic interest rate $= j/m = .06/2 = .03$, and n is the number of payments $= 2 \times 8 = 16$.

$$s_{\overline{n}|i} = s_{\overline{16}|.03}$$

From Table IV, $s_{\overline{16}|.03} = 20.156881$

Therefore, $S = R\, s_{\overline{16}|.03}$

$$S = \$300\, (20.156881)$$
$$S = \$6,047.06$$

AMOUNT OF ANNUITY OF $1 PER PERIOD

$s_{\overline{n}|i}$

n	2%	3%	4%
1	1.000 000	1.000 000	1.000 000
2	2.020 000	2.030 000	2.040 000
3	3.060 400	3.090 900	3.121 600
4	4.121 608	4.183 627	4.246 464
5	5.204 040	5.309 136	5.416 323
6	6.308 121	6.468 410	6.632 976
7	7.434 283	7.662 462	7.898 295
8	8.582 969	8.892 336	9.214 226
9	9.754 628	10.159 106	10.582 795
10	10.949 721	11.463 879	12.006 107
11	12.168 715	12.807 796	13.486 351
12	13.412 090	14.192 030	15.025 806
13	14.680 332	15.617 790	16.626 838
14	15.973 938	17.086 324	18.291 911
15	17.293 417	18.598 914	20.023 588
16	18.639 285	20.156 881	21.824 531
17	20.012 071	21.761 588	23.697 512
18	21.412 312	23.414 435	25.645 413
19	22.840 559	25.116 868	27.671 229
20	24.297 370	26.870 375	29.778 079

TABLE IV

Tables for finding the amount of an ordinary annuity are usually labeled by the symbol $s_{\overline{n}|i}$, "Amount of an Ordinary Annuity," or "Amount of an Annuity of $1 per Period." The tables are constructed by computing $\dfrac{(1 + i)^n - 1}{i}$ for *each* value of n at each value of i. Thus, the resulting factor is $s_{\overline{n}|i}$ where $s_{\overline{n}|i} = \dfrac{(1+i)^n - 1}{i}$.

When used as column 2 of the Compound Interest and Annuity Tables, it is called "Amount of 1 per Period." It represents a *future value* of periodic deposits and is therefore included in the first 3 columns of the tables.

How to Find the Present Value
of an Ordinary Annuity

The value at the beginning of the term of all periodic payments is called the *present value* of the annuity. To avoid confusion with previous formulas of present value wherein both principal and present value were designated P, we shall use A to represent present value of an ordinary annuity.

A formula for finding present value is developed in the same manner as was done for finding the amount of an ordinary annuity. Using the same symbols, we arrive at

$$A = R \, \frac{1 - (1+i)^{-n}}{i}$$

To represent the present value *if the periodic payment is 1*, we shall use the symbol $a_{\overline{n}|i}$, read as "*a* angle *n* at rate *i*" and the portion of the formula $\dfrac{1 - (1+i)^{-n}}{i}$ is abbreviated to that symbol. Therefore, symbol $a_{\overline{n}|i}$ represents the present value of $1 per period for n periods at the periodic rate i. The formula for present value A can now be written as

$$A = R \, a_{\overline{n}|i}$$

Table V represents the present value of $1 per period computed for various values of n and i. To find the present value A or an ordinary annuity of R periodic rent payments, we need only multiply the factor from the table corresponding to the proper n and i, by R.

Example:

A house is offered for sale at $20,000. The seller agrees to accept $200 per month for 10 years at 9% interest compounded monthly. The balance must be paid as a down payment. How much is the down payment?

Solution:

$$n = 12 \times 10 \text{ years} = 120$$
$$i = .09/12 = .0075$$

$$a_{\overline{n}|i} = a_{\overline{120}|.0075}$$

From Table V, $a_{\overline{120}|.0075} = 78.941693$

$$A = R\, a_{\overline{n}|i}$$
$$A = \$200\ (78.941613)$$
$$A = \$15,788.32 = \text{present value}$$

PRESENT VALUE OF $1 PER PERIOD

$$a_{\overline{n}|i}$$

n	½% .005	¾% .0075	1% .01
60	51.725 561	48.173 374	44.955 438
61	52.463 245	48.807 319	45.500 038
62	53.197 258	49.436 545	46.039 642
63	53.927 620	50.061 086	46.573 903
64	54.654 349	50.680 979	47.102 874
65	55.377 461	51.296 253	47.626 608
80	65.802 305	59.994 440	54.888 206
81	66.469 956	60.540 387	55.334 857
82	67.134 284	61.082 270	55.777 087
83	67.795 308	61.620 119	56.214 937
84	68.453 042	62.153 965	56.648 453
85	69.107 505	62.683 836	57.077 676
116	87.858 378	77.291 494	68.470 242
117	88.416 297	77.708 679	68.782 418
118	88.971 440	78.122 759	69.091 503
119	89.523 821	78.533 755	69.397 537
120	90.073 453	78.941 693	69.700 522

TABLE V

The down payment is the *difference* between the selling price of the house and the present value of the annuity. Therefore, the down payment required is $4,211.68 ($20,000 – $15,788.32).

Although the above example of a seller taking back such a mortgage is rarely encountered in real estate transactions today, it does present a good example of the use of present value of an annuity for our purposes. In addition, it offers a method of determining the down payment necessary to carry a certain mortgage at a specified monthly payment. Although mortgage companies usually dictate required down payments, the real estate professional who can specify a required down payment in order to *budget a specific monthly payment* has added much to his professionalism.

Present value of an annuity is an increasingly important element in real estate. Further applications are discussed in Chapter 10 on mortgages and in Chapter 12 on appraising.

Tables of present value are usually designated as "present Value of $1 per Period," or simply "$a_{\overline{n}|i}$". The term "Present Worth" is used interchangeably with "Present Value" as both have exactly the same meaning. In the Compound Interest and Annuity Tables it is used as column 5.

Computing the Periodic Payment of an Ordinary Annuity

The present value of an ordinary annuity, such as a mortgage, is the amount due before the first payment is made. Because this is one of the factors in our formula, and we usually know the interest rate and number of payments, we can derive a formula for finding the periodic payment or rent by solving the present value formula for R.

Therefore, from $A = R\,a_{\overline{n}|i}$, we have
$R = A/a_{\overline{n}|i}$, or more simply, $R = A(1/a_{\overline{n}|i})$.

The reciprocal of $a_{\overline{n}|i}$ is $1/a_{\overline{n}|i}$ and therefore, if we compile a table of reciprocals to $a_{\overline{n}|i}$ from the present value tables we can easily solve for rent by multiplying the factor for $1/a_{\overline{n}|i}$ by the present value of A. If a reciprocal table is not available, we can use the table for present value ($a_{\overline{n}|i}$) and find $1/a_{\overline{n}|i}$ by dividing as indicated.

We shall call the table of $1/a_{\overline{n}|i}$ "Periodic Rent of an Annuity whose Present Value is 1." As such, it is actually the *periodic payment* that will pay interest and pay off a loan. It is therefore sometimes called "Periodic Payment to Amortize 1." It is used as column 6 in the Compound Interest and Annuity Tables.

For our example below we shall use Table V in this chapter, and divide the factor we find into 1 to obtain the reciprocal value.

Example:

A house is purchased for $40,000 with a 20% down payment. The balance is to be paid monthly on a mortgage for 10 years at 9%. What will the monthly payment of principal and interest be?

Solution:

$$n = 10 \times 12 = 120$$
$$i = .09/12 = .0075$$
$$A = \$40,000 - \$8,000 = \$32,000$$
From Table V, $a_{\overline{120}|.0075} = 78.941613$
$$R = A\,(1/a_{\overline{n}|i}) = 32,000\,(1/78.941613)$$
$$R = 32,000(.01267) = \$405.36 = \text{monthly payment}$$

The above is one method of finding the monthly payment on a mortgage or other ordinary annuity. Another method of determining periodic payments that has gained considerable acceptance in real estate and finance today is the use of the *Constant Annual Percent.*

How to Use Constant Annual Percent

Constant Annual Percent (sometimes called *annual constant*) is used almost exclusively in real estate financing. *It is the percentage of the full loan that must be paid annually to pay off the loan.* It measures the amount of money necessary each year to pay off a loan at a level monthly payment of interest and principal. *To obtain the monthly payment, find the annual constant and divide it by 12.*

The Constant Annual Percent is derived from the formulas for an ordinary annuity (when payment is in arrears or at the end of each payment period), and the table is constructed from $1/a_{\overline{n}|i}$ or column 6 of the Compound Interest and Annuity Tables. The monthly payment *factor* is found and converted to an annual percent by multiplying it by 12 (for annual) and 100 for percent. The example below shows how a Constant Annual Percent would be computed for use in a table.

Example:

What is the Constant Annual Percent on a 10 year mortgage at 9% interest with monthly mortgage payments?

Solution:

$$n = 10 \times 12 = 120$$
$$i = .09/12 = .0075$$

From Table V, $a_{\overline{n}|i} = a_{\overline{120}|.0075} = 78.941613$
$$1/a_{\overline{n}|i} = 1/78.94163 = .01267 \text{ and,}$$
$$.01267 \times 12 \times 100 = 15.20\%, \text{ therefore,}$$

Constant Annual Percent = 15.20%

Using the above Constant Annual Percent, the monthly payment and annual debt service can be found for any mortgage amount. (Debt service is the periodic amount needed to pay principal and interest on any loan or debt.) A 10 year, 9% mortgage for $20,000 will have an annual debt service of

15.20% of $20,000 = $3,040

and a monthly payment of

$3,040/12 = $253.33

The various Constant Annual Percents are compiled in tables so that it is not necessary to compute them as in the above example. Once the particular Constant Annual Percent is found from the tables, it is applied to the mortgage amount to find the necessary information. A table of selected Constant Annual Percents is included in the Appendix.

APPLICATIONS TO SINKING FUNDS AND AMORTIZATION

Sinking Funds and *amortization* are two methods generally used for making periodic payments in order to pay off long-term debt. In real estate, both are involved in appraising, investing, depreciation, and financing. Both constitute annuities in which the mathematical problem is determining the necessary value of each periodic payment or rent.

The Meaning of Amortization

Literally, the word amortization means the death of a debt. In modern real estate usage it means payment of a debt, including principal and interest, by a sequence of equal payments at equal intervals. The amortized payments on a mortgage form an ordinary annuity and, therefore, the periodic payment is found by use of the formula $R = A/a_{\overline{n}|i}$, various tables, or by use of the Constant Annual Percent, all of which have been discussed in the preceding sections.

From each equal payment, a portion is allocated to interest, and a portion is allocated to the reduction of principal. Each payment must therefore be sufficient to pay these portions and retire the debt obligation at the end of the term.

It is sometimes necessary, in amortization, to determine the outstanding debt or balance of the principal *at the end of a specific time*. The outstanding debt is equivalent to the payments yet to be made. Therefore, the outstanding debt at *any time* is the *present value* of the annuity consisting of the payments yet to be made. The formula $A = Ra_{\overline{n}|i}$ for present value and the tables for $a_{\overline{n}|i}$ are used.

Example:

What is the outstanding principal on a 9%, monthly payment, 10 year, $20,000 mortgage after 3 years? Monthly payments are $253.35.

Solution:

Since 36 payments (3 years $\times$ 12 months) have been made in 3 years, there are 84 payments remaining (120 – 36 = 84). We must find the present value (after 3 years) of an annuity consisting of 84 payments of $253.35 each (R = $253.35).

$$n = 84, \text{ and } i = .09/12 = .0075$$
$$\text{Therefore, } a_{\overline{n}|i} = a_{\overline{84}|.0075}, \text{ and, from Table V,}$$
$$a_{\overline{84}|.0075} = 62.153965.$$
$$A = R\,a_{\overline{n}|i}$$
$$A = \$253.35\,(62.153965)$$
$$A = \$15,746.71 = \text{the outstanding}$$
principal or balance of the debt.

How Amortization Schedules are Compiled

An *amortization schedule* gives a complete record of the progress of the amortization of a debt and is a basic source of information about a transaction. It shows the allocation of all payments to principal and interest and the total of the outstanding debt.

Each step in the amortization process is shown for each payment made. Although amortization is a compound interest and annuity function, the process of amortization can be shown by using simple interest. In the preceding example, the first payment is $253.35, and the outstanding balance is $20,000. The interest rate is 9%, so the interest rate per period (month) is 1/12 of 9%, or, .0075. We can schedule each payment as follows:

Payment #1: From the simple interest formula,
I = Pi = 20,000 × .0075 = $150.

Interest due is therefore $150, so, from the first payment $150 is applied to interest and the balance of $103.35 ($253.35 – $150.00) is applied to reduce the principal to $19,896.65 ($20,000 – $103.35).

Payment #2: Find the interest; I = Pi = $19,896.65 × .0075
= $149.22.

The interest portion on the second payment is deducted from the payment and the balance of the payment ($104.13) is applied to reduce the principal to $19,792.52 ($19,896.65 – $104.13).

Our schedule at this point would appear as:

Payment Number	Amount	Applied to Interest	Applied to Principal	Unpaid Balance
1	$253.35	$150.00	$103.35	$19,896.65
2	253.35	149.22	104.13	19,792.52

The computations are continued until the schedule has been completed for all 120 payments which is the total of payments on this mortgage. Of course, the use of high-speed computers today precludes the necessity of any individual preparation of amortization schedules. An understanding of the process for preparation, however, is essential to an understanding of its usage.

The Meaning of Sinking Fund

A *sinking fund* is a savings fund or an accumulation of money made in equal periodic deposits at compound interest for the purpose of accumulating sufficient funds to meet an obligation at a specified date. Sinking funds are used to replace depreciated assets or other capital losses, to meet bond obligations or real estate mortgages, or to pay off any debt that will fall due at a later date. The difference from amortization is that the principal or debt in a sinking fund does not earn interest and remains constant to maturity.

Some creditors dislike the amortization method of paying a debt, since the periodic payments include both interest and only a small or partial return of principal, which is usually difficult to reinvest. It is obvious, therefore, that many creditors will usually accept a lower interest rate with a sinking fund than he would on an amortized loan. The debtor would have to consider which would be cheaper for him.

In the sinking fund method, the debtor makes periodic deposits into a fund to earn compound interest so that the sum of the deposits and interest earned at the specified date will equal the obligation. He also pays the interest on the original debt at each interest period. The interest payments are therefore always the same.

Computations with Sinking Funds

The interest to be paid on the debt is computed using the simple interest formula $I = Pi$. The deposit to be made to the sinking fund is obtained by solving for periodic payment R in the annuity formula $S = R\, s_{\overline{n}|i}$. This is derived as

$$R = S/s_{\overline{n}|i} \text{ or, } R = S(1/s_{\overline{n}|i})$$

We can use Table IV to find the value of $s_{\overline{n}|i}$, and then find its reciprocal by dividing.

Example:

A loan of $10,000 is obtained from a bank for a 10 year period at 6% interest based on annual deposits into a sinking fund that accumulates at 3%. What is the total of the annual deposit and interest payment to the bank?

Solution:

$$I = Pi = \$10,000 \times .06 = \$600.$$
The annual interest payment to the bank is $600.
$$n = 1 \times 10 = 10 \text{ and, } i = .03/1 = .03$$
From Table IV, $s_{\overline{n}|i} = s_{\overline{10}|.03} = 11.463879$
$$R = S(1/s_{\overline{n}|i}) = \$10,000(1/11.463879)$$
$$R = \$10,000(.087231) = \$872.31 = \text{annual deposit}$$
The total payment is $600 interest plus $872.31 deposit or,
$1,472.31.

The sinking fund is the reciprocal of the Amount of 1 per Period (column 2) and is therefore used as column 3 in the Compound Interest and Annuity Tables. It is called simply "Sinking Fund."

Book Value of a Sinking Fund

The *book value* of a sinking fund is the difference between the total amount due and the amount in the sinking fund. In the above example, the book value of the debt at the end of the first year is $10,000 - $872.31 = $9,127.69. After the second year the total in the sinking fund will be the first deposit ($872.31) plus the interest earned at 3% on the deposit ($26.17), plus the total of the second deposit. The amount in the sinking fund would therefore be $872.31 + $26.17 + $872.31 = $1,770.79. The book value after the second deposit becomes $10,000 - $1,770.79 = $8,229.21.

4

How to Work with Commissions

COMMISSIONS AND BROKERAGE

Commission or brokerage is the amount of money paid to an agent for buying or selling something. Brokerage does not involve possession of goods whereas commission could include possession on a consignment basis, such as a *commission merchant*. The real estate business then, is not a commission business, but a brokerage business that pays commissions for services rendered.

All persons engaged in real estate brokerage are familiar with commissions as their primary source of income. Because *income* is the "name of the game," we devote this short chapter to the *proper* computation of commission income.

Commission rates vary throughout the country and the prevailing commission rate in any area is usually established by local realty boards or by custom and traditional practice.

MEANINGS AND TYPES
OF COMMISSION

In real estate, commission means a percentage of the gross selling price of a property, percentage of gross rental on a lease, or other *percentage remuneration* for services rendered.

The computation of commission is simply the solution of a percentage problem where commission is the percentage P, selling price or other gross amount is the base B, and the rate of commission is the percentage rate R. All commission formulas are therefore derived from the standard percentage formula

$$P = BR$$

To more readily identify the variables in the formula with commission problems, we will change the designated variables in accordance with the above paragraph. Percentage (P) becomes Commission C, base (B) becomes Gross Selling Price S, and rate (R) retains its identity as commission rate R. The formula now reads

COMMISSION = GROSS SELLING PRICE × RATE OF COMMISSION

or

$$C = SR$$

This commission formula can be used for all types of commission problems or computations. The same procedures are followed whether the commission involves rental leases, management fees or allowances, mortgage placement, or insurance policies.

Because of the wide variations in office policy and methods in which commissions are paid, it would not be feasible to show all possible commission problems. We will limit our explanations to the most common systems in use.

COMPUTING STRAIGHT COMMISSION

Straight commission means that the remuneration is on commissions only and no other allowances are made. Computing straight commission is simply a matter of substituting the values into the formula and finding the unknown variable. The standard commission formula is used to find the commission.

Example:

What is the commission on a $37,500 sale if the commission rate is 8%?

Solution:

$$C = SR$$
$$C = \$37,500 \times .08$$
$$C = \$3,000$$

Finding Selling Price

We can derive the formula for finding selling price by transforming the standard formula, by solving for S, into

$$S = C/R$$

Thus, gross selling price is found by dividing the commission by the rate of commission.

Example:

A salesman earned a $1,575 commission on the sale of a house. If the commission rate was 6%, what was the selling price of the house?

Solution:

$$S = C/R$$
$$S = \$1,575/.06 = \$26,250$$

Finding Commission Rate

By solving for rate R in the basic formula, we can derive a formula for finding commission rate when the other two variables are known. The formula for commission rate becomes

$$R = C/S \text{ or,}$$

to find the commission rate, divide the commission by the gross selling price.

Example:

A house sold for $42,500 and the broker earned a commission of $2,762.50. What was the commission rate?

Solution:

$$R = C/S$$
$$R = \$2,762.50/\$42,500$$
$$R = .065 = 6\tfrac{1}{2}\%$$

GRADUATED COMMISSIONS

Straight commissions are sometimes paid on a graduated scale. The commission rate changes as the value of a lease or sale changes. Normally the rate will decrease as the value of the gross selling price or lease increases. This procedure is more common with leases than with sales. The computations are done for each graduation or change in rate and value, and the sum of the computations is the resulting total commission.

Example:

A 20 year lease is arranged by a broker at an annual rental of $12,500 for the first 10 years and $9,500 for the next 10 years. The commission rate is 6% for the first year, 3% for the next 4 years, 2% for the next 5 years and 1% thereafter. What is the total earned commission?

Solution:

First year: $C = SR = \$12,500 \times .06 = \$750.$
Next 4 years: $C = \$12,500 \times .03 = \$375$ per year
        $\$375 \times 4$ years = $1,500 total
Next 5 years: $C = \$12,500 \times .02 = \$250$ per year
        $\$250 \times 5$ years = $1,250 total
Next 10 years: $C = \$9,500 \times .01 = \$95$ per year
        $\$95 \times 10$ years = $950 total
Full Commission earned:
        $\$750 + \$1,500 + \$1,250 + \$950 = \$4,450$

SPLIT COMMISSIONS

Salespersons on straight commission are usually paid a percentage or fractional part of the gross commission, using a specified rate for listing a property and a specified rate for the actual sale. The simplest approach to finding the salesperson's commission when percentage is used is to convert the rate to a percentage rate of the gross sales price. If a fraction is used, the fractional part of the gross commission is found rather than percentage rate of gross sales price.

Example:

A salesman receives 20% of the gross commission for listing and 40% for selling a property. If he lists and sells a property for $37,500 at 8% gross commision, how much does he earn?

Solution:

Convert salesman's commission to a rate of selling price:

Listing   = 20% of 8% = .20 X .08 = .016 = 1.6%
Selling   = 40% of 8% = .40 X .08 = .032 = 3.2%
Combined = 60% of 8% = .60 X .08 = .048 = 4.8%

He will therefore receive 4.8% of the gross selling price:

$$C = SR = \$37,500 \times .048 = \$1,800$$

If he had listed only and had not sold the property, he would have received 1.6% of the selling price:

$$C = SR = \$37,500 \times .016 = \$600$$

If he had sold the property but had not listed it, he would have received 3.2% of the selling price:

$$C = SR = \$37,500 \times .032 = \$1,200$$

The above method, although very simplified, is the same method used for split commissions with cooperating brokers who sell a property listed exclusively with another broker. The gross commissions are usually split 50/50 in such a case, but other arrangements are also made. A 50/50 split is also commonly used for salespersons in some offices. In such cases, a portion of the commission must be allocated for listing.

THE 100 PERCENT COMMISSION PLAN

For years, salespersons were usually compensated on a 50/50 commission split with the broker as mentioned above. A new concept has recently developed in some areas of the country wherein the salesperson will earn 100% of the gross commission and pay the broker a pro-rata share of office operating expenses plus a management fee to compensate the broker for supervising the operation.

The purpose of the system is to eliminate non-producers and the additional overhead costs they incur. In effect, the plan reduces the broker's overhead to zero. The broker receives income from his own sales and the management fees.

Example:

Four salespersons and a broker are on the 100% Commission Plan and share an office with annual overhead expenses of $20,000. The overhead is shared equally by the 4 salespersons, each paying 25%. The management fee for each salesperson is $400 per month. What will a salesman's annual net earnings be if he had $500,000 of sales for the year at a commission rate of 6%?

Solution:

Find annual expenses:

Pro-rata overhead expense = 25% of $20,000 = $5,000.
Total management fees = $400 × 12 months =   4,800.
                        Total annual expenses = $9,800.

Find Gross Commissions:

$500,000 × .06 = $30,000

Find Net Earnings:

$30,000 – $9,800 = $20,200

On the normal 50/50 plan, the salesman would have earned $15,000 net ($500,000 × .03).

The broker received *all* his overhead ($20,000) for a zero overhead cost, plus management fees of $19,200 ($400 × 4 × 12). He also received 100% of any commissions he earned on his own sales.

DRAWING ACCOUNT AGAINST COMMISSION

In order to retain good salespersons, some offices offer a draw against commission. This allows payment of a weekly amount until a specified time when settlement on the account is made. If the difference between draw and commissions earned results in a deficiency in the account, the deficiency is usually carried over to the next settlement date. If the salesperson is discharged because of lack of commission production, he normally does not have to pay back the deficiency.

Example:

A saleswoman draws $250 per week. A settlement is made after 10 weeks during which time she earned commissions of $3,648. How much is she due?

Solution:

$250 per week X 10 weeks = $2,500
Earnings for 10 weeks   = $3,648

The difference of $1,148 ($3,648 – $2,500) is the amount due her providing there was no deficiency to make up from the prior settlement period.

FINDING SELLING PRICE
FOR A NET SALE

A common mathematics problem in real estate brokerage is calculating a proper selling price in order for the seller to net a given amount after payment of the broker's commission and other costs. This procedure is known as a *net sale* and is also discussed in Chapter 5.

The best method is to use the *percentage rate* that corresponds to the net amount instead of *commission rate* in the formula. The gross sales price is 100% and the net price is the difference between that and the commission rate. The percentage rate *after* commission rate is subtracted from 100% is used as the rate R in the formula.

The percentage rate R in this case no longer represents *commission* but is the percentage of the gross selling price corresponding to the *net proceeds*. The C in the formula is commission *only* when the *rate* is *commission rate*. In this case, the C is the *net* proceeds and proper substitution must be made. The variables must *always correspond* in the formula. Therefore, the amount of net proceeds needed is substituted for commission C.

Example:

A seller must net $30,000 after settlement on the sale of his property. If the sales commission is 7% and the additional selling costs involved total $940, for how much must the property be sold?

Solution:

Net proceeds corresponds to 93% of gross sales price (100% - 7% = 93%), so *rate* is 93%. The net proceeds after commission must total $30,940 ($30,000 + $940), so C represents $30,940. Therefore:

$$S = C/R$$
$$S = \$30,940/.93 = \$33,268.82$$

or, gross selling price is $33,270. (rounded)

5

Finding and Using Profit and Loss
in Real Estate

DEFINITIONS

There are two different aspects of profit and loss with which we will deal in this chapter. One is the profit or loss involved in the actual sale of real estate not involving investment applications and the other is the matter of over-all profit and loss in the operation of a real estate partnership. The mathematical applications of investments in real estate involving rates of return, capitalization, leverage, etc., are covered in Chapter 15.

Our concern in the first aspect of profit and loss is only in finding the solutions to profit and loss problems of simple real estate transactions.

It is the usual custom, unless stated otherwise, to compute the profit or loss on *cost*. The tendency in modern accounting, however, is to compute profit based on *selling price*. This tendency developed because selling price is used in determining commissions, certain taxes, discount, assessments, etc. It is also a better basis of comparison for past and future transactions. Loss, however, is usually always expressed as a percent of the cost.

For simplicity and continuity, we will consider profit and loss as *based on cost*, but the mathematical applications of both methods will be shown.

HOW TO FIND PROFIT AND LOSS
BASED ON COST

Because we are working with percentage, the standard percentage formulas and procedures are used. From the simple equation
Profit (or Loss) = Cost × Rate of Profit (or Loss), we have the formula

$$P = BR$$

where the amount of profit or loss is the percentage P, the original investment or cost is the base B, and the percent of profit or loss is the rate R. Finding profit or loss is simply a matter of finding the product of its rate multiplied by the base. Note that *rate* of profit or loss is the same as *percent* of profit or loss and the terms can be used interchangeably.

Example:

A house sold at a profit of 20% on cost. If it cost $24,000, how much is the profit?

Solution:

P = BR = $24,000 × .20 = $4,800 profit

Example:

A house sold at a loss of 12% on cost. If it cost $24,000, how much is the loss?

Solution:

P = BR = $24,000 × .12 = $2,880 loss

It is important to remember that corresponding values must always be used. When P represents *profit*, then R must be rate or percent of *profit*, and when P represents *loss*, then R must be rate or percent of *loss*.

Finding Selling Price

Finding selling price, given cost and *profit,* is accomplished by *adding* the profit to the cost in order to obtain the selling price. In the first preceding example, the profit of $4,800 is added to the cost of $24,000 ($4,800 + $24,000) to find the selling price of $28,800.

To find the selling price given cost and *loss, subtract* the loss from the cost and the difference is the selling price. In the second preceding example, the loss of $2,880 is subtracted from the cost of $24,000 ($24,000 – $2,880) to obtain the selling price of $21,120.

Shortcuts

If it is not necessary to find the amount of profit or loss, but selling price is needed, and we know the cost and rate of profit or loss, we can use one of our basic percentage principles for a shortcut method to find selling price.

When profit or loss is based on cost, cost is always considered as 100% (or 1). If the profit is 20%, then the selling price (cost + profit) would have to be 120% of the cost (100% + 20%). Or, as an equation,

Selling Price = Cost × (1 + Rate of Profit)

Therefore, in our first example, we can substitute and find,

$$\text{Selling Price} = \$24,000 \times (1 + .20)$$
$$= \$24,000 \times 1.20$$
$$= \$28,800$$

In the second example we can also use this shortcut. However, we know that the selling price is 12% *less* than the cost *because it is a loss.* Therefore, the selling price would be 88% of the cost (100% – 12% = 88%). Or, if we solve by equation we would have,

$$\text{Selling Price} = \text{Cost} \times (1 - \text{Rate of Loss})$$
$$= \$24,000 \times .88 = \$21,120$$

Finding Rate or Percent of Profit or Loss

To find percent of profit or loss, given cost and amount of profit or loss, we solve our percentage formula for R and find

$$R = P/B$$

This can also be simply stated as: *To find percent of profit or loss, divide the amount of profit or loss by the cost.* In other words, the percent of profit or loss is the *ratio* of profit or loss to cost.

Example:

A property was purchased for $24,000 and sold for $32,000. What was the percent of profit?

Solution:

$$\text{Profit} = \$32,000 - \$24,000 = \$8,000$$

$$R = P/B = \frac{\$8,000}{\$24,000} = \frac{1}{3} = 33\ 1/3\% \text{ profit}$$

Example:

A building lot was purchased for $10,000 and later had to be auctioned off at a loss of $2,000. What was the percent of loss?

Solution:

$$R = P/B = \frac{\$2,000}{\$10,000} = \frac{1}{5} = 20\% \text{ loss}$$

Finding Cost

To find the cost (base), given percent of profit or loss, and the amount of profit or loss, we solve our original percentage formula for B and find

$$B = P/R$$

Example:

A house was sold at a profit of $3,000. The profit was 25%. What was the cost of the house?

Solution:

$$B = P/R = \$3,000/.25 = \$12,000.$$

If the above example had involved a loss, the same procedure would have been followed and we would have found that the cost was the same, $12,000. The only change would have been selling price. In the example of profit, the selling price was $15,000 ($12,000 + $3,000) and with a loss, the selling price would have been $9,000 ($12,000 – $3,000).

It might be necessary to find cost knowing only the selling price and the percent of profit or loss. Using the preceding example, we know the selling price is $15,000 when the profit is 25%, and we want to find the cost.

We can use the selling price as P in the formula providing we use the corresponding value for rate R. Once again, if cost is 100% or 1, then the selling price is cost + profit, or, in this case, 125% (100% + 25%) of cost. The 125% is the corresponding rate of selling price to use in the formula B = P/R. The formula for cost becomes

$$\text{Cost} = \frac{\text{Selling Price}}{(1 + \text{Rate})} \text{ and, by substitution,}$$

$$\text{Cost} = \frac{\$15,000}{1.25} = \$12,000$$

This same procedure is used to find cost when a rate or loss and the selling price are given. Because it involves a loss, the selling price must be *less* than cost. Cost is 100%, so selling price is equivalent to the cost minus the percent loss. In our equation we use *1 – rate* as the corresponding percent of loss for the selling price. The formula becomes

$$\text{Cost} = \frac{\text{Selling Price}}{(1 - \text{Rate})}$$

Example:

A property was sold at a loss for $10,350. The rate of loss was 10%. What was the cost?

Solution:

$$\text{Cost} = \frac{\$10,350}{(1 - .10)} = \frac{\$10,350}{.90} = \$11,500$$

HOW TO FIND PROFIT AND LOSS
BASED ON SELLING PRICE

If we change the base B from cost to selling price, the most important effect is that selling price becomes the 100% factor rather than cost. The basic percentage formulas remain the same with the exception that all results are based on sales and expressed in terms of selling price. The basic equation changes to

**Profit (or Loss) = Selling Price × Rate of Profit (or Loss)
and the formula, P = BR, is used with corresponding values of
*selling price.***

Example:

What is the profit on a property sold for $20,000 if the percent profit is 15% on selling price?

Solution:

$$P = BR = \$20,000 \times .15 = \$3,000$$

Example:

A property is sold for $35,000 at a 20% loss on selling price. How much is the loss?

Solution:

$$P = BR = \$35,000. \times .20 = \$7,000$$

Finding Rate or Percent of Profit or Loss

To find percent of profit or loss, given selling price and amount of profit or loss, divide the amount of profit or loss by the selling price. This is the same as the formula

$$R = P/B$$

Example:

A farm is sold for $80,000, amounting to a profit of $16,000. What is the rate of profit on the selling price?

Solution:

$$R = P/B = \frac{\$16,000}{\$80,000} = 1/5 = .20 = 20\%$$

Finding Cost

Because selling price is the base, the cost is found by *subtracting the profit* from the selling price or *adding the loss* to the selling price.

Example:

A house sold for $12,000 at a profit of 20% on selling price. What did the house cost?

Solution:

1. Find profit.

$P = BR = \$12,000 \times .20 = \$2,400.$

2. Find Cost:

$\$12,000 - \$2,400 = \$9,600.$

Example:

A vacant lot sold for $6,000 representing a 10% loss on selling price. What did the lot cost?

Solution:

1. Find loss:

$P = BR = \$6,000. \times .10 = \$600.$

2. Find cost:

$\$6,000 + \$600 = \$6,600.$

Shortcuts

The solutions of the above examples can be reduced to one step. For instance, in the first example, we know that selling price is 100% and the profit is 20%. The *cost*, being the difference of the two, is

80% of the selling price (100% – 20% = 80%). We have only to find 80% of the selling price to find cost. In equation form this would be

Cost = Selling Price × (1 – rate of profit)

Substituting in the above equation, we have

Cost = $12,000 × (1 – .20) = $12,000. × .80 = $9,600

We can do the same for the second example. However, the cost is *more* than the selling price because the property was sold for a loss. If the selling price is 100%, then the cost would have to be 100% plus the rate of loss and would be represented in the equation by *1 + rate of loss*. The formula then becomes

Cost = Selling Price × (1 + rate of loss)

Using the information from the second example above, we can substitute and find

Cost = $6,000 × (1 + .10) = $6,000. × 1.10 = $6,600.

Finding Selling Price

In this case, selling price is the base B and we use the same percentage formula for finding base, $B = P/R$.

Example:

What was the selling price of a commercial property if it was sold at a profit of $6,000 representing 15% of the selling price?

Solution:

$B = P/R = \$6,000/.15 = \$40,000$

The method of finding selling price when only the cost and percent of profit or loss is given is similar to finding cost when profit and loss are based on cost. If selling price is 100% or 1, then the cost is equal to selling price minus profit, or, 100% – percent of profit. And, in the case of loss, cost is equal to selling price plus loss, or, 100% + percent loss. Using these relationships accordingly, we derive the equations:

$$\text{Selling Price} = \frac{\text{Cost}}{(1 - \text{rate of profit})} \text{ and}$$

$$\text{Selling Price} = \frac{\text{Cost}}{(1 + \text{rate of loss})}$$

Example:

If a property cost $24,000, what must it sell for to make a 20% profit on selling price?

Solution:

$$\text{Selling Price} = \frac{\$24,000}{(1 - .20)} = \frac{\$24,000}{.80} = \$30,000$$

Example:

What did the above property sell for if the sale resulted in a 20% loss on selling price?

Solution:

$$\text{Selling Price} = \frac{\$24,000}{(1 + .20)} = \frac{\$24,000}{1.20} = \$20,000$$

COMPARISONS AND CONVERSIONS

In comparing profit and loss based on cost with profit and loss based on selling price, it can be seen that the percent of profit or loss will vary according to the method used.

Where profits are concerned, the percent of selling price is smaller than the percent of cost. Where losses are concerned, the percent of selling price is larger than the percent of cost.

From common business practice we know that a profit of 100% on cost is equal to a profit of 50% on selling price. This is obtained mathematically by using the ratio of the percent of profit or loss by one method to the base of the other method in terms of percent of the first method.

For instance, the profit of 50% on selling price is found by using 100% profit on cost as the ratio numerator and using percent selling price *in terms of cost* (100% of cost plus percent of profit on cost) as the ratio denominator. Thus, the numerator is 100% and the denominator is 200% (100% + 100%). The ratio appears as $\frac{100\%}{200\%}$ or $\frac{1}{2}$, which equals .50, or 50% of selling price.

To avoid confusion and lengthy formulas, the procedures can be summarized in the following statements:

1. To change percent of profit on selling price to percent of profit on cost, *divide the rate of profit on selling price by 1 minus the rate.*

Example:

A 40% profit on selling price is equal to what percent profit on cost?

Solution:

$$\text{Percent profit on cost} = \frac{.40}{1-.40} = \frac{.40}{.60} = \frac{2}{3} = 66\ 2/3\%$$

Note that 1 − .40 (100% − 40%), or .60 (60%), is the *cost* in terms of selling price. That is, if the percent of profit on selling price is 40%, then the *cost* is 60% of the selling price.

2. To change percent of loss on selling price to percent of loss on cost, *divide the rate of loss on selling price by 1 plus the rate.*

Example:

A 20% loss on selling price is equal to what percent loss on cost?

Solution:

$$\text{Percent loss on cost} = \frac{.20}{1+.20} = \frac{.20}{1.20} = .16666 = 16\ 2/3\%$$

3. To change percent of profit on cost to percent of profit on selling price, *divide the rate of profit on cost by 1 plus the rate.*

Example:

A 25% profit on cost is equal to what percent profit on selling price?

Solution:

$$\text{Percent profit on selling price} = \frac{.25}{1+.25} = \frac{.25}{1.25} = .20 = 20\%$$

4. To change percent of loss on cost to percent of loss on selling price, *divide the rate of loss on cost by 1 minus the rate.*

Example:

What percent of loss on selling price is equal to a 33 1/3% loss on cost?

Solution:

Percent loss on selling price =

$$\frac{.33\ 1/3}{1-.33\ 1/3} = \frac{.33\ 1/3}{.66\ 2/3} = \frac{1}{2} = .50 = 50\%$$

PARTNERSHIPS AND PROFIT AND LOSS

The proper computation of division of profits or loss by partners constitutes a problem frequently encountered in the real estate business.

In a sole proprietorship there is little problem because the entire profit or loss belongs to the individual owner. A corporation shares profit or loss in accordance with the ratio of stock held by the stockholders.

Only in a partnership, by virtue of the endless number of possible arrangements that could be made, is it necessary to define the method of distribution upon formation of the partnership. It should be noted that unless the partnership contract states otherwise, and regardless of any differences in capital investment, experience, etc., profits and losses must be shared equally by all partners. The Articles of Partnership should therefore define the method to be used for distribution.

Our purpose is to familiarize the real estate professional with the mathematics involved in the more common methods of distribution and the proper computation of that method.

This section is not intended for replacement of any established accounting procedures. The following examples will show the most common methods of profit and loss sharing.

Division of Profits by Ratios

Because of the possible variations in capital invested, duties involved, business experience, and other matters, division of profit and loss is usually agreed to on the basis of a specific ratio. Ratio is the simplest way to divide proportionately, so the common methods used involve ratio.

Arbitrary Ratio

The partners agree to the ratio or proportion that they believe suits their particular situation best.

Example:

Three partners invest capital of $60,000, $40,000, and $20,000, and agree to divide the profits and losses on a ratio of 5:3:2. How is the profit of $12,000 divided?

Solution:

$$5 + 3 + 2 = 10 \text{ parts}$$

Partner #1 = 5/10 of profit = ½ × $12,000. = $6,000
Partner #2 = 3/10 of profit = .3 × $12,000. = $3,600
Partner #3 = 2/10 of profit = .2 × $12,000. = $2,400

Example:

Two partners agree that profit and loss will be divided on a fixed ratio of 30% and 70%. How is a profit of $15,680 divided?

Solution:

Partner #1 = 30% of $15,680. = .30 × $15,680. = $4,704
Partner #2 = 70% of $15,680. = .70 × $15,680. = $10,976

Ratio of Capital Invested

In this method the division of profit and loss is based strictly on the ratio of each partner's capital investment to the total investment. The investment might vary each year, or at other times, thereby changing the ratio and a new computation of ratio would be necessary before division is made.

Example:

Partner A invests $9,000 and Partner B invests $11,000 to the business. Profits are to be divided according to the ratio of capital invested. At the end of the first year, how do they divide a profit of $5,460?

Solution:

Total capital investment = $9,000 + $11,000 = $20,000

$$\text{Partner A's share} = \frac{\$9,000}{\$20,000} \times \$5,460. = \$2,457$$

$$\text{Partner B's share} = \frac{\$11,000}{\$20,000} \times \$5,460. = \$3,003$$

Example:

If, in the above example, an additional $4,000 is invested by Partner A in the second year, how would they divide a $4,200 profit?

Solution:

Total capital invested = $13,000 + $11,000 = $24,000

$$\text{Partner A's share} = \frac{\$13,000}{\$24,000} \times \$4,200 = \$2,275$$

$$\text{Partner B's share} = \frac{\$11,000}{\$24,000} \times \$4,200 = \$1,925$$

Ratio of Average Investment

An investment does not have to be made for a full year as was done in the previous method. Arrangements are sometimes made to enable partners to increase or decrease their investments during the year. The division of profit or loss is then done in ratio to their *average investments.*

The average investment can be computed for days or months. Months are generally used and taken according to the nearest first of the month. The computation is done by using *dollar-month products* (or dollar-day products).

The product of the number of dollars invested (or withdrawn) times the number of months invested equals the dollar-months. The ratio is then established computing each partner's dollar-month product to the total dollar-month product.

Example:

Partners A and B began the year with an investment of $8,000 each. On May 1, A invested an additional $3,000 and B invested an additional $2,000. On July 1, B withdrew $4,000 and on September 1, A invested an additional $2,000. How is a profit of $4,500 divided at the end of the year?

Solution:

Partner A invested $8,000 for 12 months, $3,000 for 8 months, and $2,000 for 4 months, or

$$\begin{aligned}
\$8,000 \times 12 \text{ months} &= 96,000 \text{ dollar-months} \\
\$3,000 \times 8 \text{ months} &= 24,000 \text{ dollar-months} \\
\$2,000 \times 4 \text{ months} &= \underline{8,000 \text{ dollar-months}} \\
\text{Total} &= 128,000 \text{ dollar-months}
\end{aligned}$$

Partner B invested $8,000 for 12 months, $2,000 for 8 months, and *withdrew* $4,000 for 6 months, or

$$\begin{aligned}
\$8,000 \times 12 \text{ months} &= 96,000 \text{ dollar-months} \\
\$2,000 \times 8 \text{ months} &= 16,000 \text{ dollar-months} \\
(\pm\$4,000) \times 6 \text{ months} &= \underline{(-24,000) \text{ dollar-months}} \\
\text{Total} &= 88,000 \text{ dollar-months}
\end{aligned}$$

Total dollar-months = 128,000 + 88,000 = 216,000

$$\text{Partner A's share} = \frac{128,000}{216,000} \times \$4,500 = \$2,667$$

$$\text{Partner B's share} = \frac{88,000}{216,000} \times \$4,500 = \$1,833$$

Other Methods

Another method of division of profits commonly used is the payment to each partner of interest on his investment prior to profit or loss distribution. The interest, of course, is paid out of profits, thus leaving a smaller profit to be divided. The computations involving interest are covered in Chapter 1.

Various combinations of the above methods can be used and the arrangements that can be made for division of profit and loss are almost unlimited. Although we have used division of profit only in our examples, it is obvious that division of losses is computed in the same manner.

RESIDENCE REPLACEMENT RULE ON PROFIT AND LOSS

Profit or loss sometimes plays a role in the IRS tax problems of a client and the real estate professional should have a basic understanding of the IRS "Residence Replacement Rule."

The rule is applied when a principal residence is sold and a replacement is purchased within 18 months before or after the sale. In the case of new home construction, the time allowance is 24 months.

If the replacement home costs *more* than the adjusted sales price of the former home, the total tax on the profit is deferred until a home is sold without purchase of a replacement.

Example:

A home is bought originally for $32,500 and sold for $52,000 to buy a new home for $75,000. What is the taxable profit?

Solution:

Profit = $52,000 - $32,500 = $19,500

The tax on the profit is deferred because the new home costs more than the sales price of the old home.

The deferred profit of $19,500 is deducted from the cost of the replacement home to arrive at an adjusted cost of $55,500 ($75,000 - $19,500 = $55,500) on the replacement home. If and when it is sold, the *adjusted cost* of $55,500 will be used to obtain a new profit or loss, thus carrying over the previous untaxed profit. The deferment and adjustments continue until a replacement home is *not* purchased.

Example:

In the above example, if the replacement home costing $75,000 is sold a few years later for $85,000 without purchase of another replacement home, on how much profit must taxes be paid?

Solution:

Cost basis of $75,000 home is $55,500
Taxable profit = $85,000 – $55,500 = $29,500

If the replacement home costs *less* than the adjusted sales price of the former home, tax is due on the profit *up to the difference in prices of the two homes.* If the difference in prices of the two homes is less than the profit, the tax on the difference is due and the balance of profit is deferred and used to lower the cost basis of the new home. If the difference in prices of the two homes is *more* than the profit, the taxes on the total profit are due.

Example:

A home is bought originally for $32,500 and sold for $52,000. A replacement home is bought for $43,000. How much of the profit is taxable now and what is the adjusted cost basis of the replacement home?

Solution:

Profit on first home = $52,000 – $32,500 = $19,500
Difference in prices = $52,000 – $43,000 = $9,000

Balance of profit = $10,500

The *difference in prices* is taxable now and the *balance of profit* is used to reduce the cost basis of the replacement home to $32,500 ($43,000 – $10,500 = $32,500).

If the replacement home had cost $30,000 instead of $43,000, the entire profit of $19,500 on the first home would have been taxable *now* because the difference in prices between the old home and the replacement home would have been $22,000, which is *more* than the profit.

Losses on the sale or exchange of personal residences are not tax-deductible and do not affect the cost basis of the replacement home.

6

A Simplified Approach to Insurance,
Taxes and Proration

To prorate means to divide or assess *pro-rata* or to divide proportionately. Proration is a term used almost exclusively in real estate. It is the apportionment of certain financial responsibilities of the property as of the date of closing of the transaction between buyer and seller. The items usually adjusted at the closing include insurance, taxes, and interest on a mortgage.

In order to understand the computations involved in prorating, it is necessary to understand the computation of the items to be prorated.

UNDERSTANDING FIRE INSURANCE

Practically all property today is insured against loss by fire and other damages. Mortgagees require that their interests be covered by adequate insurance. A buyer should also have his interests covered by insurance in case of a loss prior to settlement or closing.

For the past two decades, package policies (Homeowner's and Multi-Peril) have replaced many of the basic fire insurance policies. The terminology, however, is basically the same and the mathematical computations for value, premiums, cancellation, and proration are applicable to either.

Finding Premiums, Rates, and Values

The total cost of a policy for a specified period (term) is called the *premium*. This can be paid on an annual or a three year basis. The premium is determined by multiplying a *rate* by a specific amount of insurance called the *face of the policy*. The rate is usually established on the basis of a certain cost per $100 of insurance.

The various rates are determined by rating bureaus in different regions throughout the country. In the case of package policies, premiums are found directly from published tables, incorporating all the varied rates for the coverages involved, in order to simplify premium computation. (Rate-making is a complicated procedure involving the mathematics of probability and statistics and will not be approached in this chapter.)

The basic formula for premium computation is

Premium = Rate × Amount of Insurance

Rate is usually expressed as a cost per $100 and for simplicity of computation can be written in the formula as a ratio. For instance, a rate of 25 cents per $100 can be written as $\dfrac{\$.25}{\$100}$.

Example:

A property is insured for $15,000 at a rate of 32 cents per $100 for one year. What is the annual premium?

Solution:

$$\text{Premium} = \text{Rate} \times \text{Amount}$$
$$\text{Premium} = \frac{.32}{100} \times \$15,000 = \$48.00$$

Many insurance companies allow a discount on the premium if it is paid for 3 years in advance. The usual discount is 10% of the premium. To find the 3 year premium, use the factor 2.7 (10% of 3 = .3, and 3 − .3 = 2.7), and multiply 2.7 times the annual premium. The 3 year premium in the above example would be

$48. annual × 2.7 = $129.60, rounded-off to $130

To change the formula *to find rate,* divide the basic formula P = R × A on each side by A and the result is the formula for rate,

$$\text{Rate} = \frac{\text{Premium}}{\text{Amount}}$$

The rate thus found is rate per $1 and must be multiplied by 100 to find the rate per $100.

Example:

Find the rate per $100 if $10,000 of insurance costs $40 annually.

Solution:

$$\text{Rate} = \frac{P}{A} = \frac{\$40}{\$10,000} = .004$$

Therefore, rate per $100 = .004 × 100 = $.40

Using the derivation of the basic formula *to find amount of insurance,* the formula is changed to

$$\text{Amount} = \frac{\text{Premium}}{\text{Rate}} \quad \text{or} \quad A = \frac{P}{R}$$

Example:

A property is insured at a premium of $49 per year. If the rate is 35 cents per $100, for how much is the property insured?

Solution:

$$A = \frac{P}{R} = \frac{\$49}{\dfrac{.35}{100}} = \$49 \times \frac{100}{.35} = \$14,000$$

The amount of insurance carried is rarely the actual value of the property insured. A loss does not usually involve a *total* loss so the tendency for the insured, in order to save on premium costs, is to carry less insurance than the insurable value. Insurance companies have developed the principle of *coinsurance* to take care of this contingency.

Coinsurance and Contributing Insurance

Coinsurance is the obligation of the insured to share in the losses. A coinsurance clause is used in practically all fire insurance policies with the exception of the standard dwelling policy. The purpose of the clause is to enforce on the insured the amount of insurance upon which a certain rate is based. (Rates are usually predicated on full insurance to value.) The clause states that the insured must carry at least a certain percentage (usually 80%) of insurance to value or he becomes a coinsurer. If a loss is sustained, he will only be paid in the *proportion* that the amount of insurance taken bears to the insurance required, up to the face of the policy, or amount of actual loss, whichever is smaller.

The formula for computing amount of loss paid (settlement) is

$$\text{Settlement} = \text{actual loss} \times \frac{\text{insurance carried}}{\text{insurance required}}$$

Example:

A $10,000 insurance policy with an 80% coinsurance clause is carried on a property valued at $20,000. A fire causes damages of $4,000. How much does the insurance company pay on the loss?

Solution:

$$\text{Insurance required} = 80\% \text{ of } \$20,000 = \$16,000$$

$$\text{Settlement} = \text{actual loss} \times \frac{\text{insurance carried}}{\text{insurance required}}$$

$$\text{Settlement} = \$4,000 \times \frac{\$10,000}{\$16,000} = \$2,500$$

Because insufficient insurance was carried to meet the 80% coinsurance requirement, only $2,500 of the $4,000 loss is paid. If more than the required amount of insurance is carried, the settlement is limited to the actual amount of the loss.

Example:

On an inventory of $30,000 of merchandise, insurance with an 80% coinsurance clause is carried for $28,000. If a fire loss of $10,000 occurs, how much is paid in settlement?

Solution:

Insurance required = 80% of $30,000 = $24,000.

Settlement = $10,000 $\times \dfrac{\$28,000}{\$24,000}$ = $11,666

Therefore, paid settlement = $10,000

Contributing Insurance is the spread of the risk with more than one insurance company. This is done for many reasons: a risk might be larger than a company is willing to insure and it will therefore be willing to share the risk with other companies; or, the insured might want to insure with several companies or agents for various personal or business reasons.

In the case of contributing insurance, *each company is liable only for the loss in the ratio that the amount of its policy bears to the total insurance carried.* The company pays only its proportionate share of the loss and in no case can the insured collect more than the face value of the policies. The contributing insurance ratio is expressed as the formula

$$\textbf{Company share of loss = Loss } \times \frac{\textbf{Amount of Policy}}{\textbf{Total insurance carried}}$$

Example:

A building was valued at $600,000 and insurance with an 80% coinsurance clause was carried with 3 companies. Company A carried $200,000, Company B carried $150,000, and Company C carried $180,000. A fire caused a loss of $200,000. For how much was each Company liable?

Solution:

Insurance required = 80% of $600,000. = $480,000.
Total insurance carried = $200,000 + $150,000
+ 180,000 = $530,000
Loss to be paid in full as requirements of coinsurance met.

$$\text{Company A pays} = \$200,000 \times \frac{\$200,000}{\$530,000} = \$75,472$$

$$\text{Company B pays} = \$200,000 \times \frac{\$150,000}{\$530,000} = \$56,604$$

$$\text{Company C pays} = \$200,000 \times \frac{\$180,000}{\$530,000} = \underline{\$67,924}$$

$$\text{Total paid} = \$200,000$$

Cancellation Rates

The insurance company or the insured can cancel a policy (within certain restrictions by law in some states). The method of determining the *earned premium* or what amount of premium the insurance company retains depends upon who cancels.

Pro-rata cancellation is used when the insurance company cancels a policy. By law, in most states, the company can only retain the exact pro-rata portion of the premium for the time the policy was in force.

In determining the pro-rata portion, the ratio of *exact* number of days in force to the *exact* number of days in the policy term is used. The balance must be returned to the insured if it has been paid in advance. The product of the pro-rata ratio times the term premium is the amount that can be retained by the insurance company.

Example:

A one year policy dated March 3 with a premium of $120 is cancelled pro-rata on October 14. What is the earned premium?

Solution:

March 3 to October 14 = 225 days

$$\text{Earned premium} = \$120 \times \frac{225}{365}$$

Earned premium = $73.97, rounded-off to $74

Short-rate cancellation is used when the insured cancels a policy, for whatever reason, prior to its expiration date. If an insured wants coverage for a shorter term than one year, the short-rate would apply to the time the insurance was in force.

Term

Policy In Force Days	% Prem. Earned 12 Mo. Term	Policy In Force Days	% Prem. Earned 12 Mo. Term	Policy In Force Days	% Prem. Earned 12 Mo. Term	Policy In Force Days	% Prem. Earned 12 Mo. Term
1	5	70–73	30	161–164	55	270–273	80
2	6	74–76	31	165–167	56	274–278	81
3–4	7	77–80	32	168–171	57	279–282	82
5–6	8	81–83	33	172–175	58	283–287	83
7–8	9	84–87	34	176–178	59	288–291	84
9–10	10	88–91	35	179–182	60	292–296	85
11–12	11	92–94	36	183–187	61	297–301	86
13–14	12	95–98	37	188–191	62	302–305	87
15–16	13	99–102	38	192–196	63	306–310	88
17–18	14	103–105	39	197–200	64	311–314	89
19–20	15	106–109	40	201–205	65	315–319	90
21–22	16	110–113	41	206–209	66	320–323	91
23–25	17	114–116	42	210–214	67	324–328	92
26–29	18	117–120	43	215–218	68	329–332	93
30–32	19	121–124	44	219–223	69	333–337	94
33–36	20	125–127	45	224–228	70	338–342	95
37–40	21	128–131	46	229–232	71	343–346	96
41–43	22	132–135	47	233–237	72	347–351	97
44–47	23	136–138	48	238–241	73	352–355	98
48–51	24	139–142	49	242–246	74	356–360	99
52–54	25	143–146	50	247–250	75	361–365	100
55–58	26	147–149	51	251–255	76		
59–62	27	150–153	52	256–260	77		
63–65	28	154–156	53	261–264	78		
66–69	29	157–160	54	265–269	79		

SHORT RATE TABLE

Computation of short-rate is done with tables prepared by the insurance companies. The tables allow for an additional percentage of premium to be charged as a penalty to the insured for cancelling or using less than the specified term of the policy. A typical one-year short-rate table for fire insurance is shown on page 107.

To compute the short-rate premium, take the percentage shown in the table opposite the number of days for which the policy is in force, and multiply it by the annual premium.

Example:

> A policy effective June 12 at an annual premium of $160 is cancelled short-rate on November 13. What is the earned premium?

Solution:

> June 12 to November 13 = 154 days
> From the table, 154 days = 53% of annual premium
>
> .53 X $160. = $84.80 = earned premium

SIMPLIFIED REAL ESTATE TAXES

Of the many forms of taxation, the only one we are concerned with here is real property tax, or real estate tax.* The tax may be imposed by state, county, or municipal government and is determined by use of a *tax rate*, expressed as a percent, in mills, or in dollars and cents.

The tax rate is obtained by dividing the total tax budget by the total assessed valuation of the taxable real estate in the political district.

The amount of tax collected on each piece of real property is determined by multiplying the tax rate by the assessed valuation of the real property. The assessed valuation of the property is a specified percentage of its appraised value (for tax purposes) and is called the *tax ratio*.

---

*The general distinction between real property and real estate is that real estate means the land and improvements attached thereto whereas real property includes all the rights involved in the ownership of the real estate.

Determining Tax Rates and Millage

The tax rate of a community or political district is found by the formula

$$\text{Tax Rate} = \frac{\text{Taxes to be collected}}{\text{Total Assessed Valuation}}$$

Example:

A municipality has a tax budget of $1,398,525 and the assessed valuation of the taxable real estate in the municipality is $60,425,300. What is the tax rate?

Solution:

$$\text{Tax Rate} = \frac{\$1,398,525.00}{\$60,425,300.00} = .0231446$$

The tax rate thus computed is a *decimal rate* that is a bit unwieldy and therefore must be shortened. The accepted rule is that tax rates are never *rounded-off* but for each digit dropped (regardless of how small), the remaining digit, or the last one to be kept, is raised by one. Of course, if the tax rate has few digits and no remainder, there is none to drop. There are various ways in which the tax rate can be expressed after some of the digits are dropped.

Expressions of Tax Rates

The most common method of tax rate expression is by *millage*. A mill is 1/10 of a cent ($.001). Ten mills therefore equal one cent. The above tax rate expressed as mills is 24 mills or 23.15 mills, depending upon how many decimal places are desired. A tax rate expressed in mills is called a *mill levy*.

The simple rule for changing *mills to cents* is to move the decimal point 3 places to the *left;* and, to change *cents to mills,* move the decimal point 3 places to the *right.* For example, 12 mills = $.012, 2.5 mills = $.0025, $.028 = 28 mills, etc.

In addition to millage, tax rates can be expressed as percents or in dollars and cents. The above tax rate, expressed as a percent to the thousandths place would be 2.315%. Following the rule for dropping digits, it would be 2.32% to the hundredths place, or 2.4% to the tenths place.

Tax rates in dollars and cents can be expressed either as a rate per $100 or $1,000 of assessed valuation. In the foregoing example, multiply the tax rate by 100 to obtain $2.32 per $100 of assessed valuation or multiply by 1,000 to obtain $23.15 per $1,000 of assessed valuation.

The formula for finding tax rate can be applied to finding the tax rate of an individual property.

Example:

What is the tax rate on a property if its assessed valuation is $10,000 and the real estate tax due is $370?

Solution:

$$\text{Tax Rate} = \frac{\text{Tax}}{\text{Assessed valuation}} = \frac{\$370}{\$10,000} = .037$$

The tax rate is 37 mills or $3.70 per $100 of assessed valuation.

Finding Assessments

The assessed valuation of real property is determined by a tax appraiser or assessor. According to area custom, the assessor will make either a direct valuation for assessment on the property, or use a current market value appraisal with a specified tax ratio (usually 25% to 60%) to determine assessed valuation. If a property is appraised at $25,000 market value, a tax ratio of 50% would result in an assessed valuation of $12,500 for tax purposes. Mathematical computations used for appraising and assessing are covered in Chapter 12.

By rearranging the formula for tax rate when tax and tax rate are known, a formula for finding Assessed Valuation can be derived. The formula becomes

$$\text{Assessed Valuation} = \frac{\text{Tax}}{\text{Tax Rate}}$$

Example:

The real estate tax on a property is $287.50 and the tax rate is 23 mills. What is the assessed valuation of the property?

Solution:

$$\text{Assessed Valuation} = \frac{\$287.50}{.023} = \$12,500$$

Because assessed valuation is a percentage of appraised value, use is made of the standard percentage formula $B = P/R$ to find the appraised value. The appraised value is the base B, assessed valuation is the percentage P, and tax ratio is the rate R. By substitution,

$$\textbf{Appraised Value} = \frac{\textbf{Assessed Valuation}}{\textbf{Tax Ratio}}$$

If the tax ratio in the above example is 40% (assessment = 40% of appraised value), by substitution we find

$$\textbf{Appraised Value} = \frac{\$12,500}{.40} = \$31,250$$

Finding Taxes Due

It is obvious that the tax due is the product of assessed valuation and tax rate, and the formula for tax due, by derivation, is

$$\textbf{Tax} = \textbf{Assessed Valuation} \times \textbf{Tax Rate}$$

Example:

How much tax is due on a property assessed at $8,750 if the tax rate is 3.243%

Solution:

3.243% = $.03243 per dollar of assessed valuation
Tax = $8,750 × $.03243 = $283.76

Any of the various expressions of tax rate could have been used to solve the above example. The percent as given, 3.243%, used as a decimal is .03243 and if multiplied by $8,750, results in the same answer, $283.76.

Example:

The appraised market value of a property is $36,500. The tax rate is $4.63 per $100 of assessed valuation. If the property is assessed at 55% of its appraised value, what is the tax payment?

Solution:

$$\text{Assessed valuation} = 55\% \text{ of } \$36,500$$
$$= .55 \times \$36,500 = \$20,075$$
$$\text{Tax rate} = \$4.63 \text{ per } \$100 = \frac{\$4.63}{\$100} = .0463$$
$$\text{Tax} = \$20,075. \times .0463 = \$929.48$$

COMPUTING PRORATION

Prorations for insurance premiums, utilities, real estate taxes, and existing mortgage interest are generally made using the *statutory year* (30 days per month and 360 days per year). For prorations of less than a month, the actual number of days is used. Prorations of interest on *new mortgages* are computed using *exact time.*

Prorations are made up to and *including* the day of settlement. The buyer therefore becomes responsible on the day *after* settlement for items that are prorated between buyer and seller. Items prorated for the buyer only become the responsibility of the buyer as of the day of settlement. Credits to the buyer include any items owed, but not paid, by the seller. The seller receives credit for items that have been prepaid.

Insurance Prorations

When a policy is transferred or assigned to the buyer, he must credit the seller with the unearned premium remaining on the policy from the day of settlement to the expiration date of the policy. This is done on a *pro-rata* basis.

The procedure is to find the unused time remaining on the

APPROACH TO INSURANCE, TAXES AND PRORATION   113

policy and multiply the ratio for unused time to total term of the policy by the total premium. The result thus found will be the credit due the seller for the unused premium. This can be shown by formula as

$$\text{Credit Due} = \frac{\text{Unused time in days}}{\text{Policy term in days}} \times \text{Total Policy Premium,}$$

where unused time = Expiration Date minus Settlement Date

Example:

A one year policy expiring on December 5 is transferred to the buyer at settlement on August 18. The premium is $130. How much is credited to the seller?

Solution:

	Month	Day		Month	Day
Unused Time =	12	5	=	11	35
(Statutory)	-8	18	=	-8	18
			=	3 months	17 days

The unused time is 3 months and 17 days for a total of 90 (3 X 30) + 17, or 107 days of unearned premium.

$$\text{Credit Due} = \frac{107}{360} \times \$130. = \$38.638, \text{ rounded-off to } \$38.64$$

Note: Always compute to three decimal places until the final re-result, then round-off.

If the policy is for more than a one year term, divide the premium by the policy term and find the premium due for each year.

Example:

Settlement date is June 15, 1977. A Homeowner's policy expiring on November 8, 1979 with a prepaid 3 year premium of $450 is to be assigned to the buyer. How much of the premium will be credited to the seller at settlement?

Solution:

Year	Month	Day		Year	Month	Day
1979	11	8	=	1979	10	38
-1977	6	15	=	-1977	6	15
				2	4	23

Unused Time = 2 years 4 months 23 days = 2 years 143 days

Premium each year = $\dfrac{\$450}{3}$ = $150.

Credit due for 2 years = $300.

Credit due for 143 days = $\dfrac{143}{360}$ × $150. = $49.583

Total credit due = $300.00 + $59.58 = $359.58

Tax Prorations

Because settlement or closing rarely occurs on the date that taxes are due, proration of taxes is practically always required at settlement. Tax due dates vary considerably so the date for payment of taxes must be known.

Sometimes the actual tax for the current year will not be known. In that case, the tax amount for the previous year is used for the computation.

There are several methods in use for prorating taxes. One common method uses the ratio of the number of tax days for which the seller or buyer will receive a credit to days in the year (360). This ratio multiplied by the annual tax will result in the tax proration for the number of tax days used.

Example:

Taxes on an apartment building amounting to $1,560 were paid when due on May 1, 1977. The building was sold and settlement held on November 15, 1977. How much is credited to the seller?

Solution:

Because taxes were prepaid, the seller will receive a credit for the period November 16, 1977, to May 1, 1978. (Seller is responsible for taxes on November 15.)

Subtract to find total tax days:

1978	5	1	=	1977	16	31
-1977	11	16	=	-1977	11	16

Tax days = 5 mo. 15 days = 165 days

Tax Proration = $\dfrac{165}{360}$ × $1,560. = $714.999 = $715.

In the above example, the taxes were prepaid and the seller received a credit (buyer received a debit). In the case where the taxes have *not* been paid for the year, the buyer will receive a credit for the period of time for which the seller owes the taxes. It is necessary then to subtract the tax due date from the settlement date. However, because the settlement date *must* be included, one day is added to the difference in days. (Note that in the preceding example it was not necessary to add one day because the minuend of May 1, 1978 was the next tax due date and was not included in the total tax days credited.)

Example:

Taxes due on a property July 1, 1976, amounting to $940 have not been paid. The property is sold and the transaction is closed on January 20, 1977. What credit does the buyer receive?

Solution:

Add one day to January 20, 1977 before subtracting:

1977	1	21	=	1976	13	21
-1976	7	1	=	-1976	7	1

Tax days = 6 mo. 20 days = 200 days

$$\text{Tax Proration} = \frac{200}{360} \times \$940. = \$522.222 = \$522.22$$

Buyer will receive a credit (and seller a debit) of $522.22 because the seller owes that amount of tax for the period July 1, 1976 to January 20, 1977.

Another common method of prorating taxes is becoming more widely accepted and used now because of the Truth-in-Lending Act (Regulation Z), and The Real Estate Settlement Procedures Act (RESPA). The disclosure and settlement statements required by the Acts list all settlement charges including taxes. The taxes are specified on a *monthly* basis. Because the monthly tax *must* be computed, it is advantageous to use the monthly basis for prorating taxes.

In this method the annual tax is divided by 12 to find the monthly tax. The daily tax is then found by dividing the monthly by 30. Once these taxes have been found, the appropriate time element in terms of months and days must be computed. The number of months computed is multiplied by the monthly tax and the number of days is multiplied by the daily tax. The sum of the two will be the tax proration to be credited.

In order to compare the two methods, the preceding example will be used again with the monthly method.

Example:

Same information as the preceding example.

Solution:

By subtraction, the time element was found to be 6 months and 20 days.

Monthly Tax = $940. ÷ 12 = $78.333
Daily Tax = $78.333 ÷ 30 = $2.611
Multiply: 6 months X $78.333 = $469.998
          20 days   X $ 2.611 = +$52.220
          Tax Proration = Sum = $522.218 = $522.22

Mortgage Interest Prorations

RESPA, as implemented in conjunction with Regulation Z, requires that all prepaid finance charges be listed both on the Advance Disclosure of Costs and on the Statement of Actual Costs.

Prorated mortgage interest is an essential part of the Prepaid Finance Charge and is used to compute the Annual Percentage Rate (APR) of the mortgage loan.

The *daily rate* of interest to be charged by the lender from the date of settlement to the first day of the following month is also usually shown on the various forms and can be used to compute the mortgage interest proration.

Daily interest is found by computing the interest for one day on the principal amount of the mortgage at the specified mortgage rate (see Chapter 1). The mortgage interest proration is the product of the daily interest multiplied by the number of days from settlement (including date of settlement) to the first day of the following month.

Example:

Find the mortgage interest proration on a mortgage of $15,200 at 9¼% if settlement is on August 18.

Solution:

$$\text{Daily Interest} = \frac{\$15,200. \times .0925}{365} = \$3.852 = \$3.85$$

Exact Time from August 18 to September 1 = 14 days
(September 1 is not counted because it will be the
first day of the new interest period.)
Mortgage Interest Proration = $3.85 × 14 days = $53.90

Accurate Interest was used in the above example and is used in all cases of interest proration on *new mortgages. Statutory Time* is used for computing mortgage interest prorations when real estate is transferred subject to an existing mortgage.

Because interest on existing mortgages accrues prior to the payment due date, the seller must credit the buyer for interest accrued but not yet due on the mortgage. A monthly mortgage payment of principal and interest due September 1 will include interest on the principal balance remaining for the month of August. If settlement for the property occurs during the month of August, the buyer will make a mortgage payment on September 1 and his payment will include interest accrued for the entire month of August. He must therefore be *credited* with the interest accrued during that portion of the month for which he was not the owner.

Example:

A home is purchased subject to an existing mortgage. Settlement is on July 16 and the mortgage balance after payment on July 1 was $18,600. Interest on the mortgage is 8%. How much is the mortgage interest proration credited to the buyer?

Solution:

Actual number of days from July 1 to July 16 including *both* days = 16 days.

$$\text{Daily interest} = \frac{\$18,600 \times .08}{360} = \$4.133$$

Mortgage interest proration = $4.133 × 16 days
$$= \$66.128 = \$66.13$$

7

Understanding Figures and
Linear Measure

DESCRIPTION OF LINEAR
MEASUREMENTS

Linear measurement is used to determine the distance between two points on the surface of the earth. All real property has specified boundaries and the determination of such boundaries must be exact. The boundaries are established by linear measurements in specified directions to specific points.

The determination of the boundaries for a parcel of real estate is done by *surveying,* wherein various instruments are used to measure the lengths and determine the exact locations of the points. The lines and points are mapped and, once determined, are transcribed into written language and become the legal description of the property. (See Chapter 8)

Even though the earth is actually a spheroid, linear measurements of land are made assuming a horizontal plane surface. Because of the relatively short distances involved, curvature of the earth is not considered, although there will be some degree of error. Geodetic surveys of extensive areas do consider curvature. These will rarely be

encountered in normal real estate transactions and, therefore, will
not be discussed in this book.

The Units of Linear Measurement

Linear measure consists of linear units used to measure distances along straight lines. In the United States and Great Britain the
linear unit most commonly used is the foot, and the unit of area is
the acre, which is 43,560 sq. ft. The metric system, which is in common usage throughout the remainder of the world, uses the meter as
its linear unit.

The metric system will ultimately be used in the United States
and is now in the process of introductory voluntary usage. The
United States Coast and Geodetic Survey uses the metric system in
all its surveys, although the published results of leveling are expressed
in feet. (See Appendix for full discussion of the metric system.)

The linear units of inches, feet, yards, and miles are in constant,
everyday use and, therefore, require little introduction here. We are
all familiar with the common *Table of Linear Measure* which lists

> 1 foot = 12 inches
> 1 yard = 3 feet = 36 inches
> 1 mile = 5,280 feet = 1,760 yards.

Because we are involved in land measure, we encounter the
basic unit of length used in all U.S. government land surveys and
known as the *Gunter's Chain*.

The Gunter's chain is 66 feet long and is divided into 100 *links*,
each of which is 0.66 ft., or 7.92 inches long. Although the actual
use of chains for linear measurement is obsolete, the chain unit of
length is still expressed by utilizing steel tapes graduated in chains
and links.

The chain unit of length has been retained because of its convenience in computing linear measurements in accordance with the
English system of feet and miles. A chain is 1/80 of a mile and, therefore, one mile equals 80 chains. It simplifies computations expressed
in acres because one acre equals ten square chains. The chain is
further broken down into *rods* (also called *perches*). The rod is 1/4
of a chain and it follows that four rods equals one chain. These measurements are added to the Table of Linear Measure and are sometimes called "Surveyors' Measure."

> 1 link = 7.92 inches or 0.66 ft.
> 1 chain = 100 links = 4 rods = 66 feet

1 rod   = 16½ ft. = 5½ yards
1 mile = 80 chains = 320 rods = 5,280 feet

Chain measurement is used extensively in the survey of public lands and farm land descriptions. Most other surveying operations today are done in units of feet and decimal parts of a foot. The real estate professional will encounter both methods at various times.

Another unit of linear measurement of real estate in the Southwestern part of the U.S. is the *vara*. Lengths of property boundaries are expressed in this unit in areas that came under the Spanish influence. The vara is *about* 33 inches long and its exact length will vary in different sections of the Southwest. Its use is limited and it is found mostly on older maps, plots, and descriptions of real property.

Horizontal Distance

The measurement of length must be done in the horizontal or *level* plane. Measuring length on a slope will not result in a true measurement because the horizontal distance will vary with the degree of slope. Therefore, the measurement is done as shown in Figure 7-1.

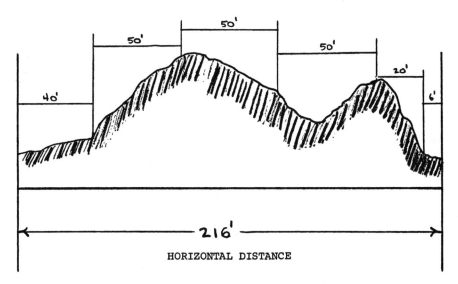

HORIZONTAL DISTANCE

FIGURE 7-1

A legal description of property will always relate the distance or lengths involved as horizontal distances, without the actual mention of the same. It is important to note that the configuration of the slope is not measured and only the horizontal distance or length is considered. If we were to pace off the ground in Figure 7–1, going up and down the hills, we would pace off the entire 216 feet at about 1/3 of the distance *short* of the true horizontal distance of 216 feet.

Another example of this is shown in Figure 7–2. The slope is straight but is not level, thus forming a triangle with the horizontal plane and the perpendicular elevation of the land above the level measurement. In this figure, the actual distance measured on the sloping ground is 200 feet but the horizontal distance is only 160 feet. Therefore, if the piece of ground were described as 200 feet in length, there would be an error of 40 feet in actual measurement.

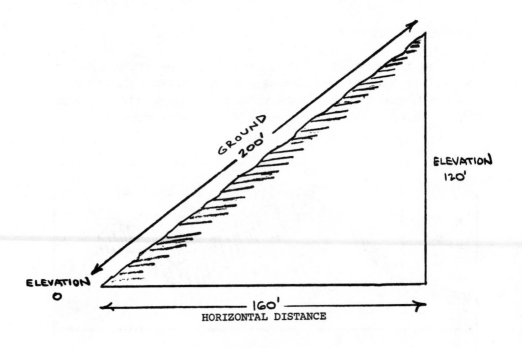

FIGURE 7-2

It can thus be seen that true linear measurement can only be done accurately on a level surface and, therefore, the measurement of land must be done only in reference to the horizontal or level plane.

The methods of obtaining correct measurements of horizontal distances are determined by surveying and are beyond the scope of this book.

Conversions and Computations

Once two points have been established, the distance between them (on a horizontal plane) can be measured using any of the units of length previously mentioned. The real estate professional will rarely be involved in actual measurement of land or buildings. He will, however, be required to understand measurements used in legal descriptions of real property, and on maps, plots, layouts, and blueprints.

Conversion of various units of length is the first requirement to an understanding of linear measurement. Later, these same conversions will be needed in determining areas and volumes.

Most linear distances are expressed in feet and *decimal* parts of a foot. The exceptions to this, of course, are in construction lay-outs and plans of structures. Decimal subdivisions of linear units are more convenient and easier to compute. They are therefore becoming more common, both in construction and trade usage.

Decimal and Fractional Parts

When computing measure problems, all measurements must be converted to the same unit of measurement. Feet cannot be multiplied by yards, inches cannot be multiplied by feet, and chains cannot be multiplied by links. Conversion to the larger unit of measurement is preferred because the computation will be in smaller numbers. If the smaller unit cannot readily be converted to a decimal part of the larger, computation in the smaller unit then becomes acceptable. In such a case, after completion of the computation, the smaller units would have to be converted again to the larger units. Because of the common usage and availability today of the mini-calculator, conversion of all units to decimal equivalents has become the accepted practice in measurement computations. Fractional parts, however, are still used in some cases and should not be neglected.

Example:

Express 4′6″ decimally.

Solution:

6″ is, by fractional part, 6/12 of a foot.
6/12 = 1/2 and the decimal equivalent of 1/2 is .5
Therefore, 4′6″ = 4.5′

The above can also be expressed fractionally as 4½′ and used for computation providing that all other units are also expressed fractionally.

Example:

Express 4′7″ decimally.

Solution:

7″ is 7/12 of a foot.
The decimal equivalent of 7/12 is .58333$\overline{33}$
Therefore, 4′7″ = 4.583′

(Reminder: The decimal equivalent is obtained by dividing the denominator into the numerator. In the above example, 7 divided by 12 equals. .58333333 and because it is a *repeating decimal* it is rounded-off to as many places as desired.)

If we were computing in fractional parts, the above example of 4′7″ would be changed to 4 7/12′ and, to calculate as a product or a quotient, would have to be changed to an improper fraction, or 55/12. This, however, becomes a bit unwieldy and is usually discouraged.

How to Convert Units

It can be seen from the foregoing that in order to change inches to feet, it is necessary to *divide the inches by 12,* the number of inches in a foot. From this we can conclude that:

To change a unit of measure into larger units, divide the smaller unit by the number of times it is contained in the larger unit.

To change inches to feet, divide inches by 12 (12″ = 1′)

Example:

How many feet are there in 112 inches?

Solution:

112 divided by 12 equals 9.333 feet.

Notice that this method automatically gives us the larger unit *and* the *decimal part* as the remainder. The alternate method would involve finding the number of feet (9′) and the number of inches as a remainder (4″). The answer using this method would be 9′4″, which is the same as (or sufficiently approximate to) 9.333′.

To change feet to yards, divide the number of feet by 3 (3 feet = 1 yard).

Example:

How many yards are there in 38 feet?

Solution:

38 divided by 3 equals 12.666 yards
(or 12 yards 2 feet, or 12 2/3 yards)

The same method is used for conversion of any of the units of linear measure:

Yards to miles (1,760 yards = 1 mile: divide by 1,760)
Links to chains (100 links = 1 chain: divide by 100)
Rods to chains (4 rods = 1 chain: divide by 4)
Chains to miles (80 chains = 1 mile: divide by 80)
Feet to chains (66 feet = 1 chain: divide by 66)

For conversion from larger units to smaller units the opposite operation (multiplication) is used and, therefore:

To change a unit of measurement into smaller units, multiply the larger unit by the number of smaller units it contains.

Changing feet to inches requires multiplying the number of feet by 12.

Example:

How many inches are contained in 46 feet?

Solution:

46 × 12 = 552 inches

To change chains to feet, multiply the number of chains by 66.

Example:

Eight chains equals how many feet?

Solution:

$$8 \times 66 = 528 \text{ feet}$$

Using the same procedures, it becomes a simple matter to change any of the units of linear measurement into smaller units.

THE DIRECTION OF A LINE

Measurement of length of a real property boundary line is meaningless unless the *direction* of that line is known. The subject of property descriptions such as Rectangular Survey and Metes and Bounds, covered in Chapter 8, assumes an understanding of line directions. Line directions in real estate are based on meridians, angles, and bearings.

Meridians

The earth is divided into *meridians* (lines of geographic longitude) which run north and south and converge at the poles. *True Meridians* converge at the exact north and south poles of the earth and are fixed in position. *Magnetic meridians* converge at the magnetic poles and vary in direction. Although used in mapping, the magnetic meridians will not be discussed further here. The true meridians determine the true north and south directions of property lines and are the meridians with which we are concerned.

For the purposes of legal property descriptions and plane surveying to the limited extent that would involve real property or small areas, an *assumed meridian* is used for convenience. This is used as a line of reference and is *assumed* to be in the general direction of the true meridian.

Meridians are used in the development of *grids*. A grid is a pattern of intersecting parallel lines on a map or plot used as a reference for locating points and directions of lines. All north-south lines in a grid are considered parallel to the meridian used as a reference, whether it is true or assumed, for that particular grid. These parallel lines are known as *grid meridians*.

The true meridians are the basis for the state grid systems (called the State Plane Coordinate Systems) in use in the United States. Control monuments, used to determine the true meridians, have been established by the federal agencies involved in land surveys in order to fix positions for mapping and land descriptions.

In addition to the monuments used for true meridians, other monuments erected for use in land descriptions and locations of boundaries include: *corner monuments,* to fix the position of the corners of a rectangular survey system; *control monuments* used in municipal surveys; *property monuments;* and *metes and bounds monuments.* These different types of land descriptions are covered in Chapter 8.

The Units of Angle Measurement

In the same way that linear measure consists of linear units to measure distances along straight lines, *angle measure* consists of the units of *degrees* to measure the space within two lines diverging from a common point called *the vertex.* The angle formed by the two lines increases as one line rotates away from the other line. A complete rotation of the line forms a circle.

The circle has been divided into 360 degrees. A half-circle (semi-circle) would contain 180 degrees. Each degree is further divided into 60 minutes and each minute into 60 seconds. The symbol for a degree is °, a minute is ′, and a second is ″. A measure of 12 degrees, 40 minutes, and 2 seconds would therefore be shown as 12°40′2″.

Azimuths and Measurement of Angles

If a line is drawn representing the north-south meridian and passing through point 0, a line rotating in a *clockwise* direction from north would, at any position, form an angle with the north meridian. The angle thus formed would measure from 0° to 360°. East would be represented by a 90° rotation, south by 180°, west by 270°, and north would be both 0° and 360°. Figure 7–3 shows a N-S meridian with various lines emanating from point 0 and the degrees that each line has formed. Line OB is 90° clockwise from north and therefore represents east.

An *azimuth* of a line is the number of degrees to the line measured from a N-S reference line. In Figure 7–3, line OA has an azimuth of 45°, OB of 90°, OC of 200°, and OD of 300°. The azimuth takes on the name of the reference line from which it is measured. If the line NS were a true meridian, the azimuths would be called *true azimuths*. If line NS were an assumed meridian, the azimuths would be *assumed azimuths,* and so on.

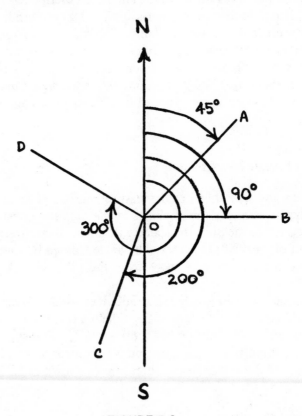

FIGURE 7-3

Bearing of a Line

A circle is divided into four parts by the directions north, south, east, and west. Each part is called a *quadrant* and contains 90°. Many property descriptions will use these quadrants as the basis for the direction of property lines.

A bearing angle is never greater than 90°. The bearing of a line gives the direction of the line relative to a reference meridian within its quadrant. The bearing is measured only *from* north or south and states whether it is measured *towards* east or west.

A line with a bearing of N40°E (called north 40° east) is measured 40° *from* north *towards* east. Likewise, a bearing of S40°E is measured 40° from south towards east.

Example:

In Figure 7–4, name the bearings of lines OA, OB, OC, and OD.

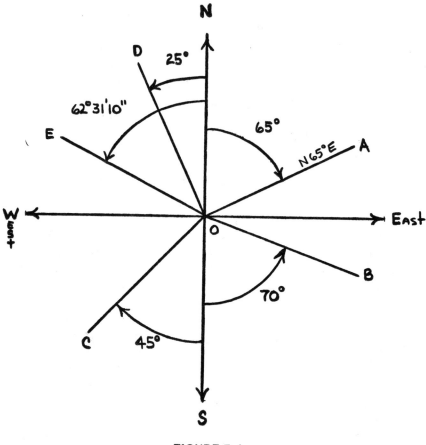

FIGURE 7–4

Solution:

Line OA measures 65° from north towards the east and would therefore be named N65°E.

Line OB measures 70° from south towards east and would therefore be named S70 E.

Line OC measures 45° from south towards west and would therefore be named S45 W.

Line OD measures 25° from north towards west and would therefore be named N25 W.

In addition to degrees, the bearings may be divided into minutes and seconds. Rarely does a bearing line measure an exact number of degrees. It will usually fall somewhere between the degrees and require the use of minutes. As previously mentioned, each degree contains 60 minutes. If the line falls between the measured minutes, the minute divisions of 60 seconds must be used. Bearing line OE in Figure 7–4 measures westward 62 degrees, 31 minutes, and 10 seconds from north. It is therefore designated as N62°31'10"W.

Rectangular Coordinates

A position is fixed on a grid by the intersection of a north-south line (vertical) and an east-west line (horizontal). Once a point has been determined, the perpendicular lines drawn through the point, or intersecting at the point, are called the *coordinates* of the point. Usually only the first quadrant, north to east, is used for locating coordinates. They are located by their distance and direction from the reference lines, which in the first quadrant would be the north and east lines.

Because the coordinate lines would be parallel to each of their reference lines and perpendicular to each other, they form a rectangle with the reference lines and are called *rectangular coordinates*. Coordinate locations are given by two numbers, the *first* being the distance from the north or vertical line in the easterly direction, and the *second* the distance from the east or horizontal line, in the northerly direction.

In Figure 7–5, the coordinates of point A are 3 and 2 (3,2), and the coordinates of point B are 5 and 6 (5,6). The points were located in order to determine the position of line AB.

Example:

Using Figure 7–5, name the coordinates of Points C and D.

Solution:

Point C is two units easterly and three units northerly. Coordinates = (2,3).

Point D is one unit easterly and five units northerly. Coordinates = (1,5)

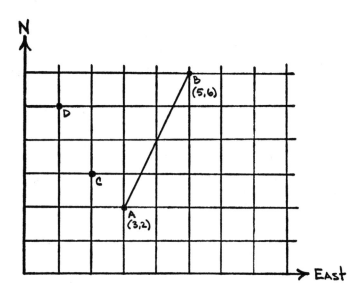

RECTANGULAR COORDINATES

FIGURE 7-5

MEASURING TO SCALE

A map, layout, plan, or blueprint cannot accurately represent the land, object, or structure unless it is drawn in exact proportion or ratio to the real object. This ratio is known as the *scale* of the drawing.

A *scale length* is the length of a segment in a scale drawing. A *real length* is the length of a segment in the actual or real object. *The scale is the ratio of scale length to real length. The first term of a scale is always the scale length and the second term is always the real length.*

A scale can be expressed in terms of length on the drawing in one unit of measurement and in terms of length of the real object in another unit of measurement. For instance, a scale may be expressed as 1 inch = 200 feet, or 1 inch = 2 miles. The scale can also be expressed as a direct ratio, such as 1:2000, or as a fraction, such as 1/2000. When expressed as a direct ratio or fraction, the units of measurement used for scale length and real length are the same. Therefore, 1/2000 is a scale of 1 *inch* on the drawing to 2000 *inches* on the real object. When a scale is expressed as a fraction, the fraction is referred to as the *representative fraction* because it represents the direct unit to unit measurement ratio.

$$\frac{\text{Scale Length}}{\text{Real Length}} = \text{Representative Fraction}$$

Example:

What is the representative fraction of a layout if it has a scale of $1'' = 10'$?

Solution:

The units of measurement must be the same, so $10'$ must be converted to inches.

$$1 \text{ foot} = 12 \text{ inches, and } 10 \times 12'' = 120''$$
$$\text{Representative fraction} = 1''/10' = 1/120$$

The numerator of the representative fraction must be stated as unity (1). If the scale were $\frac{1}{2}'' = 10'$, then the $\frac{1}{2}''$ must be expressed as $1''$.

Example:

Convert a scale of $\frac{1}{2}'' = 10'$ to its representative fraction.

Solution:

Change to the same units (inches):

$$\frac{\frac{1}{2}''}{10 \times 12''} = \frac{\frac{1}{2}''}{120''}$$

Multiply the numerator and denominator by the necessary equivalent fraction of 1 (multiplicative identity).

$$\frac{\frac{1}{2}''}{120''} \times \frac{2}{2} = \frac{1''}{240''}$$

Representative fraction = 1/240

The scale to which a map or drawing is made depends primarily on the purpose of the map or drawing, or the accuracy needed. Other factors considered are the largest real length needed to be represented and the necessary size of the drawing, or limitations of paper size. Using a smaller representative fraction (in value) allows for the representation of a larger area on the drawing. More of the real length can be shown on a scale of 1/5000 than on a scale of 1/5.

How to Find Scale or Real Length

The rules of proportion (see Appendix) are used for finding scale length or real length when only one is known.

Example:

If the scale on a drawing is $\frac{1}{4}'' = 10'$, what scale length represents a 30' real length?

Solution:

Let n = scale length and convert feet to inches.

The ratio $\dfrac{\text{Scale length}}{\text{Real Length}} = \dfrac{n}{360'' \ (30' \times 12'')}$

Representative fraction $= \dfrac{\frac{1}{4}''}{120''} \times \dfrac{4}{4} = \dfrac{1}{480}$

Thus, by proportion, $n/360'' = 1/480$, and

$$480 \times n = 360 \times 1$$
$$n = 360/480 = 3/4''$$

The same procedure would be followed to find real length if scale length is known.

Example:

What would the real length be if the scale length of a wall in a drawing is 3'' and the scale is $\frac{1}{4}'' = 1'$?

Solution:

Let n = the real length. Convert feet to inches.

The ratio $\dfrac{\text{Scale length}}{\text{Real length}} = \dfrac{3''}{n}$

Representative fraction $= \dfrac{\frac{1}{4}''}{12''} \times \dfrac{4}{4} = \dfrac{1}{48}$

Thus, by proportion, $3''/n = 1/48$, and

$$1 \times n = 3'' \times 48$$
$$n = 144'' = 12'$$

DESCRIPTIONS OF GEOMETRIC FIGURES

The preceding paragraphs have discussed the ideas of points and lines. By adding a third idea—space—we approach the basic concepts of geometry; that is, points, lines, and surfaces in space. Real estate and geometry have much in common; both deal with the fundamental elements of points, lines, and space.

The word "geometry," from the ancient Greeks, means "earth-measurement" and originally only dealt with land measurement. It later divided itself into two branches; *metric geometry,* involving measurement, and *nonmetric geometry,* involving form and space.

Our concern in real estate is not the geometry of form and space, but of measurement. We will therefore deal here with metric geometry and only touch on form and space as is necessary to understand the measurements of land and structures.

The basic geometric figures are those composed of *closed broken lines.* The term "closed" refers to a line that starts at a point and returns to the point without crossing itself. Figures created by these closed broken lines are called *polygons.* We are all familiar with the three-sided polygon called the *triangle.*

The triangle is the basic unit of metric geometry because it can be combined with other triangles to form different polygons. It is used as the basis for trigonometry and indirect measurement.

Many difficult-to-measure parcels of land can be divided into triangles to simplify measurement.

Triangulation is used by surveyors to determine locations.

Triangles are important in construction because of their rigidity; their shape cannot be changed regardless of the pressure applied to the sides.

Other polygonal structures do not have this utilitarian characteristic.

As mentioned above, the triangle has three sides and therefore has three angles. The sum of the angles of a triangle equals 180°. The *base* of a triangle is the side upon which it appears to rest. A *vertex* of a triangle is the point of intersection of any two sides.

Figure 7–6 shows a triangle (ABC) and its parts. The triangle shown is called a *right triangle* because it contains one angle of 90° (a right angle). The side opposite the right angle is called the *hypotenuse.* The other two sides are called the legs. Either leg is shorter in length than the hypotenuse. Other types of triangles include: an *equilateral triangle,* having three sides of equal length; an *isosceles triangle,* having two sides of equal length; and a *scalene triangle,* having three sides of unequal lengths.

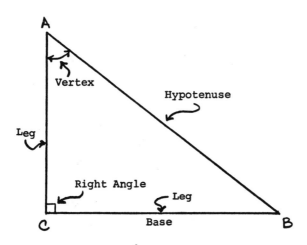

A RIGHT TRIANGLE

FIGURE 7–6

A *quadrilateral* is a four-sided polygon. These figures are also familiar to us and are shown in Figure 7–7. They are classified as follows:

A *parallelogram* is a quadrilateral having both pairs of opposite sides parallel.

A *rectangle* is a parallelogram with four right angles and opposite sides of equal length.

A *square* is a parallelogram with four sides of equal length and with four right angles.

A *rhombus* is a parallelogram with four sides of equal length.

A *trapezoid* is a quadrilateral with one, and only one, pair of parallel sides.

Other polygons with which we are familiar include the *pentagon* (5 sides), the *hexagon* (6 sides), and the *octagon* (8 sides). A regular polygon is any polygon with equal sides. A regular pentagon has 5 equal sides, a regular hexagon has 6 equal sides, and so on.

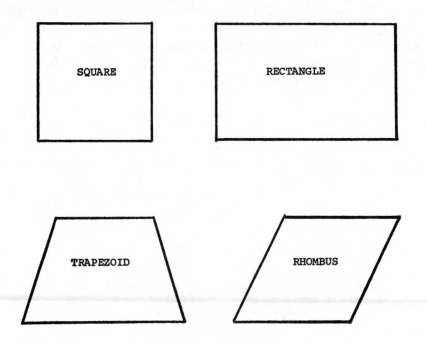

GEOMETRIC FIGURES

FIGURE 7-7

HOW TO FIND PERIMETERS

A *perimeter* is the total distance around a geometric figure. (*Peri* means around and *meter* means measure.) The perimeter of a polygon is the sum of the lengths of its sides.

If the definitions or basic concepts of each of the geometric figures is known, finding perimeter is simply a matter of applying the definitions to find a sum of the sides.

Example:

What is the perimeter of a square if one side measures 12 feet in length?

Solution:

A square, by definition, has four equal sides. Therefore, if one side equals 12 feet, then 4 times 12 feet will equal the sum of the sides.

$$4 \times 12' = 48' = \text{perimeter}$$

Formulas can be derived for perimeters by using the definitions of the figures. If **P** represents perimeter and *s* represents one side of a square, we can derive a formula for the above example by stating

P = s + s + s + s, or
P = 4s

The formula for finding the perimeter of a square will always be P = 4s.

A rectangle has equal opposite sides. If *l* represents the equal long sides or *length,* and *w* represents the equal short sides or *width,* then the perimeter of a rectangle is

P = l + w + l + w, or
P = 2l + 2w or, P = 2(l + w)

Note that length and width are not always the long and short sides respectively, but are used as examples in this case. However, the sides are always designated as *l* (length) and *w* (width) for finding perimeter.

Example:

A rectangular lot measures 112' × 64'. If a fence were to be erected completely around the lot, how many feet of fencing would be required?

Solution:

Perimeter = total fencing needed.

P = 2l + 2w
P = 2(112') + 2(64')
P = 224' + 128' = 352' of fencing

There are many varied and numerous types of triangles and it would be superfluous here to develop perimeter formulas for each type of triangle. Rather, we will designate each side of the triangle as a, b, or c. The designations should be in accordance with the name of the opposite angle, if such is also designated. For instance, side a is designated as the side opposite the designated angle A. The sum of the sides, or perimeter, would therefore be

$$P = a + b + c$$

Because this is simply a matter of adding the linear measures of each of the three sides to obtain their sum, an example is not necessary.

Any perimeter of any geometric figure can be determined by finding the sum of the measures of all the sides of the figure.

8

Application of Surface and Land Measure to Real Estate

POLYGONS, QUADRILATERALS AND REAL ESTATE

The application of surface and land measure to real estate involves finding the areas of various shapes, geometric figures, or combinations thereof. Quadrilaterals, as one of the basic polygonal figures discussed in Chapter 7, form the basis for most of the area measurement with which we are concerned. For ease in surveying, mapping, and subdividing, attempts are usually made to plot or plan divisions of land or property boundaries using a quadrilateral shape.

Shapes other than quadrilaterals, however, are used, or formed by necessity, in order to conform to natural boundary lines, land configuration, or legal requirements. The measurement of land area therefore requires not only computations for squares and rectangles, but for all other possible shapes.

It would be neither feasible nor desirable in this chapter to demonstrate the computations of area for all possible shapes. Proper usage of combinations of figures and some geometric imagination will allow for almost any possible configuration by using the computations we will describe here.

COMPUTATIONS OF AREAS

The number of times a unit of measure will fit *into* a geometric figure is known as *area* and is designated by square units of measure. A *square unit of measure* is the geometric square formed with each side equivalent to a *linear unit* of the measure. One square inch is shown in Figure 8–1. Each side of the square measures one inch and the total area is one *square* inch. Thus, length is a one dimensional measure whereas area is a two dimensional measure.

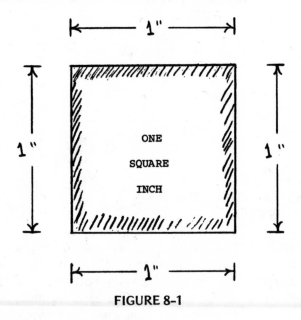

FIGURE 8–1

Areas of Rectangles and Squares

Computing the area of a square or the area of a rectangle are similar operations. Square area is found by multiplying the number of units on one side (length) by the number of units on the other side (width). The product would be the total number of square units contained in the figure (see Figure 8–2).

Because the sides of the rectangle or a square are perpendicular, the product represents the *exact* number of square units within the geometric figure. If the sides were not perpendicular, there would be some *partial* units inside and the product of length times width would not be exact. Therefore, the method of multiplying length times width will only be correct in the case of a rectangle or square.

From the above, it is obvious that the formula for finding the area of a rectangle, using l for length and w for width, is

$$A = l \times w, \text{ or } A = lw$$

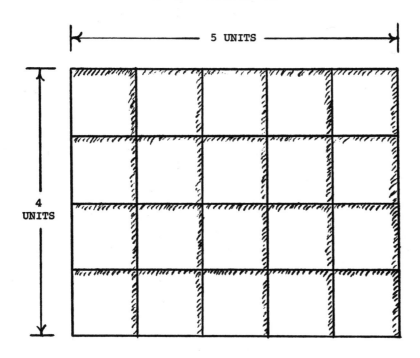

TOTAL AREA = 5 X 4 = 20 UNITS

FIGURE 8-2

Example:

What is the total area of a building lot that measures 112′ X 200′?

Solution:

$$A = lw$$
$$A = 200' \times 112'$$
$$A = 22{,}400 \text{ square feet}$$

Because all the sides of a square are of equal length, we need only know the length of one side in order to perform the multiplication of length times width. The area of a square, as stated above is

l X w. If all the sides are equal in length, however, we can designate each side as s, and of course, $l = s$ and $w = s$. The formula for the area of a square can then be derived as

A = s X s, and, more suitably, A = s^2

Example:

Tiles are to be laid on a square floor measuring 18' X 18'. How many square feet of tiles are needed?

Solution:

$$A = s^2$$
$$A = 18 \text{ X } 18$$
$$A = 324 \text{ square feet of tiles.}$$

The units that are multiplied must be the same linear units of measure. Inches cannot be multiplied by feet, and so on. Conversions to the same unit must be made as discussed in Chapter 7.

Example:

How many square feet of paving is needed to pave a driveway measuring 10'3" X 96'6"?

Solution:

$$10'3" = 10.25 \text{ feet}$$
$$96'6" = 96.5 \text{ feet}$$
$$A = lw = 96.5 \text{ X } 10.25$$
$$A = 989.125 \text{ square feet.}$$

The above answer can be changed to 989 1/8 square feet or rounded-off to 989 square feet.

To find the width or length of a rectangle if the area and only one of the dimensions is known, divide the area by the known dimension and the result (quotient) will be the other dimension.

Example:

A lot has an area of 11,040 square feet. If the frontage of the lot is 92', what is the depth?

Solution:

$$A = lw$$
$$11,040 = l \times 92'$$
$$\frac{11,040}{92} = l$$
$$120' = l, \text{ or depth of lot}$$

If the area of a square is known, the linear measurement of a side can be found by taking the *square root* of the area.

Area of a Parallelogram

In Chapter 7 we described a quadrilateral as a four-sided figure and a parallelogram as a quadrilateral whose opposite sides are parallel. Squares and rectangles are quadrilaterals or parallelograms in which all four angles are right angles.

If none of the angles are right angles however, we have a quadrilateral which can only be described as a parallelogram. (A rhombus is a parallelogram with four equal sides.) Figure 8–3 shows a parallelogram.

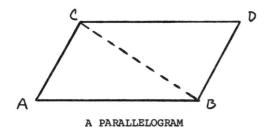

A PARALLELOGRAM

FIGURE 8-3

To find its area, we can use some geometric imagination and transform it into a rectangle. In Figure 8–4, if we draw a perpendicular line from C to the base of the parallelogram, we form a triangle ACE. We extend the base AB to F and draw another perpendicular, forming triangle BDF. If we were to imagine cutting off triangle ACE from the figure, we would find that it fits *exactly* into triangle BDF and the resulting figure is transformed into a rectangle CDFE. The area of a rectangle is *lw*. If we use *b* (base) to represent *l*, and *h* (height) to represent w, the area of the parallelogram can be formulated to

$$A = b \times h, \text{ or } A = bh$$

Height (h) is the perpendicular distance between the base and its opposite parallel side.

Although the area of a parallelogram has limited use in real estate, finding its area is necessary because of the additional geometric figures that can be created from it. By knowing the formula for the area of a parallelogram, we can derive a formula for finding the area of the ubiquitous triangle.

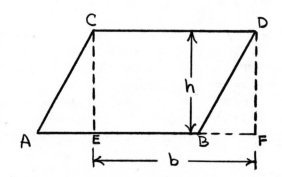

THE AREA OF A PARALLELOGRAM IS BASE X HEIGHT

FIGURE 8-4

Area of a Triangle

If a diagonal line is drawn in a parallelogram from one angle to its opposite angle, two triangles are formed. In Figure 8-3, the diagonal line CB divides the parallelogram into two triangles. One of these is shown in Figure 8-5. The triangles combined have the same area as the parallelogram and the triangles themselves have the same shapes and sizes. Therefore, their areas must be equal, and the area of each must be half of the area of the parallelogram. Since the area of a parallelogram is given by the product of the length of the base and the height of the parallelogram, the area of the triangle must be one half of this product, or $\frac{1}{2}bh$. The formula for the area of a triangle then, is

$$A = \frac{1}{2}bh$$

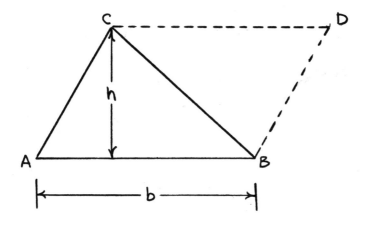

THE AREA OF A TRIANGLE IS HALF

THE AREA OF A PARALLELOGRAM OR

$$\frac{\text{base X height}}{2}$$

FIGURE 8-5

Example:

A triangular tract of land has a base of 65 yards and a height of 50 yards. How many square yards are contained in the tract?

Solution:

$A = \frac{1}{2}bh$
$A = \frac{1}{2}(65 \times 50) = \frac{1}{2}(3,250)$
$A = 1,625$ square yards

Although the above formula for area of a triangle is the one with which most real estate personnel are familiar, its usage is limited because the height (h) of a triangular tract of land is rarely known. Usually, the only dimensions of a triangular tract that are known are the linear dimensions of the sides or boundaries of the tract.

A formula, known as Hero's Formula, is useful for finding the area of a triangle when three sides are known. (The formula first appeared in the writings of Hero, a mathematician who lived in Alexandria about 125 B.C. and it is named for him.) The formula is frequently used in surveying and appraising. The proof, or derivation of the formula, would require many pages of explanation and therefore is presented here without derivation. It does require computation of square roots and, therefore, a review of such computations and square root tables can be found in the Appendix.

The area of a triangle whose sides are a, b, and c is given by the formula

$$A = \sqrt{s(s-a)\,(s-b)\,(s-c)}, \text{ where } s = \tfrac{1}{2}(a+b+c)$$

Note that a + b + c is also the perimeter of the triangle so it can also be stated that *s* equals half the perimeter of the triangle.

Example:

A tract of farm land forming a triangle has boundaries which measure 8, 15, and 17 rods. What is the area of the tract?

Solution:

$$s = \tfrac{1}{2}(a+b+c) = \tfrac{1}{2}(8+15+17) = 20$$
$$A = \sqrt{s(s-a)\,(s-b)\,(s-c)}$$
$$A = \sqrt{20(20-8)\,(20-15)\,(20-17)}$$
$$A = \sqrt{20(12)\,(5)\,(3)}$$
$$A = \sqrt{3{,}600}$$
$$A = 60 \text{ square rods}$$

Area of a Trapezoid

Another geometric figure formed by boundary lines is the trapezoid. The figure is the most common figure formed by most irregular lots. The trapezoid has two parallel sides (called bases) and two non-parallel sides. The height (h) is the perpendicular distance between the two bases. The formula for its area is derived in the same manner as the formula for the area of a parallelogram. The exception is that each side forms a separate and distinct triangle usually of a *different* shape and size than the other triangle. Figure 8–6 shows a typical trapezoid with the two bases designated b and B respectively.

The area of a trapezoid is found by taking ½ of the product of the linear unit measurement of the height and the sum of the linear measures of the bases. By formula, this is

$$A = \tfrac{1}{2}h(b + B)$$

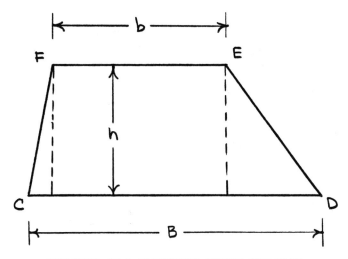

THE AREA OF A TRAPEZOID EQUALS ONE-HALF

THE HEIGHT TIMES THE SUM OF THE BASES.

FIGURE 8-6

Example:

An irregular lot is 150 feet on one of the parallel sides and 80 feet on the other. It is 50 feet wide. What is the area of the lot?

Solution:

The lot forms a trapezoid.

$$A = \tfrac{1}{2}h(b + B)$$
$$A = \tfrac{1}{2}(50)(150 + 80)$$
$$A = (25)(230)$$
$$A = 5{,}750 \text{ square feet}$$

As mentioned previously, the geometric figure formed by a parcel of land is not always a rectangle, triangle, or trapezoid. Areas of most parcels, however, can be computed by dividing the figure formed into geometric shapes and combinations of such shapes. The areas of the individual shapes are then added to give the total area involved.

Example:

Find the area of the irregular shaped lot ABCDE in Figure 8-7.

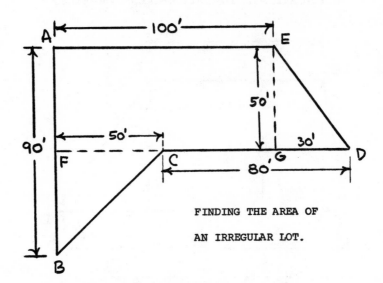

FINDING THE AREA OF

AN IRREGULAR LOT.

FIGURE 8-7

Solution:

The lot is divided into one rectangle and two right triangles by drawing perpendicular lines CF and EG. The dimensions of the various lines are either scaled from the plot or figured by deduction from the given measurements.

Rectangle AFGE:

$$A = lw = 100 \times 50 = 5,000 \text{ square feet}$$

Triangle BCF:

$$A = \tfrac{1}{2}bh = \tfrac{1}{2}(40 \times 50) = \tfrac{1}{2}(2,000) = 1,000 \text{ square feet}$$

Triangle DEG:

$$A = \tfrac{1}{2}bh = \tfrac{1}{2}(50 \times 30) = \tfrac{1}{2}(1,500) = 750 \text{ square feet}$$

Total Area = 5,000 + 1,000 + 750 = 6,750 square feet

Curved Boundaries and the Trapezoidal Rule

The method shown in the previous paragraph is limited to figures which are bounded by straight lines. If a figure is very irregular, as would be the case if it were adjacent to a stream or body of water, another system must be used because of the curved boundary.

Of course, more advanced methods are used when more than one boundary is curved or if portions of circles are involved. Such areas are measured by surveyors with the use of an instrument called the planimeter, and computations are done using trigonometry. Normal real estate transactions will not involve such complicated or detailed computations of area and they are therefore beyond the scope of this book.

Finding the approximate area of a figure with *one* curved boundary is common, however, and is of sufficient importance to be shown here.

An example of an area with a curved boundary is shown in Figure 8–8. To find its area, we divide line AB into any number of equal segments (or *common spacing*) of length x, and at the points of division draw perpendiculars (called *offsets*) to line AB and extend them to the curved boundary line. The irregular shape can now be considered to consist of a series of trapezoids.

The formula for the Trapezoidal Rule is

$$S = x\left(\frac{y_1 + y_n}{2} + y_2 + y_3 + y_4 + \ldots y_{n-1}\right)$$

wherein S is used (instead of A) for Area, x is the common spacing of the offsets, n is the number of offsets, y_1 is the first offset, with each offset numbered consecutively as $y_2, y_3, \ldots$, and y_n designating the last offset.

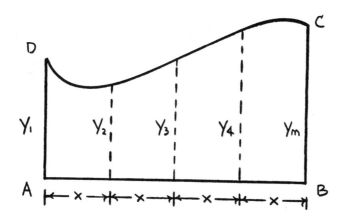

THE TRAPEZOIDAL RULE

FIGURE 8-8

Example:

Figure 8-9 shows a parcel of land bounded by the Delaware River, First Avenue, and two perpendiculars to First Avenue, designated AD and BC. What is the area of the parcel?

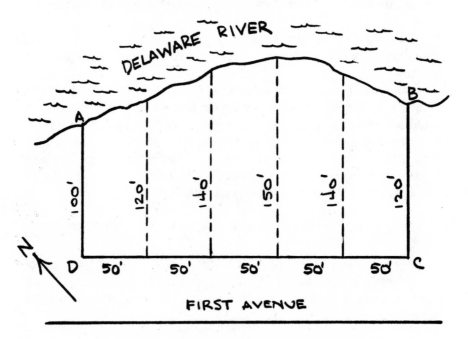

FINDING AREA WITH ONE CURVED BOUNDARY

FIGURE 8-9

Solution:

$$S = x\left(\frac{y_1 + y_6}{2} + y_2 + y_3 + y_4 + y_5\right)$$

$$S = 50\left(\frac{100 + 120}{2} + 120 + 140 + 150 + 140\right)$$

$$S = 50(110 + 120 + 140 + 150 + 140)$$

$$S = 50(660)$$

$$S = 33,000 \text{ square feet (approximate)}$$

Although the area found is approximate, it is significantly close enough to an accurate area to be considered accurate in most instances. The accuracy of the computation would depend upon the number of offsets used and the actual curvature of the boundary.

Equivalent Measurements

The measurement of areas differs from linear measure because the units involved are *square units* containing two dimensions. A rectangle with an area of 10 square feet can have dimensions of 1' × 10', 2' × 5', 2½' × 4', or any other rational factors of ten. The dimensions of the sides, l and w, could also be expressed in inches, for example, 24" × 60".

If, however, 24" is multiplied by 60", the resulting area is computed at 1,440 square *inches,* which must be equal to 10 square feet. A square with a side equal to 12" will have an area of 144 square inches. Changing the side of 12" to an equivalent linear unit measurement of 1 foot would result in an area of 1 square foot. It follows then that an area of 1 square foot is equivalent to an area of 144 square inches, or

1 square foot = 144 square inches

Likewise, a square with one side having a linear unit measurement of 1 yard would have an area of 1 square yard. Changing the 1 yard linear unit to its equivalent unit in feet would result in one side being 3 feet and the area (3' × 3') would be expressed as 9 square feet. Both squares have exactly the same linear and area measurements expressed in different but equivalent terms. Therefore, because 1 yard = 3 feet,

1 square yard = 9 square feet

The rules for changing area measures to equivalent area measures are the same as for linear measure. That is, *divide* to obtain *larger* units and *multiply* to obtain *smaller* units.

To change square inches to square feet, divide by 144.

To change square feet to square yards, divide by 9.

To change square feet to square inches, multiply by 144.

To change square yards to square feet, multiply by 9.

Example:

How many square yards are contained in a rectangle measuring 14' × 28'?

Solution:

Area = l × w = 14 × 28 = 392 square feet
392 divided by 9 = 43.55 square yards

From the Table of Linear Measure in Chapter 7, it can be seen that other square units of measure are needed. Although the *chain* unit of measure is common in linear measurement, it is retained almost exclusively for linear measure, being replaced by the equivalent units of *rods* in area measure. A square tract of land measuring one chain per side would theoretically contain one square chain. One chain contains 4 rods so the same area would have an area measurement of 16 square rods (4 × 4 = 16) and would be stated as such, rather than using the term of one square chain.

From the table, we have 16½ feet = 1 rod, 5½ yards = 1 rod, and 320 rods = 1 mile. Converting these to square or area measure, we find

272.25 square feet   = 1 square rod
30.25 square yards = 1 square rod
102,400 square rods = 1 square mile.

These units are cumbersome and difficult to manage, and therefore, the unit of an *acre* has been retained as the basic unit of area measurement in real estate.

THE ACRE

The original meaning of acre was "open country." As a measure of land, it was first defined as the amount a yoke of oxen could plow in one day. Statutory values were enacted at various times and in 1878 it was defined as containing 4,840 square yards. This definition is still used today in this country although it is usually expressed in equivalent square feet (43,560) rather than square yards.

The acre is a unit of square measure having no linear units of measure. It contains only *square* units of feet, yards, or rods. Acreage is the common term applied in real estate when the acre unit is used. It is used in practically all aspects of real estate when land measurement of any kind is indicated.

Because it is defined as 4,840 square yards, the acre can be readily converted to more convenient equivalents. If the number of square yards in an acre is divided by the number of square yards in a square rod, the result will be the number of square rods in an acre.

$$4,840/30.25 = 160 \text{ square rods} = 1 \text{ acre}$$

We have previously determined that there are 102,400 square rods in one square mile. Therefore, if we divide 102,400 square rods by the number of square rods in an acre, we will find the number of acres in a square mile.

$$102,400/160 = 640 \text{ acres} = \text{one square mile}$$

These equivalents can be used in forming a Table of Acreage as follows:

1 acre = 43,560 square feet
1 acre = 160 square rods
640 acres = 1 square mile

How to Compute Acreage

By using the above Table and equivalents, computations involving acreage are simplified. *To find acreage,* divide the given units of area by the number of the *same* units contained in *one* acre.

Example:

Three rectangular lots are sold. Lot #1 measures 320' X 290', lot #2 is 165' X 140', and lot #3 is 220' X 130'. How many acres are involved in the sale?

Solution:

Lot #1 = 320 X 290 = 92,800 square feet
Lot #2 = 165 X 140 = 23,100 square feet
Lot #3 = 220 X 130 = 28,600 square feet
Total = 144,500 square feet
There are 43,560 square feet in 1 acre, so
$$\frac{144,500}{43,560} = 3.32 \text{ acres (3 1/3 acres)}$$

Fractional or decimal parts of an acre are found in the same manner.

Example:

Ground is subdivided into lots, each containing 16,300 square feet. How many acres are there in each lot?

Solution:

$$\frac{16,300}{43,560} = .374 \text{ acres}$$

The fractional acreage will vary, depending on how the decimal .374 is used. If rounded-off to tenths, it would equal .4, or 2/5 of an acre. If not rounded-off, it could be stated as approximately 3/8 of an acre. (3/8 = .375)

The conversion of square miles to acres is also computed similarly provided that the number of *square miles in an acre* is used as the divisor or denominator. Because 640 acres = 1 square mile, there are 1/640 square miles in an acre.

Example:

Convert 4 square miles to acres.

Solution:

$$\frac{4}{1/640} = \frac{4}{1} \times \frac{640}{1} = 2,560 \text{ acres}$$

The above method of converting square miles to acres was used to provide consistency of computation (units of area divided by units in *one* acre). Conversion of square miles to acres, as shown in the above example, is done by multiplying the number of square miles by 640. (The division of fractions and inversion of denominator, if a fraction, results in multiplication.)

To convert acres to any other unit of area, multiply the number of acres by the number of units of area contained in one acre.

Example:

How many square feet are contained in 4 acres?

Solution:

$$1 \text{ acre } = 43,560 \text{ square feet}$$
$$4 \text{ acres} = 43,560 \times 4$$
$$4 \text{ acres} = 174,240 \text{ square feet}$$

PROPERTY DESCRIPTIONS

The purpose of a property description in a deed is to identify the land being conveyed. The description must be accurate enough for a surveyor to establish the definitive boundaries of the property.

Although there are four common types of property descriptions in use throughout the country, government surveying and mapping organizations, notably the U.S. Coast and Geodetic Survey, have attempted to establish more definite and accurate controls for precisely locating land on the ground. A description which is satisfactory for title purposes may be inadequate for a field location of the property because of obliteration of monuments, trees, stones, or other landmarks. This situation is being rectified by the State Plane Coordinate Systems.

State Plane Coordinate Systems

All fifty states have now established coordinate systems (grids) within their state which constitute a national network and tie-in of horizontal control monuments with the federal system of surveying. These monuments, in the form of surveying stations, are being constantly filled in and added to by the government.

Every control point throughout the country bears a definite relationship of one to another. This network of controls allows surveyors to incorporate their own surveys for purposes of coordination, checking, and reestablishing lost points. Because of the extent of the network and the incorporation of surveys into it, property landmarks can be permanently located and thus become indestructible. The location of a property described by use of the state coordinate system will always be exact and therefore alleviate any question in the deed as to identification or location.

Many areas of the country, however, are still not covered by the federal network and it will require many years before the State Plane Coordinate System is completely utilized.

Property descriptions, therefore, are still dependent upon the description as given in the original deed. The types of descriptions generally used are the Rectangular Survey, lot number on plot or map, and metes and bounds descriptions. Descriptions by monuments or landmarks only are still used in some rural areas but are vague and, in many cases, considered void.

Rectangular Survey

The objective of the U.S. Rectangular Survey system was the locating on the ground and fixing for all time, the legal subdivisions of land under the public domain of the U.S. The system is also known as U.S. Public Land Surveys.

Because it became law in 1785, all property deeded prior to that date was not affected. The system has been used in 31 states including Alaska. The first such survey now forms part of the state of Ohio.

The law provided for *townships* 6 miles square, containing 36 sections 1 mile square. The sections were numbered from 1 to 36, starting with number one in the northeast corner and ending with number thirty-six in the southeast corner. Figure 8–10 shows the method of numbering sections. This method of numbering sections is still in use.

The law was amended several times after its inception, causing some variations in detail. Therefore, some older property descriptions may not conform exactly to a more recent survey of the subject land.

The survey is begun by the establishment of an *initial point.* The exact position of this point is determined astronomically so that it becomes permanent. A true meridian running through the initial point is also determined astronomically and is called the *principal meridian.* It is extended north and south through the initial point. A *base line* is extended east and west on a true parallel of latitude through the initial point to the limits of the area being surveyed. Permanent monuments mark the locations of all lines and points at intervals of 40 chains (½ mile).

At 24 mile intervals, *standard parallels* are run parallel to the base line. They are numbered from the base line concurrently in a north and south direction. The standard parallel drawn 24 miles north of the base line is called "First Standard Parallel North" and the others are named accordingly (Second, Third, and so on).

The survey is next divided into 24 mile squares by *guide meridi-ans* which are true meridians located 24 miles to the east and west of the principal meridian and continuing at 24 mile intervals in either direction. They are also numbered according to their relationship to the principal meridian.

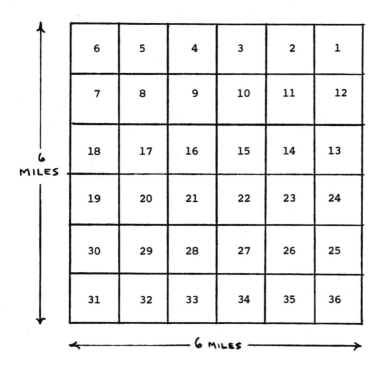

NUMBERED SECTIONS OF A TOWNSHIP

FIGURE 8-10

Each 24 mile square obtained from the above procedure is called a *check* and each check is further subdivided into 16 townships, each being 6 miles on a side.

The township of 36 square miles is divided then into *sections,* each containing one square mile (640 acres). The sections on the north and west side of the township contain the corrections made because of the curvature of the earth and might contain more or less than 640 acres. These sections are called "fractional sections." As mentioned previously, the law provides only for divisions of the township into sections. Once numbered, the government survey is completed and any further subdividing is left to the local authorities.

The townships of a survey are *numbered* east and west into *ranges* and north and south into *tiers* (or townships) with respect to the principal meridian and base line of the district. The east-west lines are called range lines and the north-south lines are called township lines.

The townships are *named* giving tier number north or south and range number east or west with respect to the applicable principal meridian. Figure 8–11 shows a Rectangular Survey of townships containing two checks. Township T2NR2E, 4th PM is the township in tier 2 north, and range 2 east, of the 4th principal meridian.

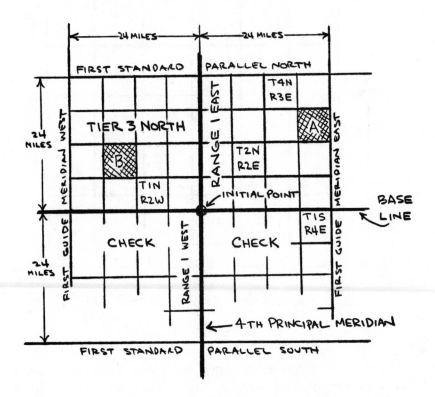

SUBDIVISION OF CHECKS INTO TOWNSHIPS

FIGURE 8-11

Example:

Name the township labelled A in Figure 8–11.

Solution:

It is in tier 3 north and range 4 east, at the 4th principal meridian. Therefore, it is

T3N R4E, 4th PM

Township B in Figure 8–11 is township T2NR3W, 4th PM and is divided into 36 sections as shown in Figure 8–10. Each numbered section contains 640 acres (1 square mile) and is subdivided first by locating the center of the section (*center-point*) and then quartered or divided into four equal parts (quarter-sections) through the center. Each *quarter-section* of 160 acres is named according to its relationship from the center-point. They are called the Northeast, Northwest, Southeast, and Southwest quarter-sections and designated as NE¼, NW¼, SE¼, and SW¼. Each quarter-section is again divided into quarters, forming parcels of 40 acres each. The rectangular system provides for the disposal of the public lands in these units of *quarter-quarter sections* of 40 acres.

Each of the quarter-quarter sections is also named according to its portion, as NE¼, etc. A quarter-quarter section in the north west corner of quarter-section NE¼ is labelled NW¼NE¼, meaning that it is the Northwest quarter-quarter section of the Northeast quarter-section.

Further subdivisions of these parcels may be made and each subdivision bears the name of the portion in which it is contained. Figure 8–12 shows the subdivisions of Section 8 of a township and some subdivisions of the quarter-quarter sections, or 40 acre parcels.

The parcel of land labelled A in Figure 8–12 is the Southwest quarter of the Northwest quarter-quarter section of the Southwest quarter-section of Section 8. It would therefore be designated as SW¼NW¼SW¼Sec8. The parcel labelled B in the figure is designated as E½NE¼NW¼NE¼Sec8. If both these parcels were to be described in a deed simultaneously, the word "and" would be used to separate them and each would still retain its own identification. This method of subdivision and designation provides a very convenient method for legal descriptions of land which is to be conveyed by deed.

Example:

What is the legal description of the parcel of land labelled C in Figure 8–12?

Solution:

It is the Southern half of the Southwest quarter-quarter section of the Southwest quarter-section. It is therefore described as

S½SW¼SE¼ Sec8, T3NR2W, 4th PM.

Accepted practice in real estate for purposes of locating a parcel and determining its acreage is to read the description from *right to left*. The section is read first as 640 acres, then each quarter-section is read using its fractional part of the preceding section. In the above example, for instance, Section 8 = 640 acres, SE¼ = 160 acres (¼ of 640), SW¼ = 40 acres (¼ of 160), and S½ = 20 acres (½ of 40 acres).

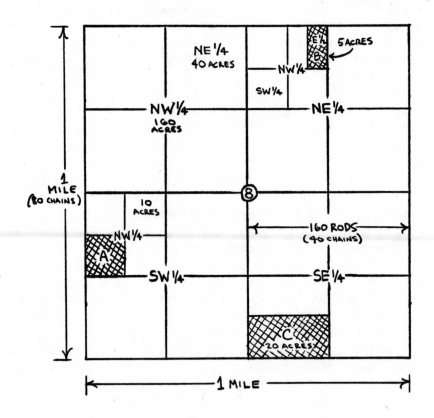

SUBDIVISION OF SECTION 8 OF T3NR2W, 4th PM.

FIGURE 8-12

Lot and Block

A building lot is usually described legally with reference to a *plat.* A plat is a map, drawing, or plot of a small geographic area. The survey of a tract is platted on paper, the plat showing all blocks, streets, lots, sizes and numbers of lots, and all other pertinent details. The plat also contains a complete written description of the tract. After it is certified and approved, it is recorded in the office of the register of deeds or similar official for the appropriate county.

The property is then easily identified in the legal description by reference to the recorded plat, giving lot number, block, and where and when recorded.

Metes and Bounds

The metes and bounds system is the oldest method of describing land and was used extensively in the original thirteen states. "Metes" are units of length and "Bounds" are directions or boundaries usually given in *bearings of a line,* as described in Chapter 7. The quantity or acreage of the land is determined by the metes while the bounds fix or confine the limits of that quantity.

The description must start with a *Point of Beginning* and give an exact description of such point, either by reference to a permanent monument, distance and direction from a dividing line or street line, or some other reliable designation. The description then proceeds *clockwise,* tracing the lines by directions and distances back to the Point of Beginning.

SIZE AND SHAPE

The size and shape of land are determined by the areas and geometric figures formed by the boundaries. Their importance in real estate does not apply as much to land measure alone as it does to the valuation and appraisal of the land.

The size, or width and depth, determines the *use* possibilities of the parcel and the shape determines *how* the lot can be advantageously developed. Size and shape include other elements that are mentioned here only because they do involve land measure. These include frontage, plottage, and topography.

Frontage is the linear units of measurement along the front of a property and is always given as the first dimension of the lot. The frontage is the prime consideration in determining value of some lots, and in some cases, the area value decreases as the depth of the lot increases.

Plottage is the added value of several lots when purchased under one ownership. The lots may be adjacent or separated.

Topography concerns the shape of the land in heights and elevations. It details the relief features or surface configuration of an area.

Because these factors are primarily matters of valuation and appraisal, they are discussed fully in Chapter 12.

9

How to Use Solid Measure in Appraising and Building

VOLUME AND CUBICAL CONTENTS

The importance of square and linear measure to real estate was discussed in Chapter 8. The mathematical aspects of area and surface measure were shown to be necessary factors in property descriptions, boundaries, and sizes. The standard unit for measuring area was the *square*.

Another form of measurement is also essential in real estate, especially in the real estate fields of appraising and construction. This aspect of measurement is known as *cubic* or *volume measure*.

If it often necessary to know the *amount of space* that an object contains or occupies. This amount of space is called its *volume*, and the standard unit for measuring volume is the *cube*.

COMPUTATIONS OF VOLUMES

A cubic unit of measure is the solid geometric cube formed with *each* of its dimensions equivalent to a linear unit of measure. *One cubic inch* is shown in Figure 9-1. Each edge of the cube is one inch long. It has a width, length, and height of one inch each, respectively.

We saw that length was a one dimensional measure and area was a two dimensional measure. *Volume is a three dimensional measure.* A cubic foot measures one foot on each dimension and a cubic yard measures one yard on each dimension.

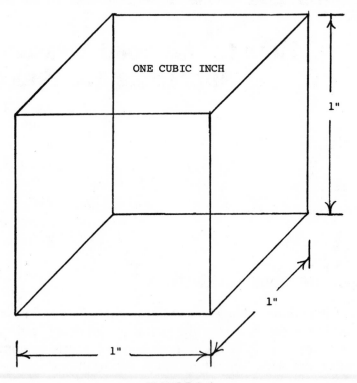

ONE CUBIC INCH

FIGURE 9–1

Volume of Rectangular Solids

In a cube, all three dimensions are the same because each surface (or face) is composed of a square of equal dimensions. The cube in Figure 9–1 is a *rectangular solid.* A building with a flat roof is also a rectangular solid.

The volume of any rectangular solid is determined by the number of cubic units of measure it contains. In Figure 9–2, we have filled the bottom of the rectangular solid with cubes which measure one unit each. The number of cubes covering the bottom can be determined by multiplying the length l (6 units) by the width w (5 units). The area of the bottom surface is therefore 30 square units. Because it also has a third dimension, or height, of one unit, the bottom layer contains 5 X 6 X 1 = 30 cubic units. If we fill the rectangular solid with cubes as in Figure 9-3, we could compute the number of cubes in the solid by multiplying the bottom layer by the height *h*, or number of layers.

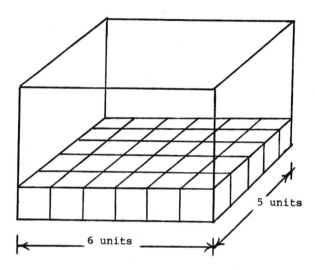

5 units

6 units

FIGURE 9-2

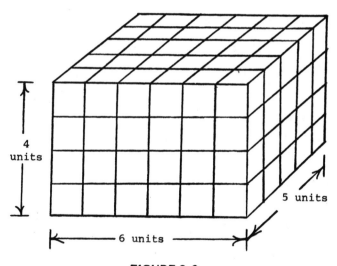

4 units

5 units

6 units

FIGURE 9-3

Thus, 5 X 6 X 4 = 120 cubic units. It can be seen that there are 120 cubes contained in the solid. The cubic content then, or volume of the solid, is 120 cubic units. It follows that the volume of any rectangular solid is found by multiplying $l \times w \times h$. By formula,

$$V = lwh$$

Example:

What is the volume of a garage building with a front of 24 feet, a length of 100 feet, and a height of 12 feet?

Solution:

$$V = lwh$$
$$V = 100' \times 24' \times 12'$$
$$V = 28,800 \text{ } cubic \text{ } feet$$

Volume of a Cylinder

The shape of a common tin can or a gas storage tank is a cylinder. Using the same reasoning as in rectangular solids, we can find the volume of a cylinder. The number of cubes necessary to cover the base of a cylinder is determined by finding the area of the base. The base is a circle and the area of a circle is πr^2 (π is called *pi* and represents the ratio of the circumference of the circle to its diameter. This ratio is approximately 3.1416 and is sometimes rounded-off to 3.14.) If we multiply the area of the base by the height of the cylinder, we will find the volume of the cylinder. By formula,

$$V = \pi r^2 h$$

which means the volume equals π(3.1416) times the radius squared times the height.

Example:

Find the volume of a cylinder that has a radius of 10 feet (diameter of 20 feet), and a height of 40 feet.

Solution:

$$V = \pi r^2 h$$
$$V = (3.14)(10^2)(40)$$
$$V = 3.14 \times 100 \times 40$$
$$V = 12,560 \text{ cubic feet}$$

Volume of a Triangular Prism

Figure 9–4 shows a triangular prism. Its bases are the triangles on either end. Using the same procedures for finding volume as above, the product of the area of the base and the height of the figure will result in the volume of the prism. To avoid confusion, the area of the base is designated B. The capital B is used to emphasize the fact that the *area* of the base is being represented. The height h is the distance between the two bases. The formula is

$$V = Bh$$

To use the formula, we must find B, the area of the triangle (Chapter 8). The area of a triangle is ½bh. (The h in the area formula is the *height* of the triangle and should not be confused with h in the volume formula which is the distance between the two bases.)

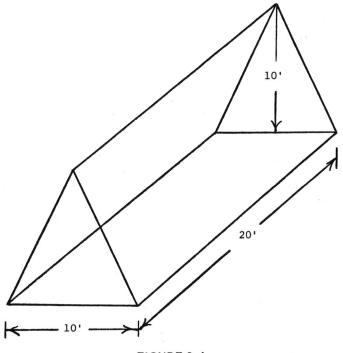

FIGURE 9-4

Example:

Using the dimensions in Figure 9-4, what is the volume of the triangular prism pictured?

Solution:

$$\text{Area of triangular base} = \tfrac{1}{2}bh = B$$
$$\text{Area} = \tfrac{1}{2}(10' \times 10') = 100/2 = 50 \text{ square feet}$$
$$\text{or, } B = 50 \text{ square feet}$$
$$\text{Volume} = Bh = 50 \times 20 = 1,000 \text{ cubic feet}$$

Other Volumes

The volume of any other geometric solid with parallel sides and bases can be found in a like manner. Find the area of either base and multiply by the height or distance between the two bases to find the volume of the solid.

The exceptions to this rule, of course, would be figures which are not constructed of parallel sides and bases. It is not necessary here to develop such formulas. Listed below are some volume formulas that might be used in real estate.

$$\text{Volume of a Sphere} = 4/3 \ \pi r^3$$
$$\text{Volume of a Pyramid} = 1/3 \ Bh$$
$$\text{Volume of a Cone} = 1/3 \ \pi r^2 h$$

Example:

A church spire is constructed in the shape of a regular square pyramid (the base is a square). Each side of the base is 10 ft. and the height of the pyramid is 33 ft. How many cubic feet of space does the spire contain?

Solution:

$$\text{Area of the Base} = B = s^2 = 10^2 = 100 \text{ square feet}$$
$$V = 1/3 \ Bh = \frac{100 \times 33}{3}$$
$$V = \frac{3300}{3} = 1,100 \text{ cubic feet}$$

EQUIVALENT MEASURES OF VOLUME

As in square measure, the units of measure that are multiplied must be the same units of measure. Inches cannot be multiplied by feet, and so on. Square inches multiplied by inches gives a product of cubic inches. But, square inches cannot be multiplied by feet unless the number of feet is changed to inches. The equivalence may be done fractionally or decimally.

Example:

A concrete wall is 24″ thick, 4 feet high, and 12′6″ long. What is the cubic content of the wall?

Solution:

Thickness = 24″ = 2 feet
Length   = 12′6″ = 12.5 feet
V = lwh
V = 12.5 × 2 × 4 = 100 cubic feet

A cube that measures 1 foot × 1 foot × 1 foot has a volume of *1 cubic foot.* Changing feet to inches, it can be seen that the dimensions change to 12 inches × 12 inches × 12 inches. The cubic foot volume in inches becomes 12 × 12 × 12, or 1,728 cubic inches. Therefore, *1 cubic foot = 1,728 cubic inches.*

Likewise, a cubic yard that measures 1 yard × 1 yard × 1 yard can be converted to feet. Thus, the dimensions become 3 feet × 3 feet × 3 feet, or 27 cubic feet. Therefore, *1 cubic yard = 27 cubic feet.*

From the foregoing we can construct a *Table of Cubic Measure* without developing all of its elements.

CUBIC MEASURES
1,728 cubic inches = 1 cubic foot
27 cubic feet = 1 cubic yard
128 cubic feet = 1 cord (wood)
40 cubic feet = 1 ton (shipping)
231 cubic inches = 1 standard gallon
1 cubic foot = 7.4805 gallons

Example:

In the previous example, we found the concrete wall to contain 100 cubic feet. Convert this to cubic yards.

Solution:

$$27 \text{ cubic feet} = 1 \text{ cubic yard}$$

$$\text{Therefore, } 100 \text{ cubic feet} = \frac{100 \text{ cubic feet}}{27 \text{ cu. ft. per cu. yd.}}$$

$$\text{and, } 100/27 = 3.70 \text{ cubic yards}$$

It can be seen that to change cubic feet to cubic yards, we *divide by 27*. Likewise, to change cubic inches to cubic feet, *divide by 1,728*. When changing from a large cubic unit to a smaller cubic unit (cubic yards to cubic feet, for instance) the opposite operation, multiplication, is performed.

COMPUTATIONS OF CUBES AND BUILDING COSTS

Cubic measure and square measure are used extensively in many aspects of building and appraising. They are each used as methods of estimating costs of entire structures as well as for estimating or accurately determining the costs of portions or units of construction.

The accuracy of the estimate or use of cubic and square measure depends upon the accuracy with which the actual measurements of the volume or area are made. A small error in a linear measurement on one side of a rectangular solid can result in a large percentage of error in the total volume.

Cubic Foot Method of Estimating

The formulas for finding volume of geometric solid figures normally represent the product of the area of the base B times the height h of the solid figure. In using this concept, the cubical content of a building can be found easily once the square foot area of the floors is determined and if each ceiling height is known. The cost is found by multiplying the estimated cost per cubic foot times the total cubical contents in feet. This procedure is known as the *Cubic Foot Method of Estimating* and is discussed more thoroughly in Chapter 14.

Example:

A structure has a square foot area of 1,200 in the basement, 2,460 on the first floor, and 2,100 on the second floor. The ceiling heights are 10 feet, 12 feet, and 9 feet, respectively. What is the cubical contents of the structure and how much will it cost to build at $1.56 per cubic foot?

Solution:

Basement:

1,200 sq. ft. X 10 ft. = 12,000 cubic feet

First Floor:

2,460 sq. ft. X 12 ft. = 29,520 cubic feet

Second Floor:

2,100 sq. ft. X   9 ft. = 18,900 cubic feet

Total Cubic Contents = 60,420 cubic feet

Building Cost:

60,420 cu. ft. X $1.56 per cu. ft. = $94,255.20

Tank Capacities

The capacity of a cylindrical tank can be computed by using cubic measure. The volume of the tank is determined by multiplying the area of its base by the length of the tank. The formula (page 166) is $V = \pi r^2 h$. To convert the volume in cubic feet to gallons of capacity, multiply the number of cubic feet by the number of gallons in one cubic foot (7.4805).

Example:

An oil tank has a diameter of 6′ and a length of 15′. How many gallons of oil can it hold?

Solution:

r = ½ diameter = ½(6) = 3′
$V = \pi r^2 h = 3.1416 \times 9' \times 15'$
V = 424.12 cubic feet
One cubic foot = 7.4805 gallons, therefore,
424.12 X 7.4805 = 3,172.6 gallons capacity of tank

A shortcut to finding area of the base is to multiply the *diameter* squared times .7854. Thus, in the above example, Volume = area

of base X height (or length) and, area of base = $(6^2)(.7854) = 28.27$.
Therefore, 28.27 times 15 (length) equals volume of 424.1 (rounded-off) cubic feet. *The constant .7854 times diameter squared will always equal the area of the circle* or base of a cylinder (to the nearest tenth).

Concrete and Excavating

The most common usage of cubic measure in building is in excavations and mass concrete, both of which are normally measured in *cubic yards.* Such measurements are used in excavating trenches and basements, and in determining costs of footings, foundations, and basement walls. Square measure is used for concrete walks and driveways where the depth is more or less constant.

In computing for volume, it is important to change cubic feet to cubic yards, or vice versa, either by changing to equivalent measures before computing cubic content, or by dividing equivalent measures after the computation. The choice depends upon which is easier to compute for the particular problem.

Example:

The cost of excavating for a foundation is $1.85 per cubic yard. If the excavation will be 360 ft. X 12 ft. X 6 ft., how much will it cost?

Solution:

Change foot measurements to yard measurements:

360 ft. = 120 yards, 12 ft. = 4 yards, and 6 ft. = 2 yards.
Then, 120 X 4 X 2 = 960 cubic yards, and
960 cubic yards X $1.85 per cubic yd. = $1,776 cost.

In finding areas or volumes for construction, fractional measurements are usually increased to the next half or whole unit *before computing.* This allows for easier computations and makes an additional small allowance for waste in ordering materials. (Waste and shrinkage are unavoidable when working with concrete.) The procedure should not be used, however, if the resulting error in measurement would be detrimental to the accuracy required. Some judgement would have to be exercised.

Example:

A concrete foundation is to be poured at a cost of $26.20 per cubic yard including labor. The excavation for the pour is 7'10" X 38' X 2'9". How much will the concrete cost?

Solution:

Change 7'10" to 8' and 2'9" to 3'
Find cubic content:
    8' X 38' X 3' = 912 cubic feet, and 27 cubic
    feet = 1 cubic yard, so, 912/27 = 33.78 cubic yards.
Find the cost:
    33.78 cubic yards X $26.20 = $885.04. However, in ordering
    the concrete, the 33.78 would have to be changed to 34 cubic
    yards, making the actual cost 34 X $26.20 = $890.80.

Conversion of Inches to Feet

Many dimensions in concrete work are given in inches. As shown earlier, inches cannot be multiplied by feet to obtain cubic feet. A short cut used by many estimators and contractors in converting to *like measurements* is to convert inches to a fractional part of a foot. This is done by using the inches of dimension as the numerator and 12" (1 foot) as the denominator. Thus, 6" becomes 6"/12" or, ½ foot, and 5" becomes 5"/12", or 5/12 of a foot.

To determine the cubic foot volume of a sidewalk slab 4" deep, change the 4" to 4/12, or 1/3 of a foot, then multiply by width and length in feet. When computing the volume of odd-shaped solids, separate computations are done for each shape and the cubic contents of each shape are added to find the total volume.

Example:

How many cubic feet of concrete mix are required in the footing in Figure 9-5?

Solution:

Volume of bottom portion = lwh

$$V = 10' \times 20/12 \times 8/12 = \frac{10 \times 20 \times 8}{144} = \frac{1600}{144} = 11.11 \text{ cu. ft.}$$

Volume of Top Portion = lwh
    12/12 X 8′ X 10′ = 1 X 8 X 10 = 80 cubic feet
Total Volume = 80 + 11.11 = 91.11 cubic feet

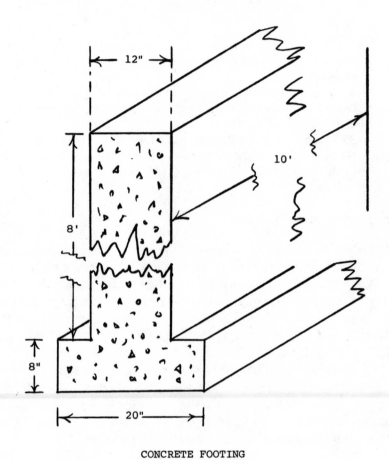

CONCRETE FOOTING

FIGURE 9-5

10

The Mathematics of Mortgages and Financing

The financing of real estate in today's market plays a large part in almost every real estate transaction, and every financing transaction involves much mathematics.

Many aspects of the mathematics of mortgages and finance have been covered elsewhere in this book. Because of the complexity of the subject and the procedures covered previously, we will attempt, in this chapter, to *simplify* the mathematical procedures involved by *consolidating* them into their usage with appropriate mortgage tables and a few formulas.

UNAMORTIZED LOAN OR STRAIGHT TERM LOAN

Although seldom used today, except in some cases of short-term mortgages, the unamortized or straight term mortgage calls for specified payments of principal and interest due on the unpaid balance at specified periods. The interest will vary according to the balance of the mortgage remaining and will be highest during the early periods of repayment. There is no amortization of the debt.

The computation is easy because it only involves the calculation of simple interest on the unpaid balance. Each payment of principal is subtracted from the balance to obtain the new outstanding balance.

Example:

A mortgage for $10,000 at 7% interest is to be repaid in 5 years on a straight term basis with annual payments of $2,000 on the principal plus the interest due on the unpaid balance. What are the first and last annual payments?

Solution:

First Payment:
  Outstanding balance = $10,000.
    Principal payment = $2,000.
    Interest = P $\times$ R = $10,000 $\times$ .07 =   700.
                    Total first annual payment $2,700.
Last Payment (5 years):
  Outstanding balance = $10,000 – $8,000
                    (4 payments made) = $2,000
    Principal payment = $2,000.
    Interest = P $\times$ R = $2,000 $\times$ .07 =   140.
                    Total last payment = $2,140.

PARTIALLY AMORTIZED MORTGAGES

If parts of the mortgage or loan are paid during the term of the mortgage, and the balance of the debt is due at the end of the term, the mortgage is called a "partially amortized mortgage." It is sometimes called a "balloon mortgage," the last payment being the largest or "balloon" payment. Its use is very limited but it is sometimes used for financing of income property where there is a limited cash flow.

AMORTIZATION

In Chapter 3, amortization was defined as the payment of a debt, including principal and interest, by a sequence of equal payments at equal intervals. The mathematics as used in amortization was also shown and will not be repeated in detail here.

With the availability of high speed computers, small electronic calculators, and the abundance of published tables, it is needless to take the time for mathematical development of complete amortization or other mortgage tables. Instead, we will show the partial development and mathematical usage of the tables.

Fully Amortized Loan

A mortgage in which the full balance is paid by equal installments spread evenly over the term of the mortgage is a fully amortized loan. No additional payments are made or required. The equal intervals may be monthly, quarterly, semi-annual, or annual. The amount paid at each interval is determined by the *Constant Annual Percent.*

Constant Annual Percent

The Constant Annual Percent was explained in Chapter 3 and defined as the *percentage* (including principal and interest) of the full loan that must be paid annually to pay off the loan. The method of finding Constant Annual Percent was also shown previously. The annual payment of principal and interest can be obtained by referring to the Constant Annual Percent Tables (see Appendix).

Example:

What is the annual payment of principal and interest necessary to pay off a $12,000, 20 year mortgage, at 9% interest?

Solution:

From the Constant Annual Percent Tables (Appendix),
find 20 years at 9%:
Annual Constant = 10.80% (rounded-off from 10.797)
Amount of mortgage X Constant Annual Percent = annual payment
$12,000 X .1080 = $1,296

Monthly Payment

The monthly payment of principal and interest is found by dividing the Constant Annual Percent by 12. The result will be the percentage of the loan necessary for the monthly payment of principal and interest.

Example:

What is the monthly payment of principal and interest on the above mortgage?

Solution:

10.80%/12 = .9% = .009
$12,000 × .009 = $108 monthly payment
Note that this can also be solved by dividing the annual
payment ($1,296) found in the preceding example by 12:
$1,296/12 = $108

For simplicity in these examples, we have used the rounded-off amounts for the Constant Annual Percent and monthly payments. In preparing an amortization table, however, as will be shown later, the Constant Annual Percent should be used to three decimal places (10.797).

CALCULATING MORTGAGE
INTEREST AND PRINCIPAL

It is sometimes necessary to know the amount of interest or principal that is included in the mortgage payment. This is particularly necessary when the annual interest must be known for tax deductions purposes or, in the case of real estate investment (Chapter 15), when determining cash flow and taxable income. The Mortgage Amortization Table (Figure 10-1) is used to determine the percentages of the *annual payment* that are applied to interest and principal. These tables are available in *The Thorndike Encyclopedia of Banking and Financial Tables* published by Warren, Gorham, and Lamont, and other financial publications.

How To Use The Mortgage
Amortization Table

The table is based on the Constant Annual Percent which is broken down for each year of the loan into the parts of it allocated to interest and to principal. (The procedure for actual computation of each annual percentage of interest and principal is briefly shown in the next section.) Tables used in various financial publications will usually list the percentage of interest and principal for each year of the mortgage term paid by a level monthly, quarterly, semi-annual, or annual payment.

More frequent payments (for instance, monthly as opposed to quarterly or semi-annual) produce a lower Constant Annual Percent because of the nature of the amortization process. That is, with each payment, the principal is reduced by the amount of the principal payment, and the next periodic payment of interest is computed on the *new* principal balance. Therefore, the *total annual interest* paid

MORTGAGE AMORTIZATION TABLE

9% Annual Interest   20 Year Term   Monthly Payments

Constant Annual Percent = 10.797 (10.80)

YEAR	ANNUAL INTEREST	ANNUAL PRINCIPAL	YEAR END BALANCE
1	8.924	1.873	98.127
2	8.748	2.049	96.079
3	8.556	2.241	93.838
4	8.346	2.451	91.388
5	8.116	2.681	88.707
6	7.865	2.932	85.775
7	7.590	3.207	82.568
8	7.289	3.508	79.060
9	6.960	3.837	75.223
10	6.600	4.197	71.026
11	6.206	4.591	66.435
12	5.776	5.021	61.414
13	5.305	5.492	55.922
14	4.789	6.008	49.914
15	4.226	6.571	43.343
16	3.609	7.188	36.155
17	2.935	7.862	28.294
18	2.198	8.599	19.694
19	1.391	9.406	10.288
20	0.509	10.288	0.000

FIGURE 10-1

on a level *monthly* payment mortgage will be *lower* than the *total annual interest* paid on a level *annual* payment mortgage.

Although the total annual interest will be lower with monthly payments, the *Annual Percentage Rate* (APR) will be higher than the mortgage nominal interest rate. As mentioned in Chapter 2, the APR was established in 1969 by the Truth in Lending Act, and as required by Regulation Z, must be disclosed in all real estate transactions. The APR will be discussed later in this chapter.

In Figure 10-1, the table is for a 20 year mortgage at 9%. The Constant Annual Percent is 10.797%. The annual interest and annual principal represent that portion of the Constant Annual Percent allocated to each and therefore totals 10.797% each year. They also represent the annual percentage of the mortgage amount applicable. For instance, in the first year, the annual interest is 8.924%. On a $15,000 mortgage, this would represent an interest payment for the first year of 8.924% of $15,000, or, .08924 × $15,000 = $1,338.60.

Example:

Using Figure 10-1, and a mortgage of $25,000, what will the annual interest and principal be in the 6th year? How much of the mortgage will be paid off by the end of the 14th year?

Solution:

Annual payment = 10.797% = .10797 × $25,000 = $2,699.25
Locate 6th year on Table:
  6th year interest = 7.865% =
    .07865 × $25,000 = $1,966.25
  6th year principal = 2.932% =
    .02932 × $25,000 = $733.00
Check: Annual payment = interest + principal =
                $1,966.25 + 733.00 = $2,699.25
Year end balance at end of 14th year = 49.914%
  Balance = .49914 × $25,000 = $12,478.50
  Paid off = $25,000.00 - $12,478.50 = $12,521.50

Mortgage Amortization Schedules

Mortgage loan amortization schedules show the principal balance remaining at the end of each period and the amounts of each payment that are applied to principal and interest in *actual* dollar amounts for a particular mortgage. The schedules are compiled as shown in Chapter 3 by using the Constant Annual Percent and the simple interest formula. The mathematical process is long and tedious and usually of little need to calculate in the real estate office.

The mortgage lender will usually supply a mortgage amortization schedule for any particular mortgage. Many tables are available for use in preparing a particular schedule if the mortgagee does not supply one, or if a computer-run is not available.

Figure 10-2 is a typical mortgage amortization schedule (abbreviated to show only the first-year monthly breakdown) prepared by using the procedure outlined before. An actual schedule would be broken down for the full 20 years, showing 240 months of payments.

MORTGAGE AMORTIZATION SCHEDULE

$10,000 Loan at 9%   Term 20 years   Monthly payments

Constant Annual Percent = 10.797

YEAR	MONTH	PAYMENT	INTEREST	PRINCIPAL	BALANCE OF LOAN
1	1	$89.98	$75.00	$14.98	$9,985.02
	2	89.98	74.89	15.09	9,969.93
	3	89.98	74.77	15.21	9,954.72
	4	89.98	74.66	15.32	9,939.40
	5	89.98	74.56	15.42	9,923.98
	6	89.98	74.43	15.55	9,908.43
	7	89.98	74.31	15.67	9,892.76
	8	89.98	74.20	15.78	9,876.98
	9	89.98	74.08	15.90	9,861.08
	10	89.98	73.96	16.02	9,845.06
	11	89.98	73.84	16.14	9,828.92
	12	89.98	73.72	16.26	9,812.66

FIGURE 10-2

Example:

Show how the amortization schedule in Figure 10-2 was prepared for the first and second months ($10,000 loan at 9% for 20 years).

Solution:

Constant Annual Percent = 10.797

Find the level monthly payment:

Monthly payment = Constant Annual Percent/12 months
= 10.797/12 = 0.8998% = .008998

Level monthly payment = .008998 × $10,000 = $89.98

Beginning balance of loan =	$10,000.00

Interest for 1 year: .09 × $10,000 = $900

Monthly interest: $900/12 = $75.00

Principal payment: $89.98 - $75.00 =	−14.98
Balance at end of first month =	$9,985.02
Second month beginning balance	$9,985.02

Interest for 1 year: .09 × $9,985.02 = $898.65

Monthly interest: $898.65/12 = $74.89

Principal payment: $89.98 - $74.89 =	−15.09
Balance at end of second month =	$9,969.93

ANNUAL PERCENTAGE RATE AND MORTGAGES

The purpose of the Annual Percentage Rate (APR) as stated by the Truth in Lending Act was to standardize the measurement of actual interest charges to arrive at the *true cost* of a loan. Other methods used prior to 1969 usually *understated* the true cost of the loan. The APR must be shown in all real estate transactions involving financing.

The APR is the ratio of all charges to the outstanding balance of the loan, or, by formula,

APR = Charges/Outstanding balance

In amortization, particularly with monthly payments, the outstanding balance will change with each periodic payment. Therefore, when determining the APR, the *total* of the monthly interest charges and the *average* of the outstanding balances for the year must be used.

Example:

Find the APR for the mortgage shown in the Amortization Schedule of Figure 10-2.

Solution:

Total of monthly charges (interest) = $892.42
Total of monthly outstanding balances = $118,798.94
Average outstanding balance = $118,798.94/12 = $9,899.91
APR = Charges/Average outstanding balance
= $892.42/$9,899.91 = .09014 = 9.014%

It can be seen that the APR is actually slightly higher than the nominal 9% interest rate. In loans other than amortized mortgage loans (installment loans, etc.), the difference between the nominal rate and the APR will be much greater.

VARIABLE RATE MORTGAGES

Because of the constant changes in prime interest rates in recent years, some controversy has developed concerning mortgage interest rates. Fluctuations in mortgage interest rates have raised havoc with mortgage lenders over what proper interest rate to demand.

The concept of variable rate mortgages is simply a matter of relating or "tying" the mortgage rate to a *reference rate* such as the *prime rate* of commercial banks or the U.S. Treasury Bill rate. The mortgagor would agree to pay a certain number of "points" above the reference rate, thereby "varying" his interest rate on a *monthly basis.*

One method of payment would involve varying the monthly payment to meet the interest rate demand *each month.* In that way, if the interest rate moved from 8% to 8.5% during the month, the monthly mortgage payment might change from $280 to $289.

Another method that has been suggested is to extend the payments by retaining a level monthly payment but adding to the term of the loan as the rate fluctuates. This could change a 120 payment mortgage to a 140 payment mortgage in order to accommodate the interest charges.

There are many mathematical problems involved in the use of the variable rate mortgage, one being that the amortization schedule would no longer be a valid real estate document. Such mathematical details are far beyond the scope of this chapter.

As a simple example, however, of the effect a monthly change might have, we can use the mortgage in Figure 10–2.

Example:

If the mortgage in Figure 10-2 were a Variable Rate Mortgage, what would the payment in the 4th month change to if the variable rate increased to 10%?

Solution:

Balance at end of 3rd month = $9,954.73
Interest for the 4th month:
$I = PR/12 = \$9,954.72 \times .10/12$
$I = \$82.956 = \$82.96$
The difference in interest of $8.30 ($82.96 - $74.66) would be added to the established or base level monthly payment of $89.98:

$$\$89.98 + \$8.30 = \$98.28$$

The monthly payment on the 4th month would be $98.28 (an increase of over 9% on the monthly payment).

CONSTRUCTION LOANS

Although usually considered as mortgages, construction loans differ from mortgages in that money is advanced to the borrower in stated amounts at definite *stages* of the construction, or monthly, as specified in the mortgage or loan agreement. A final advance is sometimes made when the work is completed.

The loans are usually short-term loans from one to five years. The interest on the loan is paid monthly on the outstanding balance. Construction loans are frequently discounted by charging points to the borrower (see Chapter 2).

Points are paid in advance, and usually are deducted from the first draw on the account. The points charged allow the lender to receive some of his interest income in advance to cover the costs of the loan. When determining the *average interest costs* of the loan, the points must be taken into consideration.

The periodic interest payments made on the loan are determined in the same manner as an amortization schedule. Of course, principal payments are not included because repayment of principal is not made until the construction has been completed.

To find the average interest rate, the simple interest formula, $R = I/P$ is used. The interest is the total monthly interest plus points paid, the principal is the total of the monthly balances, and the resulting rate will be the *monthly* rate. The monthly rate is multiplied by the number of months to determine the average interest rate.

Example:

A construction loan of $250,000 is made for a term of one year at 12% nominal interest and 1 point is charged for the loan. The entire loan will be drawn over the term of 1 year on a monthly basis and interest on the loan balance is to be paid monthly. What is the monthly breakdown and average rate?

Solution:

Monthly Interest Rate = .12(annual)/12 months = .01
Monthly draw = $250,000/12 = $20,833.33

MONTH	DRAW	LOAN BALANCE	MONTHLY INTEREST (.01 X balance)
1	$20,833	$ 20,833	$ 208.33
2	20,833	41,667	416.67
3	20,834	62,500	625.00
4	20,833	83,333	833.33
5	20,833	104,167	1,041.67
6	20,834	125,000	1,250.00
7	20,833	145,833	1,458.33
8	20,833	166,667	1,666.67
9	20,834	187,500	1,875.00
10	20,833	208,333	2,083.33
11	20,833	229,167	2,291.67
12	20,834	250,000	2,500.00
TOTAL	250,000	1,625,000	16,250.00

Total Interest = $16,250 + $2,500 (points) = $18,750.
Monthly Rate = I/P = $18,750/$1,625,000 = .01154
Annual Rate = .01154 X 12 = .13848 = 13.8%
Note that the annual rate is *also* the APR. The average loan balance is $135,417 ($1,625,000/12) and the APR =
$18,750/$135,417 = .13846 = 13.8%

MORTGAGE BANKING AND SECONDARY MARKETS

Mortgage banking involves the buying, selling, servicing, and origination of mortgages. The buying and selling of mortgages at discount is done in what is called the "Secondary Mortgage Market." The term does not refer to a *second mortgage*, but to the purchase of existing mortgages from a mortgage banker or lender, by a permanent investor. It also includes purchases by GNMA, FNMA, and private investors, of FHA, VA, and, since 1970, conventional mortgages.

When purchasing a mortgage, the investor buys the stream of payments remaining on the mortgage, at a discounted purchase price, at a certain yield rate. The discount and purchase price will depend on the yield demanded by the investor.

The mathematics of mortgage banking and the secondary mortgage market concerns itself primarily with the price to pay in order to receive a specified yield.

How to Determine Price to Pay

Because the mortgage is a stream of payments, and thus forms an annuity with regular periodic payments for a specified time at a specified interest rate, its present value can be determined by using Column 5 of the Compound Interest and Annuity Tables (Present Worth of 1 per Period). The monthly payment on the mortgage multiplied by the Present Worth factor (monthly) will result in the price to pay for the mortgage. The formula is

$$\text{PRICE} = \text{PAYMENT} \times a_{\overline{n}|i}$$

where $a_{\overline{n}|i}$ is the present value of 1 per period at the *desired* yield rate. The Payment is the regular monthly payment on the mortgage and, if not known, is determined by using the Constant Annual Percent as discussed previously. For use in the following examples, Compound Interest Tables for 8% (2/3% monthly) and 9% (3/4% monthly) are included in the Appendix.

Example:

A $10,000 mortgage at 8% for 10 years is sold on the closing date to an investor to yield 9%. What price does the investor pay for the mortgage?

Solution:

Constant Annual Percent = 14.56
Monthly Constant = 14.56/12 = 1.2133
Monthly Payment = $10,000 × .012133 = $121.33

Find present value of 1 per period for 10 years at 9%:
    10 years = 120 months; 9% = 9/12% = 3/4% = .0075 *monthly*
From Column 5:

$$a_{\overline{n}|i} = a_{\overline{120}|.0075} = 78.9417$$

Find Price to Pay:
    Price = Payment $\times$ $a_{\overline{n}|i}$ = \$121.33 $\times$ 78.9417 = \$9,577.99
The *discounted* price to pay is \$9,578.

If payments on the mortgage are made annually, then the *annual payment* and *annual factor* for $a_{\overline{n}|i}$ are used.

Sometimes a certain mortgage may be purchased at a *premium* because of its security or other factors. The same formula and procedures are used to determine the purchase price.

Example:

A \$10,000 mortgage at 9% for 10 years is sold on the closing date to an investor to yield 8%. What price does the investor pay for the mortgage?

Solution:

Constant Annual Percent = 15.21
Monthly Constant = 15.21/12 = 1.2675
Monthly payment = \$10,000 $\times$ 1.2675 = \$126.75
Find present value of 1 per period for 10 years at 8%:
    10 years = 120 months; 8% = 2/3% or .0066 monthly
    From Column 5:

$$a_{\overline{n}|i} = a_{\overline{120}|.0066} = 82.4215$$

Find Price to Pay:
    Price = Payment $\times$ $a_{\overline{n}|i}$ = \$126.75 $\times$ 82.4215 = \$10,446.90
The *premium* price to pay is \$10,447.

If necessary, the expected yield rate can be found if the price paid and the payment are known. The formula is transformed to

$$a_{\overline{n}|i} = \textbf{PRICE/PAYMENT}$$

The factor $a_{\overline{n}|i}$, as determined by solution of the formula, must then be found in the proper column by interpolation or by trial and error. It is not necessary to show this procedure here.

The above formulas can only be used when it is estimated that the mortgages will run to maturity. A *discounted* mortgage paid-off prior to maturity will return a *higher yield,* and a mortgage purchased at a *premium* will return a *lower yield* if paid-off prior to maturity.

As is the case in any investment, the true measure of yield can only be determined at the end of the investment period (see Chapter 15).

Prepayment Prices for Mortgages

Few mortgages will actually run to maturity, and the investor must therefore be prudent enough to allow for such an event when investing. Through various experience data and estimates, it is possible to estimate the average prepayment of an investment portfolio of mortgages. The data can be applied to arrive at a calculated estimate for a particular mortgage although the validity of such a calculation can be questionable. The investor can use his *prediction* to determine the price to pay for a mortgage, assuming prepayment before maturity.

When a mortgage is prepaid, a portion has been in periodic installments and the balance is paid off in a lump sum. By adding the two factors, we can arrive at a price to pay. The formula would be

$$\text{PRICE} = \text{PAYMENT} \times a_{\overline{n}|\,i} + \text{BALANCE} \times v^n,$$

where $a_{\overline{n}|\,i}$ is the present value of 1 per period, and v^n is the present value of the balance or lump sum (Column 4 of the Compound Interest and Annuity Tables). Because we have shown earlier that the discounted mortgages that are prepaid *increase* the yield, the main concern is prepayment of mortgages purchased at a premium, resulting in a *decreased* yield. Allowance should be made for this possible decrease when the purchase is made.

Example:

A $15,000 mortgage at 9% for 20 years is purchased at premium to yield 8%. What should be paid for the mortgage if it is predicted that it will be prepaid in 10 years?

Solution:

Constant Annual Percent = 10.80; Monthly = .9%
Monthly Payment = $15,000 × .009 = $135.00

Find present value of 1 per period for 10 years at 8%:

10 years = 120 months; 8% = 2/3% monthly

From Column 5:

$a_{\overline{n}|i} = a_{\overline{120}|.0066} = 82.4215$

Find present value of 1 (balance) for 10 years at 2/3%:

From Column 4: $v^n = 0.45052$

Find Balance:

From the Amortization Tables or Percent Paid-Off Tables, the percentage of loan remaining after 10 years is 71.026%

$.71026 \times \$15,000 = \$10,653.90$

Find the Price to Pay:

Price = Payment $\times$ $a_{\overline{n}|i}$ + Balance $\times$ v^n

$= (\$135 \times 82.4215) + (\$10,653.90 \times .45052)$

$= \$11,126.90 + \$4,799.79$

$= \$15,926.69 = \underline{\$15,927.}$

11

Simplification of Depreciation

MEANING OF DEPRECIATION

Depreciation is the *loss in value* of an asset due to any cause. In real estate, these causes are usually defined as *economic obsolescence, functional obsolescence,* and *physical deterioration.* Depreciation is used both in the consideration of appraised valuation of property and in the considerations of the taxable income aspects of investment of income-producing property. The *details* of its treatment in appraising and investments are covered separately in related chapters. We will be concerned here only with the *general* mathematical aspects of depreciation, including *some* of its appraising and tax considerations.

The loss in value of an asset is recognized by the Internal Revenue Service (IRS) and it therefore allows the taxpayer to recover a portion of the capital investment by deductions for depreciation. To be considered as a capital expenditure, an asset must have a useful life of more than one year and a limited life based on estimated or determinable usefulness of the asset.

Land cannot be depreciated because it does not have a limited life (land depreciation *may* be considered in some rare cases of appraisal). Depreciation, therefore, is computed only on improvements (buildings) and only if the improvements are used for business purposes or the production of income.

It is important to note here that depreciation is basically an accounting term and its applications are not limited only to uses in appraising of real estate and income tax deductions. The depreciation of capital assets is also an important element in general business decisions, planning, and evaluation.

Depreciation is usually included as an overhead expense in various businesses. It may be computed by one method for financial status reporting and by a different method for tax purposes. A third method may be used for determining the present value of a property for appraisal purposes.

For business planning, the chief function of depreciation is, theoretically, its role in financing replacement of assets. The resources for replacement are provided by the depreciation allowances out of the operating expenses of the business. Ideally, a *sinking fund* (Chapter 3) should be established and deposits made in the amount of the depreciation. This would allow for development of replacement funds for the depreciated asset at the end of its useful life.

USEFUL LIFE AND SALVAGE VALUE

The useful life for depreciation purposes is the period over which the property may reasonably be expected to be economically useful. Guidelines for acceptable useful lives are issued by the IRS. The useful lives for various buildings may vary, however, according to the particular situation. Shown below is a representative list of some guidelines as used by the IRS.

TOTAL USEFUL LIFE IN YEARS

Apartments	50	Hotels	50
Banks	67	Office Buildings	67
Dwellings	60	Stores	67
Factories	50	Theaters	50
Garages	60	Warehouses	75

Once the useful life has been decided, the *salvage value* must be determined. This determination must be made upon acquisition of the property. It is the amount that the asset will be valued at when its useful life has been exhausted. It can be a *scrap, junk,* or *resale* value. Replacement value can never be used for salvage value. The salvage value is the portion of cost that is *unrecovered* by depreciation.

The salvage value is deducted from the cost or other basis of the property *before* depreciation is computed. If an accelerated depreciation method, such as declining-balance, is used, salvage value is not considered. In no instance can assets be depreciated below salvage value, although there are special circumstances in which salvage value can be reduced by an amount not in excess of 10% of the cost or other basis of the property. These will not be considered in this chapter.

DEPRECIABLE AMOUNT

The depreciable amount is the total amount to be depreciated during the lifetime of the asset. It is equal to the original cost plus any capitalized expenses, less any adjustments, less salvage value, and in the case of real property, less the land value. It can be thought of as the *net amount* to be depreciated, or the total cost of improvements less salvage value.

DEPRECIABLE AMOUNT = TOTAL COST – SALVAGE VALUE

BOOK VALUE

The book value of an asset at any time is the difference between the depreciable amount and the total of all depreciation charged or taken to that date (*accrued* depreciation). It is the balance of depreciation remaining to be taken in the future. It represents the *present value* of the asset in terms of depreciation.

BOOK VALUE = DEPRECIABLE AMOUNT
– ACCRUED DEPRECIATION

METHODS OF CALCULATING
DEPRECIATION

Once the useful life and salvage value have been determined, selection must be made of the *method* of depreciation to be used. The *straight-line method* is the easiest to use and compute, as the depreciable amount is prorated *equally* over the years of useful life.

The other common methods involve *accelerated depreciation* which allow for more depreciation in the earlier years. This is advantageous for tax purposes and for quicker recovery of the investment. The annual allowance declines each year. The accelerated methods include *declining-balance* and *sum-of-the-digits*. Other methods that are available, not involving accelerated depreciation, include the *sinking-fund* and *annuity* methods.

Straight-Line Method

The straight-line method is also called the method of averages because it determines an average depreciation per year for the total years of useful life of the asset. The term "straight-line" is used because, when plotted on a graph, the depreciation, or line of value-decline, appears as a *straight line*. The initial cost, less the salvage value, is the total amount to be depreciated during the lifetime of the property or asset. Dividing this amount by the number of years results in the annual or average depreciation. By formula,

$$D = \frac{C - S}{n}$$

where D is annual depreciation, C is initial cost, S is salvage value, and n is number of years in the useful life. In most types of depreciation, $C - S$ is the depreciable amount. In real estate, however, the additional factor of land value must be deducted from the depreciable amount before computing.

Example:

What is the annual depreciation on a property purchased for $23,000 if the property has a useful life remaining of 20 years, a salvage value of $1,000, and a land value of $2,000?

Solution:

The initial depreciable cost is $21,000 after subtracting the land value of $2,000.

$$D = \frac{C - S}{n}$$

$$D = \frac{\$21,000 - \$1,000}{20} = \frac{\$20,000}{20} = \$1,000$$

Annual depreciation using the straight-line method is $1,000.

When using the above method, the result is always a dollar amount. It is a common practice, however, to state the annual depreciation as a *percentage* of the depreciable amount. This is a simple computation and will provide us with a method for determining other values in the straight-line method. For instance, the declining-balance method is dependent upon a *percentage* of straight line depreciation.

Using the above example, if the useful life is 20 years, the annual fractional part of 20 years is 1/20, and by converting this to a decimal and then to a percent, we find it equivalent to 5% depreciation (1/20 = .05 = 5%).

Another procedure is to divide 100% (for total useful life) by the number of years of useful life and the quotient arrived at will be the *annual percentage of depreciation.* (100% divided by 20 years = 5%).

In our example, the annual depreciation is 5% of the depreciable amount. We determined that the depreciable amount was $20,000. Therefore, 5% of $20,000 is $1,000, the annual depreciation.

As mentioned, the use of percentage allows us more flexibility in working with straight-line depreciation. The depreciable amount initially represents 100% of the depreciation. Each year, as depreciation is taken, the percentage is lowered by the amount of depreciation taken. The depreciation taken plus the book value will always be 100%.

Example:

What is the present value of a house if the depreciation is 2% annually and the original cost of the house 8 years ago was $30,000?

Solution:

Accrued Depreciation = 2% X 8 years = 16%
Present value is the same as book value, therefore,
16% + book value = 100%
book value = 100% – 16% = 84%
book value = 84% of $30,000
Present value = .84 X $30,000 = $25,200

Declining-Balance Method

The declining-balance method is also known as the *constant-percentage* method. The latter is more descriptive of the method because the basis of this method is to depreciate the asset by a constant percentage of its book value each year.

The book value will decrease each year as depreciation is charged against it. Because the book value is the balance of depreciation yet to be charged, and it will decline each year, the method is called *declining-balance.* By using a constant percentage of a decreasing amount, the annual depreciation will get smaller each year. The first year will have the largest depreciation allowance.

Regardless of method used, the total depreciation on any asset will be the same at the end of its useful life. Because the declining-balance method allows the *most* depreciation in the earlier years, it is called an *accelerated* depreciation method. It accelerates the amount of depreciation but does not change the total amount to be taken.

In using the declining-balance method, a percentage of the straight-line depreciation rate is chosen. This could be 125%, 150%, or 200%, usually dependent upon what will be allowed by the IRS for the particular property involved. Any rate may be chosen provided that it does not exceed the maximum allowable rate.

The rate selected is applied each year against the book value to determine the allowable depreciation for that particular year. The depreciation for the year reduces the book value by that amount and establishes the *new reduced book value* for the next year. The constant rate is applied year by year against the declining balance of book value to determine the annually reducing amount of depreciation.

Salvage value is not deducted in determining depreciable amount but the property cannot be depreciated to less than a *reasonable* salvage value. This rule is necessary because the method would never really end by continuously taking a percentage of a declining balance. A balance, although infinitesimally small, would always exist, even after 1,000 years.

Example:

Using the declining-balance method at a rate of 150%, what is the depreciation for the first, second, and third years on a $45,000 rental property? Land value is $5,000 and useful remaining life is 20 years.

Solution:

Find the depreciable amount:
$45,000 – $5,000 (land) = $40,000

Find the straight-line rate:
   100%/20 = 5% annual depreciation
Find the declining-balance constant percentage:
   150% of 5% = 1.50 × .05 = .075 = 7½%
The annual depreciation will be 7½% of the book value each year.
First year: 7½% of $40,000 = .075 × 40,000 = $3,000
Second year: Depreciable Amount − Depreciation = Book Value
   $40,000 − $3,000 = $37,000
   Depreciation = 7½% of $37,000 = .075 × 37,000 = $2,775
Third year: Current book value = $37,000 − 2,775 = $34,225
   Depreciation = 7½% of $34,225 = $2,566.88

The same method is used regardless of the accelerated percentage selected. If 200% declining-balance is selected, the constant percentage used would be 200% of the straight-line percentage.

Finding Book Value

A formula can be derived for finding book value at the end of *any year* in the declining-balance method. It is used to find the book value at the end of any number of years without first finding the preceding values. The formula is

$$BV_n = C(1 - d)^n$$

where n is number of years, BV_n is book value at the end of n years, C is the initial cost or depreciable amount, and d is the percentage used. Because n is exponential, large values would require logarithms or computers for solution. We can use the formula for small values of n.

Example:

What is the book value (or present value) of a property at the end of the 4th year if the constant percentage rate for declining-balance is 8% and the depreciable amount is $20,000?

Solution:

$$BV_n = C(1 - d)^n$$
$$BV_4 = 20,000(1 - .08)^4$$
$$BV_4 = 20,000(.92)^4 = 20,000(.7164)$$
$$BV_4 = \$14,328$$

Sum-of-the-Digits Method

Another accelerated method of depreciation is called the sum-of-the-digits. This method applies a fraction of constantly decreasing value against the depreciable amount.

The constant denominator of the fraction is the *sum of the digits* of the useful life. For instance, if the useful life of an asset is 5 years, the years' digits would be 5,4,3,2, and 1. The fractions would have a constant denominator of their sum which would be $5 + 4 + 3 + 2 + 1 = 15$.

The numerators of the fractions begin with the original number of years of useful life and decrease by 1 for each successive year. Therefore, in the 5 year life of the above asset, the first numerator would be 5 and the constant denominator would be 15. The fraction applied for the first year's depreciation would be 5/15. In the second year, the numerator is decreased by 1, changing it to 4, and the fraction, with the constant denominator of 15, becomes 4/15. The following years' depreciation become 3/15, 2/15, and 1/15.

The total sum of the fractions must always equal 1, which represents 100% of the depreciable amount. In the above case, the sum of the fractions is 5/15 + 4/15 + 3/15 + 2/15 + 1/15 = 15/15 = 1 = 100%.

It can be seen that the above sum is an arithmetic progression that decreases by 1/15 per year. The depreciation will therefore be reduced each year by that fractional part of the depreciable amount. If the depreciable amount is $1,500, then the first year's depreciation will be 5/15 of $1,500, or $500. This depreciation will reduce each year by 1/15 of $1,500, or $100, so the second year's depreciation will be $500 − $100 = $400. This is the same as 4/15 of $1,500.

Adding all the digits of the years to obtain the sum of the years' digits can become quite cumbersome, particularly in real estate where depreciation is taken over a considerable number of years. Because the process involves an arithmetic progression, a formula can be derived for finding the sum of the digits. The formula is

$$S = \frac{n^2 + n}{2}$$

where S is the sum, and n is the number of digits to be added, or the number of years of useful life. The sum for the 5 years above can be found by

$$S = \frac{5^2 + 5}{2} = \frac{25 + 5}{2} = 30/2 = 15,$$

instead of adding $5 + 4 + 3 + 2 + 1$.

Example:

The depreciable amount applicable to a rental property is calculated to be $75,000. It will be depreciated over a 20 year period using sum-of-the-digits method. How much depreciation will be charged off for the first and second years? How much depreciation is reduced each year?

Solution:

Sum of digits = $\dfrac{20^2 + 20}{2} = \dfrac{400 + 20}{2} = 420/2 = 210$

First year depreciation:
   20/210 X $75,000 = .09523 X 75,000 = $7,142.25
Second year depreciation:
   19/210 X $75,000 = .09047 X 75,000 = $6,785.25
Annual *reduction* in depreciation:
   1/210 X $75,000 = .00476 X 75,000 = $357.00
(The depreciation will be reduced by 1/210 or $357.00 each year. The third year's depreciation should therefore be $6,785.25 – $357. = $6,428.25. To verify this, 18/210 X $75,000 = .08571 X 75,000 = $6,428.25.)

A table of decimal equivalents for use with the sum-of-the-digits method is available from the IRS. Computations are easy, however, with any of the inexpensive electronic hand calculators now available.

Finding Book Value

The book value at the end of any year can be found by finding the sum of the digits for the remaining useful life. The sum thus obtained is used as the numerator and the sum of the digits of the total useful life is used as the denominator. The resulting fraction is the fractional part of the depreciable amount that remains to be depreciated or the book value of the asset at the end of that year.

Example:

In the preceding example, what is the book value at the end of the 8th year?

Solution:

Remaining life (book value) = 20 - 8 = 12 years

$$S \text{ (12 years)} = \frac{12^2 + 12}{2} = \frac{144 + 12}{2} = 156/2 = 78$$

Therefore, 78/210 is the fractional remaining life, and 78/210 = .37142 (or 37.1%). So, .37142 × $75,000 = $27,856.50 is the book value at the end of 8 years.

It can be seen from the above that, because of the accelerated depreciation, more than 60% of the allowable depreciation for 20 years has been written off by the end of the 8th year by using the sum-of-the-digits method.

PRORATING DEPRECIATION

For tax purposes, depreciation must be claimed each year. Unclaimed depreciation cannot be taken in any later tax year.

Rarely is an asset acquired on the first day of the tax year. Therefore, it is acceptable to prorate the depreciation of the asset for the nearest number of months in the tax year. (For simplicity and ease of computation in this chapter we are assuming that the fiscal year and calendar year are the same.) Portions of months are not commonly used, and the nearest first of the month will determine which full month to assume as acquisition of the asset.

For straight-line depreciation, the fractional part of a year comparable to the number of months in the year for which the asset is to be depreciated is used as the first year depreciation. If the asset is purchased in September, it is owned for 4/12 of the year and 4/12 of the annual depreciation will be allowed.

Example:

If the annual depreciation of an asset using the straight-line method is $250, what is the first year allowable depreciation if the asset was acquired on June 10?

Solution:

June 10 is closer to June 1 than to July 1, so it is considered as a June 1 acquisition. Number of months to end of year, including June, is 7, so 7/12 of a full year's depreciation is allowed.

$$7/12 \times \$250 = \$145.83$$

In the declining-balance method, the same procedure is followed by using a fractional part of the first year's depreciation. The book value or balance of depreciable amount for determining the depreciation for the second year is reduced only by the actual depreciation that was taken in the first year. Thus, if the annual depreciation for the full first year is computed to be $3,600 and only 3/12 (or $900) is allowable, the declining balance for the second year should be reduced only by the $900, and not $3,600.

The sum-of-the-digits method requires a double computation in the early years if the first year is prorated. This is necessary in order to obtain the full depreciation allowed. The full allowable first year depreciation is taken as a fractional or prorated portion the first year and the second year so that a full 12/12 is taken. If 3/12 of it is taken the first year, then the remaining 9/12 of its must be taken the second year. This can be seen more clearly by example:

Example:

A property acquired on October 9 has a useful life of 4 years and a depreciable amount of $2,000. Using the sum-of-the-digits method, what is the allowable depreciation for the first and second years?

Solution:

Sum of digits = $\dfrac{4^2 + 4}{2}$ = 20/2 = 10, and the fraction for the first year is therefore 4/10 and is 3/10 for the second year.

October 1 is the nearest first-of-the-month, so the prorated depreciation for the first year will be 3/12 of the full first year depreciation. First year depreciation:

   4/10 × $2,000 = $800 full first year depreciation, and
   3/12 × $800 = $200 prorated first year depreciation.

In the second year, the first months (9/12) will be at the fractional first year rate of 4/10 and the last 3 months (3/12) at the fractional second year rate of 3/10.

4/10 × $2,000 × 9/12 = $600
3/10 × $2,000 × 3/12 = 150

Total = $750 second year depreciation

The third and later years can be computed by using the fractional rate for the annual reduction in depreciation. In this case it is 1/10, so the annual depreciation is reduced 1/10 of $2,000 = $200 per year.

OTHER METHODS OF DEPRECIATION

The methods of depreciation discussed so far are used mostly for tax purposes. As mentioned earlier, one of the functions of depreciation is to make financial provision for the replacement of capital assets. This can be accomplished through the use of a *sinking fund* or *annuity method*.

Sinking-Fund Method

The sinking-fund method is similar to the straight-line method in that the annual deposits to be made remain constant. As discussed in Chapter 3, annual deposits are made into a *safe* fund to earn compound interest in order to accumulate sufficient funds to meet an obligation at a specified date. The obligation is the depreciable amount and the specified time is the end of the useful life of the property when using the sinking-fund method for depreciation. This method may be used regardless of whether or not actual funds are being deposited.

The procedure for finding the annual depreciation to be deposited is the same as the procedure explained in Chapter 3 for finding a sinking-fund payment. Use is made of the Sinking Fund Factor $(1/S_{\overline{n}|i})$ column of the Compound Interest Tables in the Appendix.

Example:

A building (excluding land) is valued at $20,000 with a remaining useful life of 20 years. What is the annual contribution to the sinking fund for depreciation if the fund earns 5% per year?

Solution:

From Column 3, Sinking Fund Factor page 308.
$1/S_{\overline{n}|i} = 1/S_{\overline{20}|.05} = .030243$
Depreciable amount = \$20,000
\$20,000 × .030243 = \$604.86 annual contribution (or depreciation)

Annuity Method

The annuity method is similar to the sinking-fund method with the exception that a higher rate, or *risk* rate, is used instead of a conservative *safe* rate. The same sinking fund factor column is used at the rate indicated for the annuity.

ACCRUED DEPRECIATION

Accrued depreciation is the depreciation that has already taken place up to a certain date. It is the difference between book value and the depreciable amount as shown by the formula in the section on book value. In the straight-line, declining-balance, and sum-of-the-digits methods, it is a simple matter of computing book value and finding the difference between that value and the depreciable amount. The result is accrued depreciation.

However, in the sinking-fund and annuity methods, the principle of *present value* as determined by the *function of interest,* or the cost of money, must be taken into account. This function is considered by using the accumulation factor ($S_{\overline{n}|i}$) from the Compound Interest Tables.

Accrued Depreciation by
Sinking-Fund Method

Two columns of the Compound Interest Tables are used in measuring accrued depreciation by this method. One, of course is the Sinking Fund Factor (column 3), and the other is the Amount of 1 per Period (column 2). The sinking fund rate is found at the designated interest for the number of years of determined useful life. The accumulation factor is taken from the Amount of 1 per Period column for the effective year in which the accrued depreciation is to be measured. The product of the two is the *percent* measure of accrued depreciation.

Example:

A sinking fund is established at 5% compound interest per annum to provide for depreciation replacement of a building with an estimated useful life of 50 years. What will the accrued depreciation be after 20 years?

Solution:

From column 3, Sinking Fund Factor, page 308:
$$1/S_{\overline{n}|i} = 1/S_{\overline{50}|.05} = .00478$$
From column 2, Amount of 1 per Period, page 308:
$$S_{\overline{n}|i} = S_{\overline{20}|.05} = 33.066$$
Multiply rate by accumulation factor:
$$.00478 \times 33.066 = .15805$$
Accrued Depreciation = 15.8%
(Note that after the 50 year useful life, the accrued depreciation will be $.00478 \times 209.35 = 1.001 = 100\%$)

Accrued Depreciation by Annuity Method

This method is used by institutional investors such as mortgage investment companies and is based more on the concept of reinvestment at rates of interest comparable to that earned by properties than on accruing depreciation losses by establishing a sinking fund. The procedures are the same except for the higher rate of interest.

Example:

What is the percent of accrued depreciation after 20 years on a property if the annuity method is used paying 8% compounded annually? The useful life of the depreciated property is 50 years.

Solution: (Similar to the previous example)

From the Tables, $1/S_{\overline{50}|.08} = .00174$, and $S_{\overline{20}|.08} = 45.762$
$.00174 \times 45.762 = .0796 = 7.9\%$
(Note that after 50 years, $.00174 \times 573.77 = .998$, and $.998 = 100\%$)

DEPRECIATION FOR TAX PURPOSES

For tax purposes, depreciation is a bookkeeping entry and does not affect cash flow. It is, however, a *tax deduction* and reflects a decline in the value of a property for that purpose. Even though the appraised value or market value of a building or property may increase because of inflation or other reasons, the depreciation for tax purposes continues.

The U.S. Tax Reform Acts of 1976 and 1969 established maximum allowable depreciation rates which may be applied to real property when using the methods of depreciation explained in the preceding pages.

The 200% declining-balance and sum-of-the-digits methods may be used only for *new residential rental property* from which at least 80% of the gross rental income is derived from rental of residential units. Other new real property may be depreciated under the straight-line or 150% declining-balance methods.

Used residential rental property with a useful life of 20 years or more may be depreciated under the 125% declining balance method. *Other used* real property may be depreciated only under the straight line method. For additional information, refer to *Publication 534, 1977 Edition,* Internal Revenue Service.

TAX SHELTERS AND DEPRECIATION

Depreciation is the primary source of a tax shelter in real estate investment. Tax shelters are methods taken to *exclude* portions of cash flow from income tax liability and are discussed more fully in Chapter 15 on real estate investments.

The tax-sheltered cash flow is created by the amount that the depreciation, which is tax deductible, exceeds loan principal repayments which are not tax deductible. The tax shelter, however, only postpones or defers taxable income because of *depreciation recapture* considerations in the tax laws.

DEPRECIATION RECAPTURE

When real estate is sold at a profit, capital gains tax is paid on the gain from the sale. Because of tax-deductible depreciation, some ordinary income has been converted to capital gains, which is taxed at a lower rate than ordinary income. In order to avoid abuses of accelerated depreciation, use is made by the IRS of *Depreciation Recapture Provisions* in the tax laws. *Recapture* is the conversion of capital gains into ordinary income for tax purposes.

The Tax Reform Acts of 1976 and 1969 require that all accelerated depreciation taken after 1975 above or in excess of the straight-line depreciation rate on all commercial and residential property (except low income housing) must be *recaptured* as ordinary income when the property is sold. Years of ownership prior to 1976 are allowed certain other recapture provisions in the Acts. Examples of depreciation recapture on investment properties are included in Chapter 15.

Future Depreciation

Future depreciation is actually *capital recapture*. It is the return or amortization of the capital invested over the remaining useful or economic life of the building. It differs from *depreciation recapture* in that it refers only to the return of capital invested without regard to the amount of depreciation that has been used as a tax deduction. As such, it is used in determining *capitalization rates*, which will be discussed in Chapter 12.

12

Computations Used in Appraisals
and Valuations

An appraisal is an *estimate of value*. There is no direct mathematical formula that can be used to obtain an appraised valuation. Judgement of the appraiser, however, is not the sole basis of an appraisal and he must use many mathematical concepts, tables, and formulas to *assist* him in formulating a proper appraisal.

The knowledge of basic appraisal mathematics is essential to anyone who has an interest in or must make decisions involving real estate. All real estate personnel are directly or indirectly concerned with the solutions of appraisal problems.

The mathematics of appraisal involves use of compound interest tables, sinking fund and annuity formulas, and various computations of capitalization, depreciation, amortization, and rents. Many of these aspects have been covered in previous chapters and, in order to avoid repetition, reference will be made to the pertinent chapters as necessary.

THE METHODS OF
PROPERTY VALUATION

There are three basic approaches used in appraising a property. These are the Cost Approach, the Market Value Approach, and the

Income Approach. Each approach represents a method used to arrive at a value and can be defined as follows:

Cost Approach: Obtaining value by estimating the current reproduction cost of a property less its accrued depreciation, consisting of physical deterioration, functional obsolescence, and economic obsolescence.

Market Value Approach: The comparison in market value data with similar properties in order to obtain an indicated current market value.

Income Approach: Determining the present value, by capitalization of income, of the future earnings of an investment in a property.

Cost Approach

The Cost Approach, as defined above, consists of five steps:
1. Determine the land value.
2. Estimate the current reproduction cost new of the buildings and other improvements.
3. Determine accrued depreciation.
4. Deduct accrued depreciation from reproduction cost estimate.
5. Add land value to develop the indicated total property value.

Breakdown Method

The appraiser must observe and *break down* the depreciation occurring in the structure attributable to physical deterioration, functional obsolescence, and economic obsolescence. The problem then becomes one of translating these *observed deficiencies* into *mathematical estimates* of accrued depreciation. Because we are concerned with the mathematics only, we will not discuss the theories used in obtaining the values of the three elements.

Once the appraiser has determined a value (dollar or percentage) for each of the elements, he deducts the total amount attributable to such depreciation from the reproduction cost new to obtain the present value. Note that these elements are also broken up into *curable* and *incurable* factors (repairable and unrepairable).

Example:

The reproduction cost new of a residential dwelling is estimated at $26,500. Land is valued at $6,500. Physical deterioration curable is estimated at $3,560 and incurable at $4,230. The functional obsolescence is estimated at $2,500 incurable. Economic obsolescence is considered to be $1,000. What is the appraised value by the Cost Approach?

Solution:

Find the total accrued depreciation:
  Physical deterioration
    Curable $3,560
    Incurable   4,230
  Functional obsolescence
    Curable   -0-
    Incurable   2,500
  Economic obsolescence   1,000
        Total Accrued Depreciation $11,290
Deduct accrued depreciation from reproduction cost:
        $26,500 – $11,290 = $15,210
Value, less depreciation (buildings and improvements) = $15,210
Add Land Value   +6,500
        Total value by Cost Approach $21,710

Effective Age Method

The appraiser may use a straight-line method of depreciation and adjust his observed depreciation accordingly. For instance, he may decide that the total useful life of a building is 50 years and reproduction cost new is $30,000. He then decides on an *effective age* of the building depending upon its condition. If the property has been poorly maintained, he may judge that its effective age is 20 years even though it may be only 15 years old *chronologically*. The effective age of 20 years will be used in determining accrued depreciation. Thus,

Straight-line depreciation = 100%/50 = 2% per year
20 years (effective age) × 2% = 40% accrued depreciation
40% of $30,000 = $12,000 accrued depreciation, and
$30,000 – $12,000 = $18,000 value of the building.

Example:

A building is estimated to have a reconstruction cost new of $150,000. Its useful life has been estimated at 80 years and its current age is 20 years. The appraiser has determined that the improvements are in better than average condition and therefore considers its effective age as 10 years. What is the value of the building by the Cost Approach?

Solution:

Straight-line depreciation = 100%/80 = 1.25% per year
Effective age 10 years X 1.25% = 12.5% depreciation
12.5% of $150,000 = $18,750 accrued depreciation

Reproduction cost	= $150,000
less accrued depreciation	−18,750
Building value by Cost Approach	= $131,250

Market Data Approach

As the name implies, the Market Data Approach to valuation is a process of comparing market data or comparable values to arrive at a probable market value or selling price of a property. Adjustments for value are made in comparing properties to allow for any dissimilarities that might affect the market value.

The mathematics of the Market Data Approach include area measurement, ratios, and percentages of various statistics and data, all of which have been discussed previously. Also commonly used are *Frontage and Depth Tables,* and *Gross Income Multipliers.*

Frontage and Depth Tables

Frontage was defined in Chapter 8 as the linear units of measurement along the front of a property. Properties are sold or valued often by their front foot value and, of course, would necessarily utilize a standard depth for that value. For instance, if the standard depth were 100 feet, a 100-foot deep lot may have a value of $80 per front foot. Its value, if it has a frontage of 50 feet, would be 50 X $80 = $4,000.

However, because lots do vary in depth, and the front is more valuable than the rear, depth tables are sometimes used to consider the relationship of depth to value. The depth tables are *guides* and are used only when other data is unobtainable. They do not normally apply to industrial lots which are usually valued according to square foot area, but are used for commercial and residential lots.

Various tables have been developed for all types of property by different individuals and by municipalities and taxing or assessing authorities. They are all based on the same mathematical problem: *to express equivalent values for one foot of frontage for lots of varying depth.* Although the percentages of value used vary in most tables, the procedures for using them is basically the same. Use of the 4-3-2-1 depth rule will therefore be an example for the use of any of the other tables.

The 4-3-2-1 Depth Rule

The accepted standard depth for practically all depth tables is 100 feet. The earliest use of such tables was called the 4-3-2-1 depth rule and it is still in use today. The 4-3-2-1 is the ratio or percentage that each *quarter* of depth bears to the frontage value. Thus, the first quarter (25 feet) represents 40% of the value, the second quarter 30%, third 20%, and fourth, 10%. The first 100 feet of depth therefore has a value of 100%. Every quarter of depth beyond the standard depth decreases in value by 1% from the last quarter. Therefore, the next 25 feet after the standard 100 feet has a value of 9%, the next 25 feet a value of 8%, and so on.

Example:

Two adjacent lots are appraised, and market data indicates a value for a standard depth lot (100 ft.) to be $92.50 per front foot. Lot A has a frontage of 60 feet and a depth of 85 feet. Lot B has a frontage of 75 feet and a depth of 125 feet. What is the value of each lot per front foot?

Solution:

Lot A depth = 85 feet:
First 75 feet valued at 40% + 30% + 20% = 90%
Next 25 feet has a value of 10% but depth of lot is only
    10 feet of the 25 feet. By proportion, find the percentage that 10
    feet bears to 25 feet at 10% value:

$$10\%/X\% = 25 \text{ feet}/10 \text{ feet}$$
$$25X = 100$$
$$X = 100/25 = 4 = 4\%$$

Percentage depth value of first 75 feet =   90%
Percentage depth value of next 10 feet =   4%
    Total depth value of 85 feet =   94%

94% of $92.50 = .94 × $92.50 = $86.95 per front foot for Lot A.
Lot B depth = 125 feet
100 feet = 100% value (40% + 30% + 20% + 10%)
The next 25 feet has 9% value. Therefore, 100% + 9% = 109%.
109% of $92.50 = 1.09 × $92.50 = $100.825 per front foot (Lot B)
Value of each lot per front foot:
Lot A = $87.00 per front foot (rounded-off)
Lot B = $101.00 per front foot (rounded off)

Note in the above example how the application of the depth rule affects the square footage value of the lots. Lot A has a value of

60 front feet × $86.95 per front foot = $5,217, and a per square foot value of
60 ft. × 85 ft. = 5,100 square feet
5,100 sq. ft./$5,217 = $.98 = $1.00 *per square foot,*

whereas Lot B has a value of

75 front feet × $100.83 per front foot = $7,562.25, and a per square foot value of
75 ft. × 125 ft. = 9,375 square feet
9,375 sq. ft./$7,562.25 = *$1.24 per square foot*

Gross Income Multipliers

The gross income multiplier is a mathematical device used by real estate appraisers and investors to convert annual or monthly gross income into an indication of market value. In appraising, it is used *only* in the market data approach as a comparison to other income-producing properties. It is not normally used in the other approaches to valuation because it is indicative of *gross income* and does not establish any reference to *net income.*

The multiplier is the *ratio* of established or estimated market value to the actual or estimated annual or monthly rental. By custom, it is used as a gross *monthly* multiplier for *residential* properties and as a gross *annual* multiplier for *commercial and industrial* properties. The ratio is shown as

$$\text{Gross Income Multiplier} = \frac{\text{Market Value}}{\text{Monthly or annual rental}}$$

Example:

Find the gross income multiplier (monthly) for a residential property valued at $25,000 with a monthly rental of $180.

Solution:

$$\text{G.I.M} = \frac{\$25,000}{\$180} = 138.9 = 139$$

For commercial and industrial properties, the annual rental must be determined and the multiplier found by formula will be the annual gross income multiplier.

Example:

Find the gross income multiplier for a commercial property with a current market value of $135,000 if the monthly rental is $875.

Solution:

Annual rental = 12 X $875 = $10,500
G.I.M. = $135,000/$10,500 = 12.85 = 13

Once the gross income multiplier is found it can be used to indicate either market value or reasonable rental if one or the other factors is known. To determine market value, multiply the G.I.M. by the gross rental income.

Example:

The gross income multiplier is 14 and the gross rental income is $12,000. What is the estimated value of a comparable property?

Solution:

G.I.M. X Annual rental = Value
14 X $12,000 = $168,000

To find the reasonable rental as compared to similar properties, divide the market value by the G.I.M.

Example:

The market value of a property is estimated at $130,000. If comparable properties have a G.I.M. of 11, what is the reasonable rental of the property by comparison?

Solution:

Market Value/G.I.M. = Rent
$130,000/11 = $11,818 = $12,000 annual rent

Income Approach

The Income Approach, as defined above, is the method of determining the present value of estimated future income based on capitalization of the net income. Application of the Income Approach involves:
1. Analyzing and forecasting gross income.
2. Analyzing and forecasting operating costs.
3. Computing the net income.
4. Estimating future depreciation (recapture), and making provision for maintaining the capital fund, and
5. Selecting and computing an appropriate capitalization rate.

It is apparent that the estimation of value by this method is basically mathematical or actuarial. Items 1, 2, and 3 are accounting procedures and will not be discussed here. They are also related to real estate investment and some discussion of them will be made in Chapter 15. The most important mathematical aspect of the Income Approach is *capitalization*.

Principles of Capitalization

Capitalization can be defined in simple terms as the *valuation of capital.* In real estate, since capital consists of income-producing land and its improvements, capitalization means the valuation of property according to its net income or earning capacity.

Capitalization is similar to *interest,* and the basic interest formula, $I = PRT$ (Chapter 1), is used as the basis for capitalization formulas. Time (T) is on the basis of *one* year and becomes an unnecessary factor here. By use of the interest formula, we know that a $100,000 investment at a 6% interest rate will produce interest (I) of $6,000 for the year. By formula,

$$I = PR = \$100,000 \times .06 = \$6,000$$

If we had to find the principal that was necessary to produce $8,000 interest at a rate of 8%, we would use the formula

$$P = I/R, \text{ and}$$
$$P = \$8,000/.08 = \$100,000$$

In comparing this to capitalization, it can be seen that interest (I) is comparable to the *income of the property*, interest rate (R) is comparable to the *capitalization rate*, and the principal (P) is the *invested capital* or the *value* of the property that produces an amount of income at a certain rate of capitalization. We can therefore use the symbol V for *value* as an equivalent to the symbol P for principal in the formula. The interest formula has now been transformed into a capitalization formula $I = VR$, and, because in appraising we are finding *value*, $V = I/R$ becomes the valuation formula, wherein V = value, I = net income, and R = captalization rate.

Example:

A property produces an annual net income of $3,800. The capitalization rate is determined to be 8%. What is the value of the property?

Solution:

$$V = I/R$$
$$V = \$3,800/.08 = \$47,500$$

Capitalization Rates

It can be seen from the above formula that the capitalization rate is the *ratio* of net income to the value or selling price of the property. As such it is a composite rate of the interest *on*, and recapture *of*, the investment.

Interest Rate + Capital Recapture Rate = Capitalization Rate

The value or selling price of the entire property includes land and buildings and the rate R is therefore considered the *overall capitalization rate.*

Overall Rate and Direct Capitalization

If the net income I, and the value, or sales price, V are known, the capitalization formula for finding rate R must be used. By solving for R, we derive the formula for rate as

$$R = I/V$$

The formula is used for computing typical rates of comparable properties in order to find the rate that compares most favorably with the subject property. The overall rate thus found applies to *both* the land and the buildings. The use of this method is called *Direct Capitalization.*

Example:

A property has a sales price of $200,000 and an annual net income of $15,000. What is the overall capitalization rate?

Solution:

$R = I/V$
$R = \$15,000/\$200,000$
$R = .075 = 7.5\%$

The overall rate found in the above problem can be used to determine the value of a comparable property.

Example:

After comparison with several properties, it is determined that an overall rate of 9% can be used for valuation of a property. If the net income of the property in question is $45,000 annually, what is its value?

Solution:

$V = I/R$
$V = \$45,000/.09 = \$500,000$

Building and Land Rate of Capitalization

The overall rate can be used *only* in the direct method of capitalization. In using the rate found, it must be remembered that the overall rate includes elements that must also be comparable; that is, interest and recapture. All other methods of capitalization require separate computations of an interest rate for land and buildings and a recapture rate of the buildings only.

In the above example, for instance, the capitalization rate of 9% used in the computation as an overall rate is composed of an interest rate on the land and an interest and recapture rate on the building. If the interest rate on the land and building can be determined, the recapture rate for the building can be computed as in the following example.

Example:

The annual rate of interest return on a property valued at $500,000 is considered to be 7%. The overall capitalization rate is 9%, land value is determined to be $120,000 and the net income is $45,000. What is the recapture rate on the building?

Solution:

Find interest on land and building:

Interest = $500,000 × .07 = $35,000 per year

Deduct interest income from annual net income to determine the amount attributable to recapture:

$45,000 – $35,000 = $10,000 annual recapture

Find recapture rate of building by using ratio of recapture income to value of building ($R = I/V$):

Building value = $500,000 – $120,000 = $380,000
Recapture rate = $10,000/$380,000 = .02777 = 2.8% (rounded)

It can be seen that in the above example, the overall rate of capitalization consisted of interest on the land and buildings of 7% and a recapture rate on the building of 2.8%.

Building rate of capitalization can therefore be defined as a composite rate of interest *on* and the recapture *of* the building investment, and can be found by the ratio of the building net income to the value of the building. Or, by formula,

$$R_b = I_b/V_b, \text{ where the } b \text{ indicates } \textit{building,}$$

The land rate of capitalization can be defined as the ratio of net income derived from the land to the sales price or value of the land, By formula,

$$R_1 = I_1/V_1, \text{ where } l \text{ indicates } land$$

Because depreciation, and hence recapture, is rarely used in land valuation, the land capitalization rate will usually be made up only of the land interest. In certain cases, such as depletion of minerals or other resources, and in some leasehold situations, depreciation is applicable. Only in those instances would a recapture rate for land be used.

Recapture Rates

It is obvious from the preceding paragraphs that recapture is the same as *future depreciation,* and basically means the return or amortization of the capital invested over the remaining economic life of the building. The recapture rate is based on the age-life methods of depreciation explained in Chapter 11.

Straight-line recapture is arrived at in the same manner as straight-line depreciation.

Example:

The estimated remaining economic life of a building is 40 years. What is the straight-line recapture rate?

Solution:

Economic life = 40 years = 100%
100%/40 = .025 = 2.5% recapture rate (or annual future depreciation)

A 2½% return of the investment is required each year in order to recapture the capital. The 2½% is the straight-line recapture rate.

The other methods used for selecting recapture rates are *The Sinking-Fund Method* and *The Annuity Method,* both of which will be discussed later in this chapter under those methods of capitalization.

Methods for Determining Interest Rates

The basic element of the capitalization rate is the interest rate which is a return *on* the investment. As such it must be high enough to attract investors. The appraiser must determine what interest rate to use in addition to the recapture rate in order to arrive at the capitalization rate. The various methods available include Comparison, Summation (of various economic factors), and the Band-of-Investment Method. The Comparison and Summation Methods involve a minimum of mathematics and therefore will not be shown here.

Band-of-Investment Method

Because most real estate today uses mortgage debt financing, the appraiser can use data on current mortgage rates of interest and equity interest rates to obtain a *composite interest rate*. The composite rate of interest is an *average* rate of the portions of value represented by equity and mortgage positions. These are the *bands of investment*.

Example:

Current market interest rate is 9% for an 80% mortgage, and equity investors are estimated to be receiving 12% returns in interest on investments. What interest rate could be used for a property with an 80% mortgage?

Solution:

$$
\begin{aligned}
\text{Value of property} &= 100\% \\
\text{Mortgage value} = 80\% \times 9\% \text{ interest} &= .80 \times .09 = \ .072 \\
\text{Equity value } = 20\% \times 12\% \text{ interest} &= .20 \times .12 = \underline{+.024} \\
\text{Composite Interest Rate} &= \ \ .096 = 9.6\%
\end{aligned}
$$

If, in the above example, an annual net income of $25,000 is to be valued, the distribution of mortgage and equity would be as follows:

$$
\begin{aligned}
\text{Value} = I/R \ \ &= \$25,000/.096 \ \ &&= \$260,416 \\
\text{Mortgage } 80\% &= \$208,333 \text{ at } 9\% \ \ &&= \ \ \$18,750 \\
\text{Equity } 20\% \ \ &= +\ 52,083 \text{ at } 12\% = \ \ &&+\ 6,250 \\
\text{Totals} \ \ &= \$260,416 \ \ &&\ \ \$25,000
\end{aligned}
$$

METHODS OF CAPITALIZATION

All methods of capitalization are based on the formula $V = I/R$ which expresses the mathematical relationship of income to value.

Because recapture is such an important part of the capitalization process when the formula is used, the methods of capitalization are named according to the method used to provide for recapture. The methods therefore are: Straight-Line Capitalization, Annuity Capitalization, and Sinking-Fund Capitalization.

Straight-Line Capitalization

In this method the straight-line recapture rate is found and added to the selected interest rate to obtain the building capitalization rate. The method for finding straight-line recapture rates was shown earlier. A land-building ratio or other method must be used in order to arrive at a value of the land. If the value of the land cannot be obtained, then the Land Residual Technique should be used. This technique will be explained later in the chapter.

Once the interest and capitalization rates have been determined, the capitalization formula can be used to obtain the value of the property.

Example:

A property produces a net annual income of $15,000. The portion of income attributable to the land is 20%. The remaining economic life of the building is estimated to be 25 years. The estimated interest rate is 8%. What is the value of the property?

Solution:

Income attributed to land value = $15,000 × .20 = $3,000
Land Capitalization Rate = Interest Rate = 8%
Land Value = V = I/R = $3,000/.08 = $37,500
Find the building capitalization rate:
  Recapture Rate = 100%/25 = 4%
                              +
  Interest Rate   = 8%
  Building Capitalization Rate = 12%
Find the building value:
  V = I/R = $12,000/.12   = $100,000
Add the land value   +   37,500
     Total Property Value   = $137,500

The above method of straight-line capitalization does not use the Compound Interest Tables. The method is usually used only on investment properties that will have a comparatively short period of income production. This method also assumes some decline in income during the life of the property.

The other methods of capitalization, to be explained below, make use of the Compound Interest Tables which can be found in the Appendix. The use of the tables, compound interest, annuities, and sinking funds were explained in Chapter 3. For the purposes of our explanations here, a familiarity with the uses of the tables and terms in Chapter 3 will be assumed.

Annuity Capitalization

The method of annuity capitalization is the process of computing the sum of the present value of future payments of an annuity wherein each payment is *discounted* for loss of interest income. The income from investment real estate is an annuity type of income. As the investment value or capital decreases each year by recapture, the interest on the remaining value also decreases. Although the interest return declines each year, the recapture increases, thereby maintaining a steady income stream.

As mentioned, a portion of income received is recapture, which is the *amortization* of the capital invested. In Chapter 3 it was shown that the sinking fund table is also used as an amortization table. It can therefore be used to determine the recapture, or amortization, of the investment capital.

The factor from the sinking fund or amortization table is used as the *recapture component* of the composite capitalization rate, the interest rate being the other component. In using the table, the interest rate for earnings of the whole property is also used as the rate for finding the factor from the table.

Example:

A property has an estimated remaining economic life of 40 years and an annual net income of $25,000. The market interest rate is determined to be 8%. By the annuity method, what is the value of the property?

Solution:

Use the Compound Interest Tables in the Appendix.
From Column 3, Sinking Fund Factor, page 314:
$1/S_{\overline{n}|i} = 1/S_{\overline{40}|.08} = .003860 =$ recapture rate
Capitalization rate = Recapture rate + Interest rate
$\qquad R = .003860 + .08 = .083860$
Value Formula:
$\quad V = I/R = \$25,000/.083860 = \$298,115$ property value.
To verify the value:

8% return on $298,115	=	$23,849.20
.003860 recapture on $298,115 =		1,150.72
Total =		$24,999.92,

rounded-off to $25,000 total income.

Inwood Method

The method of using certain tables of compound interest is sometimes named after the person who popularized its usage. The Inwood Method uses the *Present Value of 1 per Period Table* ($a_{\overline{n}|i}$) instead of the Sinking Fund Table and the table is therefore also called the *Inwood Premise Table*. The method is the same as the annuity method shown above with some simplification.

In the formula $V = I/R$, the capitalization rate R is replaced by its reciprocal, symbolized as F. By using the reciprocal, the formula is changed to multiplication instead of division, and becomes

$$V = I \times F \text{ or, } V = IF$$

The factor found in the table represents the reciprocal of the sum of interest *and* recapture and it is therefore not necessary to add the two to obtain the value of F in the formula.

Example:

Using the same valuation information as the preceding example, find the value of the property by using the Inwood Method.

Solution:

From column 5, Present Value of 1 per Period, Page 315:
$$a_{\overline{n}|i} = a_{\overline{40}|.08} = 11.9246$$
Value Formula (Inwood):
$V = IF = \$25,000 \times 11.9246 = \$298,115$ property value

It can be seen from the above that both methods produce the same results.

Sinking Fund Method of Capitalization

This method is based on the assumption that recapture payments are deposited to accumulate at interest. The recapture is thus deferred until the end of the economic life of the property when it is recaptured in a lump sum. The recapture deposit must be made into a *safe* sinking fund which, by virtue of its secure nature, will pay a relatively low rate of interest (as opposed to a *risk* rate). In view of the foregoing, the method is rarely used today.

The procedure is the same as the annuity method with the exception of the sinking fund *rate*.

Example:

Using the same valuation information as the preceding examples, find the value of the property using the sinking fund method at a sinking fund rate of 4%.

Solution:

From column 3, Sinking Fund Factor, page 306:

$$1/S_{\overline{n}|\,i} = 1/S_{\overline{40}|\,.04} = .010523$$

Capitalization Rate = R = .010523 + .08 = .090523

Value Formula:

V = I/R = \$25,000/.090523 = \$276,172 property value

Hoskold Annuity Method

The Hoskold method uses the sinking fund factor as above but utilizes the reciprocal value of R, thereby changing the value formula to V = IF as in the Inwood Method. Hoskold uses the reciprocal F as

$$F = \frac{1}{\text{interest rate} + \text{sinking fund factor}}$$

Special tables have been derived for the reciprocal values thus obtained. This method will not be shown here as it is basically the same as the above example, but uses the value formula of V = IF.

LAND-BUILDING RATIOS

For purposes of simplification in the above methods, we disregarded land valuation. The straight capitalization method included valuation of land as a percentage of income attributable to the land value. It is a normal procedure to develop such land-building ratios in all the methods and to add the land value to the final property valuation. If the ratio is established at 20/80 (land/buildings), then 20% of the income must be used to find land value. If a ratio cannot be established, and market data for comparison is not available, the Land Residual Technique can be used with any of the capitalization methods.

THE RESIDUAL TECHNIQUES

In mathematics, a *residual* is formed by the subtraction of one quantity from another. The residual is the quantity that is *left over* or remaining. In applying this to real estate, if the appraiser can determine the portion of income that is imputable to the *known* values, he can determine the *unknown* values by what is left over, or *residual* to the total. The land residual technique, for instance, is used to determine land value as the residual or remainder when the value of a building can be accurately estimated or is known.

For illustrative purposes in explaining each of the techniques, we shall use only the straight-line and annuity-capitalization methods, bearing in mind, of course, that any of the other capitalization methods could be similarly used.

Land Residual Technique

In the land residual technique, the building value is determined first and the net return of interest and recapture on the building value is deducted from the net income imputed to the entire property. The residual is attributable to the land and is therefore capitalized to arrive at an estimated land value.

Example:

Value of a building is determined to be $150,000, the estimated remaining economic life is 50 years, rate of interest is 8%, and the net annual income is $20,000. Find the property value using the straight-line and annuity capitalization methods and the land residual technique.

Solution:

(1) Straight-Line Capitalization
Determine building rate of capitalization:

Recapture rate = 100%/50 years	=	2% = .02	
Interest rate	=	8% = .08	
Total Building rate	=	10% = .10	

Find income imputable to building:

$I = VR = \$150,000 \times .10 = \$15,000$

Find income imputable to land (residual income):

$20,000 - $15,000 = $5,000

Find land value (capitalization rate = interest rate):

$V = I/R = \$5,000/.08 = \$62,500$

Find property value:

Building value + land value = $150,000 + $62,500 =

$212,500 property valuation

(2) Annuity Capitalization Method
Determine building rate of capitalization:

Recapture rate (Column 3, 50 years @ 8%)	=	.001743
Interest rate	=	+.08
Total Building rate	=	.081743

Find income imputable to building:

$I = VR = \$150,000 \times .081743 = \$12,261.$

Find income imputable to land (residual income)

$20,000 - $12,261 = $7,739.

Find land value: (Capitalization rate = interest rate)

$V = I/R = \$7,739/.08 = \$96,737.50$ or $96,738 (rounded)

Find property value:

Building value + land value = $150,000 + $96,738 =

$246,738 property valuation

The significant difference in value of $34,238 in the two methods is because of the different assumptions made in the recapture rate of each method. The straight-line method combines an interest-bearing rate of capitalization with a non-interest bearing rate of recapture. The annuity method is more accurate and is the preferred method. (The Inwood Method could also be used in the same manner.)

Building Residual Technique

When the *land value is known,* or can be established, and the *building value is unknown,* the building residual technique is used. The procedure is similar to the land residual technique, the difference being that the building value is the residual rather than the land value. Because of this similarity, our illustration will use only the annuity method, the other methods becoming obvious at this point.

Example:

The value of the land of a property is determined to be $50,000. The estimated remaining economic life is 40 years, the interest rate (land and building) is 8%, and the net annual income is $15,000. What is the value of the property by the annuity capitalization method and the building residual technique?

Solution:

Annuity Capitalization Method
Find income imputable to land:
$I = VR = \$50,000 \times .08 = \$4,000$
Find income imputable to building:
$\$15,000 - \$4,000 = \$11,000$
Determine the building rate of capitalization:

Recapture rate (column 3, 40 years @ 8%)	= .003860
Interest rate = 8%	= .08
Total building rate	= .083860

Find building value (residual):
$V = I/R = \$11,000/.083860 = \$131,170$
Find property value:
Land value + building value = $50,000 + $131,170 =
$181,170 property valuation

Reversion

Before discussing the Property Residual Technique, it is necessary to be familiar with the term *reversion.* Reversion is defined as the act of reverting or returning to a former condition. In real estate it can be defined as the return of control or possession of property after the expiration of a lease or the net proceeds from its sale after a period of ownership.

The reversionary value of real estate is the value it will have when sold or returned after a period of time. The mathematical problem in appraising is to estimate the reversionary value for the future return or sale and to convert that value to present value. Column 4, Present Value of 1, (V^n), of the Compound Interest Tables is used for this purpose. (See Chapter 3 for explanation of Present Value of 1.)

Example:

What is the present value of a parcel of land if it is estimated that it will have a value of $40,000 in 20 years and the market interest rate is 7%?

Solution:

Find the present value factor from the Compound Interest Tables, column 4, page 313 for 20 years at 7%:
Factor = .258419
Multiply the factor by the future worth to obtain present value:
$40,000 × .258419 = $10,336.76 = present value

Property Residual Technique

This technique is used when *neither* the land *nor* building value can be determined. The reversionary value of the land is used because its effect on present value will be of minimal consequence if the estimated future value is in error. The procedure in this technique is to use the overall capitalization rate to find the value of the property net income and to add to that value the present worth of the anticipated land value at some future date (reversionary value).

Example:

Remaining economic life of a property is estimated to be 40 years. The net annual income is $15,000 and the interest rate is 9%. The anticipated land value in 40 years is $60,000. Find the property value using the Annuity Method and the Property Residual Technique.

Solution:

Find the property rate of capitalization:

Recapture rate (column 3, 40 years @ 9%) = .002960
Interest rate = 9%   = .09
                    Total property rate   = .092960

Find value of property income:

$V = I/R = \$15,000/.092960 = \$161,359$

Find present value of land:

Column 4, 40 years @ 9%, Factor = .031838

$\$60,000 \times .031838 = \$1,910.28 = \$1,910$ (rounded-off)

Find property value:

Value of property income + present reversionary value of land

= $\$161,359 + \$1,910 = \underline{\$163,269}$ property valuation

13

Applying Mathematics to Leases

The mathematics of leases involves many facets of real estate mathematics. By virtue of its income-producing nature, it can be considered as real estate *investment* mathematics. Because investment must be analyzed by valuation, leasing must also be covered by real estate *appraising* mathematics.

We will attempt, in this chapter, to cover both the investment and valuation aspects of the mathematics of leasing.

DEFINITIONS

To avoid confusion in terminology, certain terms must be defined according to their usage in this chapter.

A *lease* is simply a contract, between the owner of a property and the *tenant*, which transfers the right of possession and enjoyment of the real estate to the tenant in return for *rent* on the property. The owner is called the *lessor* and the tenant is called the *lessee*.

The rights and interests of the lessor or owner of the property *in* his property, in accordance with the terms and conditions of the lease, is called the *Leased Fee*.

The *Leasehold* (or leasehold estate) is the lessee's interest in the property.

In a *Net Lease,* the lessee pays all or a substantial part of the operating costs and maintenance of the property. When the lessee pays all the expenses the lease is sometimes called a *net-net lease.* A *Gross Lease* provides only for payment of a stipulated rent and no expenses of the property.

Long-term leases are those that extend from 10 or more years and *Short-term leases* are those of under 10 years duration. Common usage varies however, and a period of 21 years is sometimes used as the demarcation between long or short term leases.

FIXED RENTAL LEASES

In the fixed rental lease (also called flat or straight lease), the rental is a fixed sum paid periodically throughout the term of the lease.

The mathematics of a fixed rental lease involves only the computations for determining the periodic rent (monthly, quarterly, semi-annually, or annually). If a lessor determines the annual rent needed from a property, he need only divide that amount by 12 (months) to find the monthly rent. In the case of commercial or industrial properties, however, where rents are often based on annual rent per square foot of area, the area computation must be made first.

Example:

An office is leased for $8.50 per square foot annually. The office is 25 feet wide by 100 feet long. What is the monthly rent?

Solution:

Area = L $\times$ W = 100' $\times$ 25' = 2,500 square feet
Annual Rent = 2,500 sq. ft. $\times$ $8.50 = $21,250
Monthly Rent = $21,250/12 = $1,770.83 = $1,771

PERCENTAGE LEASES

Although there are variations in form, the percentage lease basically requires that the lessee pay a stipulated percentage of the gross sales made on the premises as rent.

It is common practice to establish a minimum rental based on a percentage of the value of a fixed rental (40% to 80%). The percentage of gross sales required is then established, based on various factors including the type of business and the anticipated range of gross sales volume. Tables are available listing types of businesses and the range of gross sales percentages that normally apply to the type of business.

Some tables and sources for others may be found in McMichael & O'Keefe, *Leases: Percentage, Short and Long Term,* 5th Ed., 10th printing, Englewood Cliffs, NJ: Prentice-Hall, Inc., 1971. The ranges are based on the percentage that a particular type of business could afford to pay. For instance, a supermarket range might be 1 to 2%, while a parking lot may pay 60 to 75%.

Example:

A percentage lease for a shoe store calls for a minimum rental of $10,000 per annum and a percentage rental of 6% of gross volume. In 1975 the store had a gross volume of $160,000 and in 1976 it had a gross volume of $220,000. What were the annual rentals for each of those years?

Solution:

1975: $160,000 volume X .06 = $9,600
Because $9,600 is below the minimum rental of $10,000, the $10,000 would apply as the annual rent.
1976: $220,000 volume X .06 = $13,200
Annual rent would be $13,200 for 1976.

CONTRACT AND ECONOMIC RENT

Contract rent is the actual rent paid, or contracted for in the lease. *Economic rent* is the rent that a tenant should be, or is warranted in, paying according to current rentals of comparable properties in the open real estate market. The excess of economic or contract rent over the other results in a transfer of value from lessor to lessee or vice versa. These terms are important in determining Leased Fee Value and Leasehold Value.

Example:

Contract rent is $18,000 annually and the economic rent is estimated at $21,400. What benefit is derived from this situation and to whom?

Solution:

Economic Rent $21,400
Contract Rent – 18,000
Excess = $3,400

The excess of $3,400 per year is in favor of the lessee and therefore represents a value (leasehold value) to him. This amount can be capitalized into present leasehold value as will be shown later.

LEASED FEE VALUATION

The value of the leased fee (lessor's interest) is the present value of the contract rent plus the present value of the reversion of the property at the termination of the lease.

Because income from a leased property usually forms an annuity (see Chapter 3), the annuity, or Inwood Method of capitalization (see Chapter 12) is used in determining leased fee and leasehold valuations.

The Inwood Table, column 5 of the Compound Interest Tables, (or Present Worth of 1 per Period) is used with the reversion table, column 4, (or Present Worth of 1) for both valuations. (Note that when leases involve *advance payment* of rent, the annuity is an *annuity due*. To use column 5, the number of payments, n, is reduced by 1, and 1 is added to the factor from the table.)

In determining the value of the leased fee, the land is considered to have the same value at reversion as it has at present. The building must be depreciated to the end of the lease term to determine the reversionary value.

Example:

A building valued at $200,000 on land valued at $40,000 is rented on a 20 year lease for an annual rent of $21,400. The annual rental is considered a fair rental for comparable properties on the open market. The building will have depreciated in value 50% at the end of the lease. An interest rate of 8% is considered appropriate. What is the total value of the leased fee?

Solution:

Contract rent = Economic rent

Find present value of contract rent:
$\quad$ F (Inwood Factor) = $a_{\overline{n}|i}$ = $a_{\overline{20}|.08}$ = 9.818815 and,
$\quad$ V = I X F = \$21,400 X 9.81815 = \$210,108
Find present value of property reversion:
$\quad$ Land $\qquad\qquad\qquad$ = $\quad$ \$40,000
$\quad$ Building (\$200,000 X 50%) = $\quad$ 100,000

$\qquad\qquad$ Total reversion = \$140,000
Present value factor of reversion at 8% (column 4):
$\quad$ V^n = V^{20} = .214548
Present value of property reversion:
$\quad$ \$140,000 X .214548 = \$30,035.
Find value of leased fee:
$\quad$ Present value of contract rent $\qquad$ = $\quad$ \$210,108
$\quad$ Present value of property reversion = + $\quad$ 30,035

$\qquad\qquad$ Total value of leased fee = $\quad$ \$240,143

In the above example, the value of the leased fee was equal to the value of the property because the contract rent and economic rent were equal. If contract rent is less than economic rent, the loss in value to the lessor becomes *value*, or leasehold, to the lessee. By using the economic and contract rent of the preceding section, we can use the above example to show the difference in leased fee valuation.

Example:
$\quad$ Same information as the above example except for contract rent which is \$18,000 and economic rent which is \$21,400. Find the leased fee value.

Solution:
$\quad$ The present value of the property reversion is the same, \$30,000 (rounded-off).

$\quad$ Find the present value of the contract rent:
$\quad$ F = 9.81815
$\quad$ V = I X F = \$18,000 X 9.81815 = \$176,726
Find value of leased fee:
$\quad$ Present value of contract rent $\qquad$ = \$177,000 (rounded)
$\quad$ Present value of property reversion = + 30,000

$\qquad\qquad$ Total value of leased fee = \$207,000

The difference in value of $33,000 represents the value of the leasehold. The value of the leasehold may be indicated by the difference between the property value and the leased fee, but such is not always the case.

If the contract rent is more than the economic rent, then the leased fee value will be more than the total property value and will represent additional value to the lessor because of the higher rent he is receiving.

LEASEHOLD VALUATION

In theory, the leasehold has no value. However, as shown in the above paragraphs, the lessor transfers some of the value of his leased fee to the lessee when the contract rent is lower than the economic rent. Leasehold valuation can be found separately from the leased fee by *discounting* the future rights of the leasehold to present value. The present value will represent a negative or positive leasehold value depending upon the difference between economic and contract rent.

Example:

A 20 year lease requires annual payments of $9,000 in rent. If the economic rent is considered $12,000 annually, and the assumed interest rate is 7%, what is the leasehold value?

Solution:

Economic rent − contract rent = $12,000 − $9,000 = $3,000.
Present value of $3,000 for 20 years discounted at 7%:
From column 5 of the Compound Interest Tables,
$F = a_{\overline{n}|i} = a_{\overline{20}|.07} = 10.59401$ and,
$V = I \times F = \$3,000 \times 10.59401 = \$31,782$
Total Leasehold Value = $31,782

Note that in the above example, a *risk* rate of 7% was used because of the *reduced risk* in collecting contract rent that is lower than economic rent.

Leasehold value can also be created by capital investment on the part of the lessee. He may lease ground only and then erect a building on the ground. The capitalized value of the building is a leasehold value and, as such, represents a capital investment that can be mortgaged or sold.

Determination of leasehold value can therefore be an important factor for the lessee when considering sale or mortgage of an assignable or transferable lease.

GRADUATED LEASES

A graduated lease increases or decreases the annual rental at specified intervals of years. The changes may be predetermined or related to some agreed-upon index or revaluation of the real estate.

The valuation determination of graduated leases is done in the same manner as shown under leased fee and leasehold valuation. The present value of each graduation is determined separately and the sum of the present values is the total value of the leased fee or leasehold. An example is not considered necessary here as the process involves only the summation of the present values of the different rentals.

SANDWICH LEASES

If a property is subleased after it has been leased, the original lessee is sandwiched between the lessor and the sublessee and his lease is called a *sandwich lease.*

The sandwich lessee has the right to the income he obtains from the sublessee providing he meets his obligations to the original lessor. In effect then, his return on the value of his leasehold is the difference between what he receives in rent and what he pays to the original lessor.

Example:

A lessee subleases a store for $13,000 per year. His lease to the original lessor calls for a rental payment of $11,250 per year. What is his margin?

Solution.

$13,000 − $11,250 = $1,750 per year margin

As a sandwich leaseholder however, the leasehold value of his margin of $1,750 per year would be lower than the leasehold value if the same $1,750 were the difference between contract and economic rent. Because he assumes a greater risk in subleasing, the risk rate must be assumed higher, resulting in a higher rate of discount for present value.

Example:

Economic rent in the above example is $13,000 and the lease is for 20 years. Market analysis indicates a risk rate of 8% for the lessee if the store is not subleased. As a sandwich lease the risk rate is 12%. What is the leasehold value in each case?

Solution:

Economic rent − contract rent = $13,000 − $11,250 = $1,750
Present value of $1,750 for 20 years discounted at 8%:
$$F = a_{\overline{n}|i} = a_{\overline{20}|.08} = 9.81815 \text{ (column 5)}$$
$$V = I \times F = \$1,750 \times 9,81815 = \$17,181.76$$
Leasehold value = $17,200 (rounded)

As sandwich lease:
Present value of $1,750 for 20 years discounted at 12%:
$$F = a_{\overline{n}|i} = a_{\overline{20}|.12} = 7.46944$$
$$V = I \times F = \$1,750 \times 7.49644 = \$13,118.77$$
Leasehold value = $13,100 (rounded)

It can be seen from the above example that the leasehold value was diminished by $4,100 ($17,200 − $13,100) because of the increased risk of a sandwich lease. (A 4% spread in risk rate is not uncommon.)

SALE AND LEASEBACK

Although the sale and leaseback procedure is basically a financing transaction, it does fall in the category of leasing and is therefore included in this chapter.

Basically the sale-leaseback is just what the name implies. The owner of a property sells it to a party and then leases it back from that party. The purchaser is usually an organization, institution, or other group that controls a large sum of money available for investment (insurance companies, pension funds, syndicates, etc.).

In addition to many tax advantages, it is a method of 100% financing, allowing the lessee to have possession of the real estate without any investment of capital, thereby releasing the capital for other operations without creating debt.

Because we are primarily concerned only with the mathematics of sale-leaseback, an explanation of the advantages and disadvantages of the procedure to either party will not be made here.

The mathematics of the sale-leaseback can be quite involved and may require the use of mortgage and amortization tables. L. W. Ellwood has devised special tables for the procedure and a full explanation is available in his text, *Ellwood Tables for Real Estate Appraising and Financing,* published by the American Institute of Real Estate Appraisers, Chicago, Ill., (1967). We will limit ourselves to the simple mathematics without resorting to mortgage or amortization tables.

There are many variations of sale-leaseback procedures and it would be impossible to illustrate the mathematical applications of *all* the treatments. To show the basic mathematics involved, we will use a sample transaction comparing mortgage financing with the option of sale-leaseback.

Example:

A corporation has acquired a factory building at a cost of $950,000 which consists of $100,000 for land and $850,000 for the building. For depreciation purposes, the building has a useful life of 50 years. For illustrative purposes, a maximum depreciation of 200% declining balance will be used. Two options are available for handling the transaction:

Plan A. A mortgage of $700,000 at 7½% for 25 years is available for financing the transaction.

Plan B. An insurance company is willing to purchase the property, at cost, on a sale-leaseback. The lease would be for 25 years at 7½% with an option to renew the lease for an additional 25 years at 5%.

Real Estate taxes and all maintenance costs are assumed to be the same under each plan and are to be paid by lessee.

Show the mathematics involved in analyzing the cash situation under both plans.

Solution:

Plan A: $700,000 mortgage at 7½% for 25 years.
   Find the annual mortgage payment:
   Constant Annual Percent Table (Appendix) for 7½% at 25 years,
   constant = 8.98% (see Chapter 3)
            Annual payment = $700,000 X .0898 = $62,860
                        (includes principal and interest)
Find total interest cost:
   Total obligation (cash) for 25 years to pay off the mortgage:
                  $62,860 X 25 = $1,571,500
         Interest = $1,571,500 − $700,000 = $871,500
Find allowable maximum depreciation (Chapter 11):
   200% declining balance for 25 years of a 50 year useful life. Percent of balance of depreciable amount remaining = 36.0937%
   (from depreciation tables)
         Accrued depreciation = 100% − 36.0937% = 63.9063%
         $850,000 X .639063 = $543,201 (building only)

Summation Plan A:
   Total cash outlay 25 years (mortgage payments) = $1,571,500.
   Total tax deductions (52%)
      Interest ($871,500 X .52)   = $453,180
      Depreciation ($543,201 X .52) = 282,464

                                                    735,644

      Net cash outlay after deductions   = $835,856
      Initial cash investment ($950,000 − $700,000) =   250,000

                        Total cash expended = $1,085,856

Plan B: Sale and leaseback at 7½% for 25 years.
   Find annual net rental:
      Constant Annual Percent for 7½% at 25 years, constant = 8.98%
      Annual rent payment = $950,000 X .0898 = $85,310.
   Total net rent for 25 years = $85,310 X 25 = $2,132,750.

Summation Plan B:
            Total cash outlay 25 years (rent)   = $2,132,750
            Total tax deductions (52% of net rent)
                  $2,132,750 X .52   = 1,109,030

            Net cash outlay after deductions   = $1,023,720
            Initial cash investment   =   0

                        Total cash expended = $1,023,720

Although there is a difference of only $62,000 in total cash expended, the sale-leaseback required no initial cash investment and the $250,000 would be available to the corporation for other uses.

Many other factors would also have to be considered, and the above example was illustrative only for the applications of the mathematics involved.

Another mathematical consideration, however, would be in the sale-leaseback option to renew. Because of the reduced rental for the next 25 year period (5%), a substantial leasehold value is created.

If we consider the initial annual rent as economic rent, the renewal option rent will be contract rent.

From the Constant Annual Percent Table, 5% for 25 years, the constant is 7.10% and $950,000 X .0710 = $67,450 annual contract rent for the optional 25 years. This results in an annual advantage to the lessee of $17,550 which can be capitalized into the leasehold value.

From Column 5 of the Compound Interest Tables,

$F = a_{\overline{25}|.05} = 14.0939$ and,
$V = I \times F = \$17,550 \times 14.0939 = \$247,347$ leasehold value

The leasehold value of $247,000 is more than half of the depreciated building value and presents a definite advantage to the lessee. In this case, it might be possible for the lessee to mortgage or finance the leasehold if necessary.

14

The Use of Simple Mathematics in Building and Remodeling

REAL ESTATE AND CONSTRUCTION

Construction is an essential element of real estate because the processes of building and remodeling result in new real estate resources. Although the real estate professional will not usually be involved in actual construction, he will be involved in the processes of planning, development, financing, and marketing. These functions are directly related to the construction process and knowledge of the mathematical problems involved is a necessity.

The mathematical problems of construction, building, and remodeling are those that deal with the *estimated costs of labor and material,* both in quantity and quality, and the additional loadings for profit and overhead.

LETTING BIDS

Unless a contract is to be awarded without competitive bidding, bids are usually invited from several contractors. The lowest bidder is normally awarded the contract. Because estimating is only an *ap-*

proximation and not an exact science, bids can vary from 10 to 40 percent on the same plans and specifications. Allowance should be made before letting bids for the *expected range in bids*. Consideration must also be given to the bidding methods to be used. Some typical methods for submitting bids are:

1. A fixed price bid (lump-sum).
2. Cost plus profit and overhead.
3. Cost plus a maximum upper percentage.
4. Cost plus a fixed fee.

THE ESTIMATE

An estimate, by definition, involves the approximation of the value of the project, not the exact cost that will be encountered. It should always be considered only as an approximation no matter how finite the estimate is in detail. It is true that the finer the detail, the more accurate the total estimate should be, but this is not always the case. An estimate is only an estimate!

The estimate consists of a delineation of all costs for labor, all materials, profit, overhead costs, and any other factors that would necessarily make up a cost of the project or job.

It is not the purpose of this chapter to show how to prepare or evaluate an estimate. Our purpose is only to show the mathematics involved in various estimating procedures so that proper preparation or evaluation could be done if necessary.

LABOR ESTIMATING FACTORS

The estimated cost of labor is determined by the product of the number of hours of labor required and the wage scale per hour. (Wage scales normally indicate *hourly wage*.) This is usually stated as

Cost of labor = Hours required $\times$ wage scale

and is the basic premise for computing any combination of labor costs.

Many publications are available listing the manhours necessary to accomplish a given task. Such data has been collected for various trades and labor functions. The data is accumulated from various time studies by contractors, compilation of records for jobs completed, or just by the experiences of a knowledgeable contractor.

Other publications list hourly rates for various trades and include tables for adjusting these hourly wages to local prevailing hourly wage rates. (The U.S. Department of Labor publishes a periodic list of prevailing hourly wage rates, including benefits, for all trades in most areas of the United States.)

Aside from the simple arithmetic of multiplying hours by wages as mentioned above, the mathematical problem in estimating labor costs is that of finding the number of hours required to perform a given task or job.

Based on his own experience or published information, the contractor or builder will determine the *units* or amount of work that can be accomplished in *one hour*. Multiplying this by the total units or total amount of work to be done for the job will give him the total labor hours required. (The mathematics of ratio and proportion are used frequently in the examples below and may be reviewed in the Appendix.)

Example:

A carpenter estimates that his crew can hang four hollow core flush doors per hour. How many hours will be required to hang 18 doors?

Solution:

By proportion,
4 doors: 18 doors = 1 hour: X hours, and
4/18 = 1/X, so
4X = 18
X = 18/4 = 4.5, and therefore,
4.5 hours are required to install 18 doors.

To find the total labor cost in the above example, the wage scale of the carpentry crew must be determined. If the crew consists of one journeyman at $9.30 per hour, and one apprentice at $5.20 per hour, the total hourly wages for the crew would be $14.50. Therefore, the total labor cost in the above example would be

4.5 hours ✕ $14.50 = $65.25

The estimate for labor time was based on *units of work per hour* (or average output per hour). It is sometimes necessary to convert units of work per hour to *labor hours per unit of work.* This is required when using the unit in place cost system described later in this chapter. The conversion is done by using ratios and proportion as in the previous example.

Example:

A carpentry crew can install 4 doors in one hour. What is the labor time per door?

Solution:

$$4 \text{ doors:}1 \text{ door} = 1 \text{ hour:}X \text{ hours}$$
$$4/1 = 1/X$$
$$4X = 1$$
$$X = \tfrac{1}{4} \text{ hour per door}$$

The unit in place cost method also uses labor cost per unit. If the labor hours per unit of work has been determined, multiplying by the hourly wage will result in the unit cost. In the above example, the wage scale for the crew was $14.50 per hour. Therefore, the labor cost per unit (one door) is

¼ hour per door × $14.50 per hour, or
.25 × $14.50 = $3.625 <u>labor cost per door</u>

The two procedures above can be combined into a *one-step short-cut* for finding unit labor costs. To determine labor cost per unit, divide the hourly rate by the number of units per hour. The formula commonly used is

$1 = w/P$,

where l represents the cost of labor per unit, w represents the wage rate, and P represents the units per hour. The preceding example can be simplified to find the cost of labor per unit to

$1 = w/P = \$14.50/4 = \$3.625$

Once the cost of labor per unit has been established, multiplying by the total number of units will result in the total labor cost for the job. For instance, each door has a labor cost of $3.625 and, therefore, installation of 18 doors will have a total labor cost of $3.625 × 18 = $65.25, the same end result as in the foregoing methods.

Example:

Painters in the area are paid on the basis of $8.50 per hour (including benefits). It is determined that the average output of 1 painter (for one coat, brush applied to doors and windows only) is 110 square feet per hour. What is the estimated cost for painting 3,000 square feet of doors and windows?

Solution:

Determine labor cost per square foot:
l = w/P = $8.50/110 = $.0773 per square foot
Find the total cost:
3,000 sq. ft. X .0773 = $231.90 labor cost

Productivity

The manhours used in the above examples and as listed in all the manhour publications, use *average rate of work under normal working conditions.* A good estimate, however, must include *productivity efficiency percentages.* These percentages are based on the conditions existing at the time which would alter the rate of productivity, either increasing or decreasing it. Some of the conditions to be considered are:
1. The general economy
2. Physical job conditions
3. Job supervision
4. Weather
5. Local labor relations
6. Condition and availability of equipment

Because we are only concerned here with the mathematical aspects of estimating, it is not necessary to discuss or evaluate the various conditions above. It is easy to see, for instance, how good or bad weather conditions can affect average productivity under normal conditions. Each of the other conditions can be similarly analyzed to determine the applicable percentage of efficiency.

It is generally accepted that the average productivity efficiency is only 60 to 80 percent (40 to 60% is low, and 80 to 100% is high). Therefore, using the published production rate under these conditions, when considered average, would result in a 60 to 80 percent productivity. Tables of manhour production will sometimes show the productivity percentage upon which the production is based. If not,

it is safe to assume an average of 70%. If any one condition or production element is considered low, a productivity percentage of 40
to 60 should be used.

The percentages for all possible conditions are *averaged* and a
composite rate for productivity is found. For instance, if we are considering 3 conditions and decide that their respective percentages
would be 55%, 60%, and 50%, the average of the 3 percentages
would be 55% (55 + 60 + 50 = 165; 165/3 = 55%). The 55% average
is then used to select the composite rate of wages applicable for the
conditions of productivity. The composite rate selected is applied to
the estimate as shown in the following example.

Example:

After considering six conditions of productivity, an average
productivity efficiency percent is arrived at 55%. The job calls for
one foreman at $12.50 per hour, 6 carpenters at $9.20, and one
apprentice at $6.50 per hour. What composite hourly rate should be
estimated if the craft rates given are based on an average productivity
of 70%?

Solution:

Find the total composite manhour rate for the crew:

1 foreman	$12.50
6 carpenters	55.20 (6 × $9.20)
1 apprentice	6.50
	$74.20

$74.20/8 = $9.275 composite manhour rate for
average production.
Find the composite rate for 55% productivity:
$9.275 represents productivity of 70%; therefore,
55% productivity, a difference of 15%, would result
in *15% more cost* per manhour, or 115% of the
composite manhour rate.
$9.275 × 115% = 9.275 × 1.15 = $10.666
Composite rate for 55% productivity is $10.666.

If it is estimated that the job will take the crew 100 manhours
to complete, the composite rate is applied, and the labor cost is
determined to be 100 manhours × $10.666 = $1,066.60. If the pro-

ductivity efficiency had not been used, the labor cost would have been estimated at 100 × \$9.275 = \$927.50, a difference of \$139.10 in labor costs.

The above example is just one way in which the productivity efficiency percentage can be used. The estimator should decide in which manner he will use the percentage. It is an essential part in estimating labor costs because 100% productivity is rarely, if ever, achieved.

MATERIAL ESTIMATING FACTORS

Because materials are based on the measurements of the job, accurate measurements are essential when estimating. This is usually done in the preparation of specifications but must always be checked by the estimator. The estimator will prepare, from the plans or specifications, a materials list with sizes and quantities of all materials needed. This list of materials, by quantities, is known as a *quantity takeoff.*

It is beyond the scope of this chapter to describe procedures for quantity takeoffs or for estimating amounts of materials needed. It shall suffice to show that the quantity of material needed is multiplied by a current cost factor to determine the total cost per item. This can be stated as

Material cost = Cost per unit × number of units needed

Example:

Sheetrock (½″) is to be installed on all walls of a room measuring 12′ × 20′ × 8′. The cost of ½″ sheetrock is \$5.04/CSF (per 100 square feet). It is estimated that 4 lbs. of nails at \$.38/lb. and one tape and compound kit at \$4.11 per kit will also be needed. Estimate the material costs for the job.

Solution:

Find the squre feet of sheetrock needed:

Perimeter of room = 12 + 20 + 12 + 20 = 64 feet
Area of all walls = 64′ × 8′ = 512 square feet

Find the Costs:

512 sq. ft. of sheetrock @ $5.04 per 100 sq. ft. =
512 × 5.04/100 = 512 × .0504 = $25.80
4 lbs. of nails @ $.38/lb.   =   1.52
1 Kit @ $4.11   =   4.11
Total Material Cost   = $31.43

Unit costs can be computed by dividing the total cost of the material by the number of units involved in the cost. The unit costs for ½" sheetrock, for instance, could be determined from the above example:

Material needed for 512 sq. ft. of ½" sheetrock = $31.43

$31.43/512 = $.06138 per square foot, or

if units of 100 square feet were desired, .06138 × 100 = $6.138 = material cost per 100 square feet of ½" sheetrock.

Once the *unit cost* for ½" sheetrock has been established, the cost can be applied to other jobs. If 2,380 sq. ft. of ½" sheetrock were needed for another job, the total material cost would be 23.8 × $6.138 = $146.08.

Foot Board Measure

Lumber plays a large part in building and remodeling. In estimating for material, the term "board feet" of lumber is frequently encountered. Board foot means a piece of lumber one inch thick, 12 inches wide, and 12 inches long. It is equivalent to one square foot of *one inch* lumber. A piece of lumber having other dimensions is mathematically changed into board feet by multiplying thickness by width by length by number of pieces, and dividing the product by 12.

Example:

How many board feet of lumber are contained in 24 pieces of 2" × 4" lumber if each piece is 10 feet long?

Solution:

$$\frac{24 \times 2 \times 4 \times 10}{12} = \frac{1920}{12} = 160 \text{ board feet}$$

Lumber that is not purchased on the board foot basis is usually priced per square foot. A square foot of lumber does not consider thickness because it is an element of the price. Panels of ¼″ or ½″ are priced according to their thickness. This is also the case in siding, flooring, and other milled lumber. All fractional parts of a board foot, square foot, or lineal foot are counted as another foot.

When using board foot measure, the abbreviation *FBM* (Foot Board Measure) is used. Thus, 160 board feet will usually be shown as 160 FBM. This should not be confused with the abbreviation for 1,000 board feet which is *MBF* and commonly used in estimating or cost manuals. (The "M" represents 1,000 in Roman Numerals.) One MBF equals 1,000 FBM.

Lumber prices are usually quoted by the MBF or 100 FBM. To find the cost per FBM, divide by 1,000 or 100, respectively.

Example:

Find the cost of 30 pieces of 2″ × 8″ × 12′ lumber at $190 per 100 FBM.

Solution:

$$\frac{30 \times 2 \times 8 \times 12}{12} = 480 \text{ FBM}$$

$$\$190/100 = \$1.90 \text{ per FBM}$$

$$480 \text{ FBM} \times \$1.90 = \$912.00$$

Accounting For Waste

An important part of the material estimate takeoff procedure is an allowance for waste. Materials are sometimes wasted for various reasons and an allowance for such must be made in the estimate by *adding the estimated waste* to the quantity of materials needed.

Materials are sometimes purchased according to standard stock sizes that are not always suitable for the job. For instance, if 2″ × 4″ dimensional lumber is available in lengths of 10′, and one hundred 9′ pieces are needed, there will be a one foot waste from each piece of 10′ length purchased. This can amount to a sizeable difference in the estimate and must be considered. In addition to waste caused by the nature or sizing of some materials, waste must be considered for breakage, spoilage, hauling, and handling.

There are certain rules of thumb used by estimators in calculating waste and each estimator has his own system. Some estimating manuals will list the amount of waste to account for in each category of material. The mathematics used in accounting for waste is usually simple arithmetic.

Example:

Finished oak flooring is to be installed in a living room measuring 18' X 22'. It is estimated that there is 1/3 waste on installing 1" X 3" oak flooring. How much material is required for the floor?

Solution:

18' X 22' = 396 square feet
1/3 of 396 for waste = 132 square feet
Total material needed = 528 square feet of 1 X 3 oak

The labor time estimate on the above example would use 396 square feet as the amount of flooring to be laid because the balance of 132 square feet is waste.

Example:

If a carpenter can lay 1,000 FBM of oak flooring in 35 hours, how long would it take him to lay the above floor?

Solution:

1,000 FBM:396FBM = 35 hours: X hours
1,000X = 396 (35)
X = 13,860/1,000
X = 13.86 hours

PROFIT, OVERHEAD, AND MARGIN LOADINGS

The estimator, after considering labor costs, material costs, and material waste normal to the job, must add loadings for profit, overhead, and other marginal estimates. *Profit* is the fair and reasonable percentage of the cost to pay for knowledge, work, and services rendered. *Overhead* is the percentage of cost in conducting business whether related to the particular job or not. (Some jobs may require a larger percentage for overhead because of certain exceptional ratios created by the particular job.) *Margin* is the loading or leeway for any possible contingencies that might have been overlooked or not expected on the job.

The percentage used for each of the above vary considerably and would be impossible to list here. Each is usually figured separately rather than as a total percentage to be added to the estimate and may vary with each job.

Example:

A contractor figures that for a particular job he must add a profit loading of 12%, an overhead loading of 15%, and a margin loading of 5%. If the total estimated cost of labor and material is $14,560, what should he bid for the job?

Solution:

$$
\begin{aligned}
\text{Profit} &= 12\% \text{ of } \$14{,}560 = .12 \times 14{,}560 = \$1{,}747.20 \\
\text{Overhead} &= 15\% \text{ of } \$14{,}560 = .15 \times 14{,}560 = 2{,}184.00 \\
\text{Margin} &= 5\% \text{ of } \$14{,}560 = .05 \times 14{,}560 = \underline{728.00} \\
& \hspace{4.5cm} \text{Total Loadings} = \$4{,}659.20
\end{aligned}
$$

$$\$14{,}560 + \$4{,}659.20 = \underline{\$19{,}219.20 \text{ Bid}}$$

The above percentages could have been added for a total of 12 + 15 + 5 = 32%, and applied to the cost:

$$32\% \text{ of } \$14{,}560 = .32 \times 14{,}560 = \$4{,}659.20$$
$$\$14{,}560.00 + \$4{,}659.20 = \$19{,}219.20$$

Because each of the factors may vary with each job, it is the accepted custom to list and compute *each factor separately* as was done initially above.

METHODS OF ESTIMATING

As can be seen from the foregoing paragraphs, estimating can be a tedious and time-consuming job. Because each item of labor and material is listed and its cost itemized, the method shown in the preceding paragraphs is called the *Detailed Method of Estimating*. It is used by very experienced builders and contractors in new construction and most often in remodeling or to determine partial repair costs. Although it is the most accurate and dependable method, other methods are used to obtain the total replacement cost of a building. They are used to save time and when rough approximations of cost will suffice. Appraisers, for instance, do not have sufficient time nor the expertise to develop detailed estimates and must resort to other methods of estimating for value.

Each method of estimating has its special place in approximating the replacement or reproductive cost of buildings, remodeling, or partial repairs, depending upon the degree of accuracy desired.

Bay Method

The bay method is also called the sectional method because it is often used where there are similar or identical bays or sections and when the cost of one section is known or detail-estimated. *The replacement cost of the detailed section is then multiplied by the number of sections needed.* This method is useful on new construction or appraisal of factories, warehouses, motels, apartments, and institutional buildings.

Panel Method

The panel method is a semi-detailed method utilizing the unit cost system which is explained in the following paragraphs. The structure is divided into several component areas or panels and the unit cost per square yard or foot of the component is applied. The cost of constructing one square unit of wall area is determined by the detail method. The cost per unit is then applied to the number of units of wall that are in the entire structure. The same procedure is followed for flooring, roofs, partitions, etc., until all calculations are reduced to a standard unit of area measure or panel for every component in the structure. These are added for the total cost of the structure.

The panel method is more accurate than the bay method but does involve more detail and consequently more time to compile. It takes less time than the detailed estimate, but ranks next to it for accuracy.

Unit-in-Place Cost Method

This method combines the cost of labor and the cost of material needed to install a unit of material. Accuracy of both labor costs and material costs are required in order to obtain an accurate *unit cost.* The unit cost can be in square feet of painting (usually total cost per 100 square feet), squares of shingles installed (one square is 100 square feet), units of board feet of lumber installed, or by individual units such as "per receptacle" or "per door" installed.

In an earlier example in this chapter, it was determined that the labor cost of a painter for one coat of paint, brush applied to doors and windows only, was $.0773 per square foot. If it is likewise determined that the material cost is $.08 per square foot, we can combine the two costs and arrive at a total *unit-in-place cost* of .0773 + .08 = .1573 per square foot.

The unit-in-place cost is multiplied by the number of units to be completed, and the product is the *total cost of the job.* If there are 5,000 square feet of windows and doors to paint, the total cost would be $.1573 per unit times 5,000 units, or

$$.1573 \times 5,000 = \$786.50 \text{ total cost}$$

Most manuals used for estimating utilize this unit-in-place cost system. The *Dodge Manual for Building Construction* published by McGraw-Hill and the *Building Cost File* published by Construction Publishing Co. are examples of manuals available that use the unit-in-place cost system.

To obtain a unit in place cost without use of a manual, the following formula is used:

$$u = m + wR$$

where u is the unit cost to be determined, m is the cost of materials per unit, w is the wage rate, and R is the number of manhours of labor *per unit.*

Example:

What is the unit in place cost for 2″ by 8″ ceiling joists? Use 100 FBM as the unit to be determined.

Solution:

Material costs: (no waste included)

2″ × 8″, Douglas fir, costs $190 per MBF = $190.00
7 lbs. of nails per MBF @ $.40 per lb.   =   2.80
          Total material cost per MBF = $192.80
Costs per 100 FBM = 192.80/10 = $19.28

Labor costs:

One carpenter at $9.50 per hour and one laborer at
$6.20 per hour can install 58 FBM of 2″ × 8″ ceiling
joists per hour.
Labor costs = 9.50 + 6.20 = $15.70 per hour

Find hours of labor per 100 FBM:
By proportion, 58 FBM: 100 FBM = 1 hour: X hours

and,   58/100 = 1/X
                        58X = 100
                          X = 1.724 hours per 100 FBM

The formula: u = m + wR
               u = $19.28 + ($15.70 × 1.724 hours)
               u = $19.28 + $27.07
               u = $46.35 cost per 100 FBM

The unit-in-place cost of $46.35 is applied to the number of units to be installed. If a structure requires installation of 2,000 FBM of ceiling joists, the total costs for such installation will be

$46.35 per 100 × 20 hundreds = $927.00

Of course, many variations of the above method are in use. Consideration must also be given to waste factors, productivity, and the size of the job. Unit-in-place costs are usually contemplated for large jobs. On small remodeling jobs, the labor cost would have to be increased substantially because of the additional time required for a smaller unit. Other factors and variations must always be considered when estimating with this method.

Cubic and Square Foot Methods

Cubic measure and square measure are used extensively in both appraising and construction for the purpose of estimating costs. Such methods are considered *quick estimates* and involve comparison of cost data per unit of measure to the total volume or area of the structure rather than to individual items of the structure.

In using these methods, data must be available on current completed costs per unit, square or cubic, of various types of structures according to size, design, materials, equipment, and extras. If data is not available, the methods are not usable unless the estimator has complete knowledge of such costs based on the square or cubic units used.

There is much controversy concerning the two methods of measure as to the conditions under which each should be applied. The square foot method has gained acceptance by many appraisers because it is easier to compute than the cubic foot method. Some estimators, however, consider the cubic foot method as being somewhat more accurate, while others argue just the opposite. All agree that, at best, each method should be considered no more than 80 to 90 percent accurate.

Cubic Foot Method

In using this method, the known cost of a comparable building is divided by the total number of cubic feet contained within the structure. The quotient obtained is the cost per cubic foot for that particular building. This cost per cubic foot is then multiplied by the total cubic feet contained in the structure being estimated. The product is the estimated cost of that structure.

Example:

A structure containing 40,000 cubic feet costs $50,000 to build. What will a comparable structure containing 50,000 cubic feet cost to build?

Solution:

Original structure:
$$\frac{\$50,000 \text{ cost}}{40,000 \text{ cu. ft.}} = \$1.25 \text{ per cubic foot cost}$$
New or replacement structure:
$1.25 \times 50,000$ cu. ft. = $62,500

In determining the cubical contents of a building, the floor area is multiplied by the height of the structure, starting from the basement floor and continuing to the top of a flat roof building or half-way to the ridge of a slanted roof building. (See Chapter 9.)

The American Institute of Architects defines the standard cubical content of a building as ". . . the actual space within the outer surfaces of the outside or enclosing walls and contained between the outer surfaces of the roof and the finished surface of the lowest basement or cellar floor."

Open porches are included at one-half their cubic content. Any enclosed room or space is included at its full cubic content. Various publications are available that include tables, charts, and guides for using the cubic foot method.

Square Foot Method

The square foot method uses the square foot area of each floor in a building and the product of that total times a predetermined or comparable cost per square foot. The costs are developed in the same manner as for the cubic foot method.

The total floor area normally includes the total area of each floor within the building and is generally based on the foundation perimeter. Square foot prices are adjusted for differences in building perimeters, corners, and heights.

This method is considered more reliable, and therefore used more often than the cubic foot method when *the floor layouts are similar and of average uniform height.* It is used by appraisers for dwellings and two story buildings.

15

Calculations for Investments in Real Estate

The mathematics of real estate investment and real estate appraisal are closely associated because they both involve many of the same elements. These elements basically are capitalization, value, income, and rate of return, or yield, of the investment.

Where appraisal mathematics is primarily concerned with finding the *value* of a property, investment mathematics concerns itself with finding the *income* and/or *rate of return* of the investment.

In addition to the investment of capital for acquisition of real property and the income produced from rent, real estate investment can also involve mortgages and financing, where the yield is based *only* on the interest return. Some real estate investments are used only for purposes of tax advantages developed by a tax shelter. The only incentives for other investments might be the deductibility of interest paid, accelerated depreciation, or the availability of tax charges as capital gains instead of ordinary income.

It is obvious that different real estate investors have different objectives. Because of this, the mathematics of real estate investment could include an *infinite* number of variations and combinations of all possible investment factors. In this chapter we will attempt only to cover the basic premises and considerations of real estate investment mathematics.

HOW TO COMPUTE RATE
OF RETURN

Because the primary purpose of investment is to receive a return on the investment, our first consideration will be the determination of the rate, or percentage, of return. The valuation (or capitalization) formula used for appraising (Chapter 12) is also used for investments. To find the rate of return, we use the formula

$$R = I/V,$$

where R is the *Rate of Return,* I is the *Net Income,* and V is the total *Value* of the investment.

Yield is the same as rate of return but for simplicity, and because of the innumerable methods of determining yield and the different types of yield, we will presently consider the rate of return only as the ratio of net income to investment. Note that, in this case, net income can be used only when no debt service is involved. Yield will be discussed later in this chapter.

Example:

A $30,000 investment in a property produces a net annual income of $4,050. What is the rate of return on the investment?

Solution:

$$R = I/V$$
$$R = \$4,050/\$30,000$$
$$R = .135 = 13\tfrac{1}{2}\%$$

Although the rate of return as shown above is commonly referred to as "capitalization," the true process of capitalization has not been used here because provision has not been made for recapture (see Chapter 12). To simplify the process of investment mathematics, and to avoid confusion with the discussion of capitalization in Chapter 12, we will use the term "rate of return" or "yield" instead of capitalization.

HOW TO FIND PRICE OR VALUE

The *value* of the investment, or the price to pay for a certain net income at a specified rate can be determined by the value formula. Of course, the value of any investment should be determined according to the *income approach* as presented in Chapter 12. However, the formula can be used as a guide for finding value by transforming for *V*:

$$V = I/R$$

Example:

What is the largest cash investment an investor can make on a property with a $15,000 annual net income if he wants his money to earn 12%?

Solution:

$$V = I/R$$
$$V = \$15,000/.12$$
$$V = \$125,000$$

As long as no debt service is being considered, it is assumed that the cash investment in the above example is also the *total value* of the investment. In other words, the investor is paying cash in full for the property and receiving annual *cash* in return of $15,000.

FINDING ANNUAL NET INCOME

By using the same formula, and solving for *I*, the annual net income that will be realized at a specified rate of return can be found. The formula becomes I = VR, which is the *basic* form of the value or capitalization formula. Of course, the actual annual net income cannot be safely predicted by the use of any formula, but the value formula can *indicate* what the *anticipated* annual net income *should* be, based on the values given for *R* and *V*.

Example:

What should the annual net income be if an investor wants to realize a 15% rate of return on his investment of $50,000?

Solution:

$$I = VR$$
$$I = \$50,000 \times .15$$
$$I = \$7,500.$$

As seen above, in order to produce the desired rate of return, the annual net income must be $7,500 on the $50,000 investment. However, there are *many kinds* of net income and innumerable ways of determining it.

For consistency, we will consider the net income by its most frequent use as the net result left from gross income *after* deducting the vacancy and collection losses; operating, maintenance, and fixed expenses; and *before* depreciation and debt service.

In other words, net income is the annual income *after* allowable expenses but *before* debt service, income taxes, or depreciation. Mathematically, it can be expressed as:

Net Income = Gross Income − (Loss Allowances + Fixed Expenses + Operating Expenses)

For illustrative purposes in the next few paragraphs and examples, we will use the financial data of a fictitious property: *The Elkay Apartments.*

The purchase price of the Elkay Apartments is $450,000 for which a $250,000 mortgage is obtained at an 9% interest rate for a term of 20 years. Gross income consists of 14 apartments rented for $320 per month and 10 apartments rented for $280 per month. The vacancy allowance is 5%. Annual insurance premiums total $3,400, and the annual taxes are $8,120. Management costs of the apartments is 6% of the adjusted gross income. All other operating expenses total $19,400 per year.

Example:

Using the above formula for Net Income, find the annual net income of the Elkay Apartments.

Solution:

Find Gross Income:
    14 apartments @ $320 per month = $320 × 14 × 12 = $53,760
    10 apartments @ $280 per month = $280 × 10 × 12 =   33,600

                                    Total gross income = $87,360
Find Loss Allowances:
    5% vacancy allowance = .05 × $87,360 = $4,368
Find Fixed Expenses:
    Insurance + taxes = $3,400 + $8,120 = $11,520

Find Operating Expenses:

Management costs = .06 X $82,992 (adjusted gross) = $4,980
   (Adjusted Gross = $87,360 – $4,368 = $82,992)
Total operating expenses = Stated costs + management
Total operating expenses = $19,400 + $4,980 = $24,380
Apply formula for Net Income:
Net Income = $87,360 – ($4,368 + $11,520 + $24,380)
Net Income = $87,360 – $40,268 = $47,092

FINDING CASH FLOW

Net income is *not* to be confused with *Cash Flow.* The cash flow is the cash left over from net income *after* deductions are made for *debt service.* (Debt service is the payment of interest and principal on loans or mortgages.)

In real estate, the term *Cash Throwout* is sometimes used interchangeably with cash flow. Cash throwout means the cash flow at the end of the calendar year (December 31). Technically, cash flow is an *accounting term* which refers to the dollars remaining on April 15 after payment of taxes and allowing for depreciation. Our use of the term will be synonomous with cash throwout. It is important to note that cash flow is *not* the same as profit, yield, earnings, or taxable income. Mathematically, cash flow is found by the formula

Cash Flow = Net Income – Debt Service

Example:
   What is the annual cash flow at the Elkay Apartments?

Solution:

   Net income from preceding example = $47,092. Find Total Debt Service:

Mortgage of $250,000 @ 9% for 20 years (see Chapters 3 and 10)
Constant Annual Percent (from Appendix) = 10.80%
   $250,000 X .1080 = $27,000 annual debt service
Find Cash Flow from the formula:
         Cash Flow = Net Income – Debt Service
         Cash Flow = $47,092 – $27,000 = $20,092

THE OPERATING STATEMENT

With the information from the above examples, an operating statement can be prepared. The operating statement supplies most of the financial data necessary to evaluate a real estate investment. The operating statement will show all the information from the data compiled with the formulas in the examples. In addition, the statement will usually show a breakdown on the debt service of principal and interest amounts of the current mortgage payment.

Example:

Find the first year payment of principal and interest for the Elkay Apartments and prepare an operating statement.

Solution:

20 year mortgage of $250,000 at 9% interest. From Mortgage Amortization Tables (see Chapter 10): Find first year interest:

First year interest factor (per $100) = 8.924001
Mortgage amount in 100's $\times$ factor = 2500 $\times$ 8.924001
    = $22,310 first year interest (rounded).

Find first year principal:

First year principal factor (per $100) = 1.8760
Mortgage amount in 100's $\times$ factor = 2500 $\times$ 1.8760
    = $4,690 first year principal (rounded).

Mortgage breakdown for operating statement:

Interest payment	$22,310
Principal payment	4,690
Total annual payment	$27,000

The Operating Statement:

ELKAY APARTMENTS OPERATING STATEMENT

GROSS INCOME

14 Apartments @ $320 per month	$53,760
10 Apartments @ $280 per month	33,600
Less 5% vacancy allowance	− 4,368

FIGURE 15-1

	ADJUSTED GROSS INCOME		$82,992

FIXED EXPENSES

| Insurance | | $3,400 | |
| Taxes | | 8,120 | |

OPERATING EXPENSES

Management (6% of adjusted gross)		4,980	
Repairs and maintenance			
Utilities			
Supplies		19,400	
Other costs			

	TOTAL EXPENSES		- 35,900

NET INCOME $47,092

DEBT SERVICE

Mortgage payment	Interest	$22,310	
	Principal	4,690	
			- 27,000

CASH FLOW $20,092

FIGURE 15-1 CONTINUED

TAX FLOW AND TAXABLE INCOME

Tax flow is the amount on which taxes are paid, and is commonly called the *taxable income*. Normally, the net income *cannot* be the taxable income because it includes the interest portion of the debt service which is a deductible item. Cash flow *cannot* be the taxable income because it includes depreciation which is also deductible. The taxable income, or tax flow, then, is the cash flow *less* depreciation but *plus* the portion of debt service for payment of principal, which is not tax deductible. The tax flow can be shown mathematically as

Tax Flow = (Cash Flow + Payments on Principal) – Depreciation

Example:

What is the tax flow for the first year on the Elkay Apartments if depreciation is calculated at 200% declining-balance, and the useful remaining life is 50 years? Land value is $50,000.

Solution:

Find depreciation for the first year (Chapter 11):

Straight-line rate of depreciation = 100%/50 = 2%
200% declining-balance = 200% of 2% = 2.00 $\times$ .02 = .04 = 4%
Depreciable amount = $450,000 – $50,000 (land value)
                   = $400,000.
$400,000 $\times$ .04 = $16,000 first year depreciation

Principal payment from previous example = $4,690.

Tax flow = (Cash flow + payment on principal) – depreciation
Tax Flow = ($20,092 + $4,690) – $16,000
          = $24,782 – $16,000
          = $8,782 taxable income

HOW TO DETERMINE YIELD

We have mentioned that the rate of return on the investment is the *yield* and that there are various methods for determining yield. When using the capitalization formula R = I/V, as in the first part of this chapter, no consideration was given to mortgages or equity. All methods for determining yield use the same basic formula; the difference in methods being the values used for *I* and *V*. In the first method shown earlier, the ratio I/V was *net income* to *purchase price*. This method is used mostly as a rule-of-thumb method for comparing different properties without regard to mortgage debt.

Current or Equity Yield

A more realistic measure of yield is the ratio of *actual cash flow income* to the *cash investment* or *equity* in the property. The actual cash flow is measured *after* interest and amortization of mortgage debt, and the equity is the actual cash investment or down payment on the property. This yield is called *current yield* or *equity yield*.

Example:

In the Elkay Apartments, what is the current yield on the cash invested?

Solution:

The total cash investment is $200,000. To find the current yield rate, the ratio of *cash* flow to *cash* investment must be used:

$$R = I/V = \text{Cash Flow/Cash Invested}$$
$$R = \$20,092/\$200,000$$
$$R = .1004 = 10.04\%$$

(Note that net income can be used only when no debt service is involved or considered. If the net income had been used as I in the above example, the yield rate would have been indicated as

$$R = \$47,092/\$200,000 = 23.5\%, \text{ which is erroneous.}$$

The net income in the above case can only be used compatibly with the total value of the property. Thus, the *yield on the purchase price* can be determined as

$$R = I/V = \$47,092/\$450,000 = .1046 = 10.46\%$$

The numerator and denominator used in the current yield ratio can vary to meet the needs of the investor. For instance, some investors deduct income taxes from the cash flow before computing yield, and some add payments of principal to cash flow.

Regardless of method used, or mathematical procedure attempted (including Probability Theory), the yield is only an *anticipated* or *expected* yield. The *true yield* can only be determined at the *end* of the investment period.

Net Reversion and Deferred Yield

In finding the equity yield, the equity was considered as the original cash investment or down payment. This, however, is only the *original equity*. As the mortgage is amortized, the payments of principal *add* to the investor's equity.

The equity at any time is actually the cash value of the property to the investor. If the property is sold, the cash return to the investor will be the difference between sales price or market value and the balance owing on the mortgage. This equity can be considered *net reversion* because it is the *net resale* proceeds to the investor. By formula,

Equity (Net Reversion) = Market Value – Loan Balance

Example:

If the Elkay Apartments were sold after the first year for $500,000, what amount would be net reversion?

Solution:

Loan Balance after first year = $250,000 - $4,690 (payment on principal) = $245,310
Net Reversion = Market or Sale Value - Loan Balance
Net Reversion = $500,000 - $245,310 = $254,690

The equity obtained by amortization is considered as *deferred yield* because it is not taken into consideration until *reversion* or *resale* of the property. Amounts applied to principal by amortization *or* appreciation cannot be considered as additional investments but can be computed as additional *earnings* from the property at reversion. These earnings can be defined as the yield generated by amortization and property appreciation. Mathematically, the formula for deferred yield is:

Deferred Yield = Net Reversion – Original Equity

Example:

As in the preceding example, the Elkay Apartments are sold after the first year. What is the total deferred yield?

Solution:

Net Reversion = $254,690.
Deferred Yield = Net Reversion – Original Equity
= $254,690 – $200,000
= $54,690

It can be seen that the deferred yield of $54,690 consists of amortization of $4,690 and property appreciation of $50,000. If the property were not sold, the additional amortization over the years would be further increase of the deferred yield.

The deferred yield and current yield can now be combined to show the actual yield because it is the *end* of the investment period (property sold).

Current Yield + Deferred Yield = $20,092 + $54,690 = $74,782

This would result in a rate of return (before taxes) of R = I/V = $74,782/$200,000 = .373 = 37%.

Net reversion and deferred yield are used extensively in investment analysis and in the Mortgage-Equity Technique, both of which are beyond the scope of this book. Details of their usage can be found in L. L. Ellwood's *Ellwood Tables of Real Estate Appraising and Financing,* and Irvin Johnson's *The Instant Mortgage-Equity Technique.*

Investment Yield

Another method of determining yield involves the use of the Compound Interest Tables and the Inwood Factor. This method includes the deferred yield and is the total yield produced both by income and resale, similar to the method shown in the preceding paragraph. It determines the rate at which the investment cost is equal to the present value of income and reversion. It is used for purposes of capital budgeting and by life insurance and fiduciary investors, particularly in estimating yields of sale-leasebacks. The mathematics of determining investment yield in this manner is also beyond the scope of this book and can be found in *Ellwood Tables of Real Estate Appraising and Financing.*

TAX SHELTERS

Tax shelter is the amount of *cash flow* that is *sheltered* from taxes because of depreciation or other deductible expenses that do *not* affect cash flow. From the formula for tax flow, it can be seen that *without* depreciation, the taxable income will be higher than the cash flow because of the nondeductibility of principal payments.

The primary source of a tax shelter is depreciation. We can use the case of the Elkay Apartments as an example of tax shelters.

Example:
What is the amount of the tax shelter on the Elkay Apartments?

Solution:
As can be seen in the example of tax flow, the taxable income on the Elkay Apartments is $8,782. The cash flow represents taxable

income and the payments on principal are not deductible. Therefore, the only item sheltered from tax is the depreciation which, in this case, amounts to $16,000 for the first year. The $16,000 will be *actual cash income* that is not taxable during the first year.

Tax shelters defer or postpone taxable income but *do not* cancel it. When the property is sold, depreciation recapture laws will convert some of the income to capital gains, leaving the balance as ordinary income. The capital gains portion, of course, is taxed at a lower rate than ordinary income (see Chapter 11), and therefore also serves as a form of tax shelter.

LEVERAGE

Leverage is the process of using borrowed money to increase the percentage gain on the investment. Leverage is based on the assumption that more can be *earned* on borrowed money than the actual *cost* of the borrowed money. Leverage also allows for higher depreciation deductions because depreciation is taken on the entire building value and not just on the value of the investor's equity. To properly use leverage, the current yield rate should be higher than the mortgage interest rate. If not, the result will be *negative leverage*.

Negative Leverage

One of the disadvantages of leverage is that money might have to be borrowed at a rate higher than the rate of return on the property. As mentioned above, this would result in negative leverage and a loss to the investor of a percentage of the yield rate.

Example:

A property with a yield rate of 10% is purchased for $100,000. The investor can only obtain financing for 50% at a rate of 11% on the mortgage. What is the effect of this leverage on the yield rate?

Solution:

Net earnings on $100,000 @ 10% = $10,000
Cost of money = $50,000 mortgage @ 11% = $5,500
Cash flow = $10,000 – $5,500 = $4,500

Effect of Leverage:

R = I/V = $4,500/$50,000 investment = .09 = 9% yield rate

The yield rate has *decreased* 1% because of the additional cost of 1% over yield on 50% of the property.

(Note that for simplicity, only the interest portion of the debt service has been considered. The payment on principal would further reduce the current yield rate but would be added to the reversion, and converted to deferred yield. This was discussed earlier in this chapter.)

Care must be taken so that debt service does not exceed net income. If too much leverage is attempted, there will be insufficient income to meet expenses *and* debt service.

Positive Leverage

If the investor is able to obtain financing at a rate lower than the current yield rate of his investment, his yield rate will *increase*, resulting in *positive leverage*.

Example:

Using the preceding example, the investor is able to obtain financing for 50% of the purchase price at a mortgage rate of 8%. What is the effect of this leverage on the yield rate?

Solution:

Net earnings on $100,000 @ 10% = $10,000
Cost of money = $50,000 mortgage @ 8% = $4,000
Cash Flow = $10,000 - $4,000 = $6,000

Effect of Leverage:

R = I/V = $6,000/$50,000 = .12 = 12%

The yield has *increased* by 2%. This represents the full 10% yield on the entire property plus the additional 2% earnings on the money he has borrowed. The net cash flow has decreased by only 40% while the investment has decreased 50% with the leverage financing.

Of course, with $50,000 to invest, the investor has the option of purchasing a higher-valued property. Assume he is able to purchase a property valued at $150,000 with a current yield of 10%. With the same $50,000 investment as in the preceding example, he obtains a mortgage for $100,000 at 8% to cover the balance of the purchase price. He has increased his leverage because the borrowed money represents 2/3 of the property cost ($100,000/$150,000 = 2/3). This also represents a 1 to 2 leverage or *equity-mortgage ratio* ($50,000/$100,000 = 1/2). The following example will show how this ratio affects the yield rate.

Example:

Using the above information, what is the effect of the leverage on the yield rate?

Solution:

Net earnings on $150,000 @ 10% = $15,000.
Cost of money = $100,000 mortgage @ 8% = $8,000.
Cash Flow = $15,000 – $8,000 = $7,000.

Effect of Leverage:

$$R = I/V = \$7,000/\$50,000 = .14 = 14\%$$

The investor has increased the yield from 10% to 14% by using borrowed money. If he had purchased the property for cash, his yield rate would have remained at 10% and he would have had to invest $150,000 in cash. In addition to increasing the yield rate, the investor is now able to take advantage of a tax shelter.

The effect of leverage on the Elkay Apartments can also be analyzed now. If purchased for *cash,* the current yield on the purchase would have been 10.46% (net income to purchase price). The current yield with the mortgage financing was computed as 10.04% (cash flow to cash investment). Because of the high mortgage rate of 9%, the financing in this case resulted in a negative leverage of .42%. Another factor causing the negative leverage was the low leverage or equity-mortgage ratio of 1 to 1.25 ($200,000/$250,000). This negative leverage, however, is compensated for by the high tax shelter which, if in the 50% bracket, could save the investor approximately $7,000 in taxes.

If the $7,000 tax savings were applied to the yield rate, it would change the current yield rate to 13.5% and a definite positive leverage increase of 3.1%.

Current Earnings = Cash Flow + Tax Savings (additional cash)
= $20,092 + $7,000 = $27,092. Then,
R = I/V = $27,092/$200,000 = .1354 = 13½%

In using the tax savings as a factor in determining current yield, the investor has used an option mentioned earlier. That is, the factors in the rate of return formula can be adjusted to suit the needs of the investor. This is indicative of the flexibility and infinite number of combinations possible in the mathematics of real estate investment.

Appendix I

A Review of Basic Arithmetic Calculations

ARITHMETIC

It is a safe assumption that as a professional in the real estate business, you can add, subtract, multiply, and divide. It is also safe to assume that, as an average person, you tend to forget other arithmetic computations unless they are in constant use.

With the advent of the ubiquitous electronic mini-calculator that can be carried in pocket or purse, we are driven further away from computations of simple arithmetic, relying more and more on the electronic crutch.

The purpose of this Appendix is to review the often-forgotten basic arithmetic computations and to include them as a reference for those moments when you *must* use them.

COMMON FRACTIONS

A fraction indicates *division* or *ratio*. The top number is called the *numerator* and is the number being divided (dividend). The bottom number is called the *denominator* and is the number we are dividing *by* (divisor). The numerator and denominator are separated by a horizontal or slanted line which means "divide." Thus, 2/3 means "two-thirds" or 2 *divided by* 3. It can also mean the *ratio* of 2 to 3.

Common fractions are either *proper* or *improper*. A proper fraction has its numerator *smaller* than its denominator and is therefore *less* than 1 in value. The fractions 1/2, 2/3, 3/4, and 3/5 are proper fractions.

An improper fraction has a numerator *larger* than its denominator and is therefore *more* than 1 in value. The fractions 3/2, 4/3, and 22/7 are improper fractions.

A fraction in which the numerator and denominator are the same will always be equal to 1. (Any number divided by itself equals 1.) Thus, 8/8 = 1, 156/156 = 1, and so on.

A *decimal fraction* is the ratio of a number and 10 or some multiple of 10. All decimals can be converted to or expressed as a decimal fraction. The decimal .3 equals 3/10, and the decimal .57 = 57/100. Similarly, .2758 = 2758/10000.

Mixed numbers are numbers composed of a whole number and a fraction. All improper fractions can be changed to mixed numbers by performing the division. Thus, 22/7 = 22 divided by 7 = 3 1/7, because 22 divided by 7 is 3 with a remainder of 1, indicating 3 with 1/7 left over after dividing.

To change a mixed number to an improper fraction, multiply the number by the denominator and add the product to the numerator. The result is placed over the denominator. Thus, 3 1/7 = (3 × 7) + 1 over 7, or $\dfrac{21 + 1}{7} = 22/7$.

When the numerator and denominator of a fraction are both multiplied or divided by the same number, the value of the fraction is not changed. Thus,

$$\frac{1}{2} = \frac{1 \times 2}{2 \times 2} = \frac{2}{4} = \frac{2 \times 25}{4 \times 25} = \frac{50}{100} = \frac{50 \div 50}{100 \div 50} = \frac{1}{2}$$

To reduce a fraction to its *lowest terms*, divide the numerator and denominator by the *largest* number which will divide both without a remainder. When no number can divide both numerator and denominator evenly, they are *prime to each other* and the fraction is in *lowest terms*. For instance, to reduce 48/60 to its lowest terms, divide the numerator and denominator by 12:

$$\frac{48 \div 12}{60 \div 12} = \frac{4}{5}$$

There is no other number that can be divided evenly into 4 and 5, so 4/5 is the lowest terms of 48/60.

Fractions with the same denominator are called *like* (or similar) fractions and the similar denominators are called *common denominators.* If fractions have denominators that are not common, the fractions are called *unlike* fractions.

Adding and Subtracting Fractions

Just as units of measurement (inches, feet, yards, etc.) cannot be added or subtracted unless they are the same, unlike fractions, such as 1/12 and 3/4, cannot be added or subtracted unless they are changed to like fractions with common denominators. To do this, we must find the *lowest* common denominator (LCD) for the fractions.

Lowest Common Denominator

The LCD is the *lowest number* that can be evenly divided by all the denominators of the fractions being added or subtracted. In the fractions 1/12 and 3/4, 12 is the LCD.

Once the LCD has been found, each denominator is changed to the LCD by multiplying the *numerator and denominator* by the *factor necessary to obtain the LCD.*

For instance, the LCD of 1/12, 3/4, and 1/6 is 12. To change each to the LCD, the denominator 4 is multiplied by 3, and the denominator 6 is multiplied by 2. The numerators are multiplied by the same numbers:

$$\frac{3 \times 3}{4 \times 3} = \frac{9}{12}, \text{ and } \frac{1 \times 2}{6 \times 2} = \frac{2}{12}$$

As long as we multiply the numerator and denominator by the same number, we have not changed the *value* of the fraction, only its *form.* The value has not changed because we are actually multiplying by 1 (3/3 = 1, and 2/2 = 1). The product of any number and 1 is the same number.

When all the fractions have been changed to the LCD, we are ready to add or subtract.

To add or subtract fractions, add or subtract *only* the numerators, as the denominators will remain the same. Remember, you are adding or subtracting a quantity of 1/2's, 1/3's, 1/4's, 1/16's, etc.

As an example: add 3/8, 4/5, and 3/10, then subtract 9/10.

First, find the LCD which, in this case, will be 40. Change all the fractions to the LCD:

$$\frac{3 \times 5}{8 \times 5} = \frac{15}{40}, \frac{4 \times 8}{5 \times 8} = \frac{32}{40}, \text{ and } \frac{3 \times 4}{10 \times 4} = \frac{12}{40}$$

To add, we add the numerators over the common denominator:

$$\frac{15}{40} + \frac{32}{40} + \frac{12}{40} = \frac{15 + 32 + 12}{40} = \frac{59}{40}$$

To subtract, change 9/10 to a fraction with the LCD of 40:

$$\frac{9 \times 4}{10 \times 4} = \frac{36}{40},$$

then subtract the numerators over the common denominator:

$$\frac{59}{40} - \frac{36}{40} = \frac{59 - 36}{40} = \frac{23}{40}$$

To add or subtract *mixed numbers,* do the fractions separately; then add or subtract the results to or from the whole numbers.

Multiplying Fractions

To multiply fractions, multiply the numerators by the numerators and the denominators by the denominators. The product of the numerators will be the numerator and the product of the denominators will be the denominator of the resulting fraction. The fraction may then be reduced to lowest terms or changed to a mixed number.

$$\frac{1}{2} \times \frac{2}{3} = \frac{1 \times 2}{2 \times 3} = \frac{2}{6} = \frac{1}{3}$$

Change whole numbers or mixed numbers to improper fractions before multiplying.

$$3\frac{1}{2} \times 2/3 \times 6 = \frac{7}{2} \times \frac{2}{3} \times \frac{6}{1} = \frac{7 \times 2 \times 6}{2 \times 3 \times 1} = \frac{84}{6} = 14$$

A short cut in the multiplication of fractions is called *cancellation*. It is the process of dividing out (or cancelling) common factors in the numerator and denominator. Cancellation is *only* used in multiplication, *never* in addition or subtraction.

In the above fractions, $\frac{7}{2} \times \frac{2}{3} \times \frac{6}{1}$, the 2's can be cancelled out, and 3 is contained in 6 two times, therefore cancelling the 3 and leaving 2 instead of 6. The multiplication would be shortened to:

$$\frac{7}{\cancel{2}} \times \frac{\cancel{2}}{\cancel{3}} \times \frac{\cancel{6}}{1} = \frac{14}{1} = 14$$

Dividing Fractions

To divide a fraction by a fraction, *invert* (turn upside down) the fraction of the *divisor* (the fraction after the division sign), then *multiply* the fractions.

$$\frac{5}{6} \div \frac{2}{3} = \frac{5}{6} \times \frac{3}{2} = \frac{5 \times 3}{6 \times 2} = \frac{15}{12} = 1\,3/12 = 1\frac{1}{4}$$

When dividing mixed numbers and whole numbers with fractions, change the mixed numbers or whole numbers to fractions and proceed as above by inverting and then multiplying.

DECIMALS

The decimal system is a method of indicating decimal fractions by use of the *decimal point*. The decimal is read as a decimal fraction with the decimal fraction denominator (in multiples of 10) being indicated by the *number of decimal places* (amount of numbers to the right of the decimal point) in the number.

Numbers to the left of the decimal point are whole numbers. The decimal point separates the whole number and the decimal fraction. The first decimal place is tenths (.1 = 1/10) and the second place is ten times smaller, or hundredths (.01 = 1/100). Each additional place to the right is the next smaller multiple of 10. In order then, the decimal places are named tenths, hundredths, thousandths, ten-thousandths, hundred-thousandths, millionths, and so on.

.00003 = 3/100,000

A short-cut rule to remember is that the total number of decimal places equals the number of zeros in the decimal fraction denominator. Thus, 3 decimal places (.001) equal 3 zeros in the denominator (1/1,000).

To change any common fraction to a decimal, perform the indicated division and write the quotient in decimal form by placing the decimal point after the whole number in the dividend.

$$3/4 = 4\overline{)3.00} \quad \text{(.75)}$$

All electronic calculators will automatically show a decimal answer from the division of numerator by denominator in a proper fraction. Decimal equivalents are therefore easy to find and the use of tables is no longer necessary when a calculator is available.

To convert 3/32 to a decimal by using the calculator, divide **3** by 32 and the calculator will show 0.09375 as the decimal equivalent.

Any decimal can be changed to a common fraction by writing it as a decimal fraction and reducing it to lowest terms.

$$.50 = 50/100 = 1/2$$

Adding and Subtracting Decimals

Decimals are added or subtracted in the same manner as whole numbers by lining up the digit places in a column. To do this easily with decimals, place the numbers in a column with the *decimal points lined up* in a column. The decimal point must be kept in the proper column in the answer.

```
    2.68
   30.2                32.049
    1.046     or,    – 2.300
 +   .002             28.749
   33.928
```

Multiplying Decimals

To multiply decimals, proceed as in whole number multiplication. When the product is obtained, *count-off the number of decimal places* that were multiplied and *point-off the same number* of decimal places in the answer, counting from the right to left.

$$\begin{array}{r} 3.24 \\ \times \quad .01 \\ \hline .0324 \end{array}$$ (Total of 4 places)

(4 places in answer)

If there are insufficient places in the answer for proper placement of the decimal point, add (or prefix) as many zeros to the left end as are needed to place the decimal point.

.324 × .12 = (5 places needed in answer, but digits of answer has only 4) 3888; add a zero to the left end and place the decimal point in the proper position = .03888.

Dividing Decimals

Division of decimals is the same as in whole numbers, except for determining the proper placement of the decimal point in the quotient (answer).

For simplification, the divisor should always be made a whole number. If it is already a whole number, place the decimal point in the quotient directly above the decimal point in the dividend.

$$\begin{array}{r} .6 \\ 6\overline{)3.6} \end{array}$$

If the divisor is a decimal, it must be made a whole number by moving the decimal point to the right. By moving the decimal point to the right you are multiplying it by a multiple of 10. The number of places moved indicates the number of zeros in the multiplier.

.23 × 10 = 2.3, and .23 × 100 = 23.

The decimal point in the dividend must be moved the same number of places as the decimal point in the divisor was moved. In effect, each is being multiplied by the same multiple of 10, which does not change the value.

$$\frac{3.6}{.6} \times \frac{10}{10} = \frac{36}{6} = 6$$

After the divisor has been changed to a whole number, proceed as in division by a whole number.

$$\begin{array}{r} 6. \\ .6\overline{)3.6} = 6.\overline{)36.} \end{array}$$

If necessary, zeros can be added to the dividend in order to move the decimal point to the right for the proper number of places.

$$.12)\overline{48.} = 12.)\overline{4800.}$$

with quotient 400.

PERCENTAGE

Percent means *per hundredths* and is indicated by the percent sign (%). As hundredths, it means the number of parts of a whole quantity which is divided into *100 equal parts*.

Hundredths can therefore be expressed as a common or decimal fraction (1/100), a decimal (.01), or as a percent (1%). Because they are equal, they can be expressed in any of the forms interchangeably.

To change percent to a decimal, drop the percent sign and move the decimal point *two places to the left*.

$$35\% = .35, \text{ and } 2.6\% = .026$$

To change percent to a fraction, divide the percent by 100 and reduce to lowest terms.

$$10\% = 10/100 = 1/10, \text{ and } 75\% = 75/100 = 3/4$$

To change a decimal to percent, move the decimal point *two places to the right* and add the percent sign.

$$.25 = 25\%, \text{ and } .825 = 82.5\%$$

The percent sign cannot be used when making computations. (Percents can be added or subtracted as percents, however, as 12% + 3% = 15%.) When using a percent for calculations it *must* be changed to a decimal or a fraction.

The Percentage Formula

A percent is the rate or the fractional part of a whole thing. The number that results from taking a fractional or decimal part of the whole is called the *percentage*. The percentage is found by multiplying the whole (called the *base*) by the percent or hundredth part of the whole (called the *rate*).

Thus, to find 50% of 10, multiply rate (.50 or ½) by the base (10) and the result will be 5 (.50 × 10 = 5), or the percentage. By formula, this would be

$$P = BR$$

where P is percentage, B is base, and R is rate. Any of the three variables in the formula can be found when the other two variables are known. By transposing the variables, the formula can be arranged to find the unknown variable. Thus,

$$P = BR, B = P/R, \text{ and } R = P/B$$

To find a percentage of a number, given the rate and base, multiply base times rate:

Find 15% of $750.
$$P = BR = .15 \times \$750 = \$112.50$$

To find what percent (rate) one number is of another, given the base and percentage, use R = P/B:

75 is what percent of 150?
$$R = P/B = 75/150 = 1/2 = .50 = 50\%$$

To find a number when a percent of that number is known, given rate and percentage, use B = P/R:

40 is 20% of what number?
$$B = P/R = 40/.20 = 200$$

The only difficulty in solving percentage problems is the proper identification of *percentage, base,* and *rate.* Remember that the rate is the given percent and is the ratio of percentage to base. The base is the whole quantity of which some percent is taken. The percentage is the result obtained by taking a given part of the base.

A short-cut method for finding any one variable when the other two are given is shown in the last section of this Appendix.

RATIO AND PROPORTION

A ratio is a fraction that compares two like numbers, values, or quantities. It may be written as a fraction or with a colon (:) as the ratio sign. Because it is a fraction, it retains all the features of a fraction. It indicates division, can be reduced to lowest terms, and will not change in value when the denominator and numerator are multiplied or divided by the same number. The ratio of 2 to 5 can be written as 2/5 or 2:5.

Adding the terms of a ratio results in the total number of parts, and each term of the ratio represents that fractional part of the whole. For instance, in a ratio of 2 to 3 (2/3 or 2:3), we add the terms (2 + 3) and obtain 5, which means that there are 5 fractional parts. The first term (2) therefore represents 2/5 of the total and the second term (3) represents 3/5 of the total. If we had to distribute $1,000 in a ratio of 2:3, it would be split into 2/5 and 3/5, or

$$2/5 \text{ of } \$1,000 = \$400, \text{ and}$$
$$3/5 \text{ of } \$1,000 = \$600.$$

This represents the correct ratio of 2:3.

Two or more equal ratios are called *proportions.* Because of their equality, a proportion can be written as

$$\frac{2}{5} = \frac{6}{15}$$

A proportion can also be symbolized by a double colon (::) or proportion sign.

$$2:5::6:15$$

Both of the above examples are read "2 *is to* 5 *as* 6 *is to* 15".

The end numbers of any proportion are called the *extremes* and the inside numbers are called the *means.* In the proportion 2:5::6:15, the numbers 2 and 15 are the extremes and the numbers 5 and 6 are the means.

The basic rule of proportion is: *The product of the means is equal to the product of the extremes.* Thus,

$$\text{means} = 5 \times 6 = 30, \text{ and}$$
$$\text{extremes} = 2 \times 15 = 30.$$

The proportion is a true proportion because the products of the means and extremes are equal (both equal 30).

When written as fractions, the means and extremes are diagonally opposite each other. They can be "connected" by drawing an "X" through the equality sign:

$$\frac{2}{5} \diagup\!\!\!\!\!\diagdown \frac{6}{15}$$

To multiply the means and the extremes, multiply the connected numbers:

$$\text{means} = 5 \times 6 = 30, \text{ and}$$
$$\text{extremes} = 2 \times 15 = 30.$$

If one of the quantities is unknown, an equation can be formed in order to solve for the unknown. For instance, to find the unknown (use "x") in the proportion 2:10::x:30, first multiply the means and extremes:

$$30(2) = 60, \text{ and } 10(x) = 10x$$

Now, because the product of the means is equal to the product of the extremes, we have an equation:

$$10x = 60$$

(Note that x as used here is an unknown number and does not indicate multiplication. As such it is an algebraic equation but can be solved without any knowledge of algebra.)

The equation means that 10 times some number (x) is equal to 60. The inverse (opposite) operation of multiplication is division, so to eliminate the 10 from 10x, we *divide* 10x by 10 (10x/10) and the result is "x" (the 10's *cancel* out). The only rule of equations to remember is that if an operation (in this case, division) is done to one side of the equation, it must also be done equally to the other side. Therefore,

$$\frac{10x}{10} = \frac{60}{10}, \text{ and by cancellation,}$$
$$x = 6.$$

We have found the unknown number to be 6.

Example:

If 12 acres of land sells for $1,500, what will 20 acres cost?

Solution:

Set up the proportion as

$$\frac{12 \text{ acres}}{20 \text{ acres}} = \frac{\$1,500}{x \text{ dollars}}, \text{ or } 12:20::1,500:x$$

Multiply means and extremes to establish the equation:

$$\frac{12}{20} = \frac{1500}{x} \text{ (or use } 12:20::1500:x)$$
$$12x = 20(1500)$$
$$12x = 30,000, \text{ and, dividing both sides by 12,}$$
$$x = 30,000/12 = \$2,500.$$

THREE VARIABLE FORMULAS

The percentage formula and all similar 3 variable formulas sometimes cause difficulty when transposing the variables to find any of the unknowns. It is not necessary to memorize all the forms of the formulas, however, if the basic formula is known.

The system that has been widely used in transposing such formulas uses circles with the variables placed so that by covering the unknown, the operations for the other variables becomes obvious.

Most 3 variable formulas are derived from, or are representative of, the basic percentage formula P = BR. We will therefore use that formula for our example.

In all of the 3 variable formulas, the basic formula has one variable equal to the product of the other two. This variable is placed in the top half of a circle and the other two variables are placed in adjacent quarters of the bottom half of the circle. Figure A–1 shows how the relationships of the variables can be visualized by their positions in the circle.

The line (diameter) that divides the circle into top and bottom is the *division* line, and the line (radius) that divides the bottom half into quarter circles is the *multiplication* line. In Figure A–1, if P is the unknown variable, we can cover it with our finger and the variables that are uncovered indicate B *multiplied* by R. Therefore, to find P, multiply B by R, or, by formula, $P = B \times R$.

Likewise, if B (base) is the unknown variable, we cover it with our finger and see that P and R are left. P is on the top of the horizontal line (divide) and R is on the bottom. Therefore, to find B, divide P by R or, $B = P/R$ (B = P over R).

To find R, cover R and the formula indicated is "P over B" or, R = P/B.

Every 3 variable formula can be set up in the same manner. Figure A–2 shows the Interest Formula (I = PR). If P (principal) were the unknown, we would cover it and the remaining variables would be indicated as "I over R" or, P = I/R.

Figure A–3 shows the Income or Capitalization Formula (I = V × R). If the formula for finding R (rate) were needed, we would cover R, and the variables remaining would be "I over V" and would indicate the formula R = I/V. The Value Formula (for finding V) can easily be seen as "I over R" or V = I/R.

Figure A–4 lists many of the formulas for which this system can be used. By using the system, it is only necessary to know the basic formula, as the other two can easily be derived from the circle.

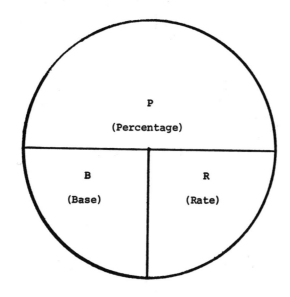

The Percentage Formula

$$P = B \times R$$

FIGURE A-1

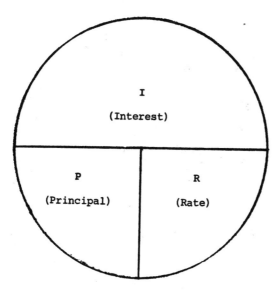

INTEREST FORMULA

$$I = P \times R$$

FIGURE A-2

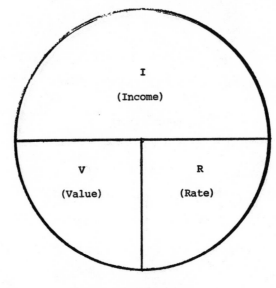

The Income Formula

$$I = V \times R$$

FIGURE A-3

COMMON THREE VARIABLE FORMULAS

Percentage	= Base × Rate	$P = B \times R$
Interest	= Principal × Rate	$I = P \times R$
Income	= Value × Rate	$I = V \times R$
Value	= Income × Factor	$V = I \times F$
	(Hoskold or Inwood Factor)	
Commission	= Gross Selling Price × Rate	$C = S \times R$
Tax	= Assessed Value × Tax Rate	$T = A \times R$
Area	= Length × Width	$A = L \times W$

FIGURE A-4

Appendix II

Using the Metric System

Our system of money is based on the decimal (units of 10) system. Because of the simplicity of the system, almost everyone can count and compute with money regardless of their mathematical ability.

The metric system is also based on the decimal system and is just as simple to learn as our money system. The reluctance and apprehension of the public to "going metric" is because of the fears and complications of *converting* from our customary system (inches, feet, yards, quarts, gallons, etc.) to the metric system.

As the use of the metric system increases in this country, most of the customary units will disappear from use and conversion to metric units, for the most part, will no longer be necessary. Some customary units, however, will continue to be used because of their non-international nature.

Real estate is rarely exchanged internationally and land therefore will probably continue to be sold in acres rather than *hectares*. The linear measurement of land, however, will be done in meters and kilometers, and the real estate professional will find conversion from metric units to the customary units of acres a necessity.

DEFINITIONS

The modernized version of the metric system is called "The International System of Units" (SI) and was established by international agreement. It provides a logical and interconnected framework for all measurements in science, industry, and commerce. The entire SI system is built upon a foundation of only *seven base units* (and two supplementary units).

The base units most frequently used are the *meter* (for length, area, and volume) and the *gram* (for weight). The *liter*, although not an official SI unit, is commonly used to measure *fluid* volume. Temperature is commonly measured in *degrees Celsius* but the base unit for temperature in SI units is the *kelvin*.

For our purposes in real estate, we need only know the base unit for length: the *meter* (m). The meter is exactly 39.37 inches or slightly longer than a yard (about 1.1 yards).

In any metric measurement, the base unit may be used by itself or it may be combined with a *prefix*.

PREFIXES

A prefix can be used with *any* base unit and indicates multiples or submultiples of the units. The most commonly used prefixes and the multiplication factors they indicate are:

milli = one thousandth (1/1000 or 0.001)
centi = one hundredth (1/100 or 0.01)
kilo = one thousand (1,000)

Thus, the term *millimeter* (mm) means 1/1000 of a meter; a *centimeter* (cm) is 1/100 of a meter; and a *kilometer* (km) is 1,000 meters. There are, therefore, 1,000 millimeters in a meter, and 100 centimeters in a meter.

When used with *grams* (g), the term milligram (mg) means 1/1000 of a gram; a centigram (cg) is 1/100 of a gram; and a kilogram is 1,000 grams.

Other prefixes sometimes used include:

deka = ten (10)
hecto = one hundred (100)
mega = one million (1,000,000)

Thus, a dekameter is 10 meters, a hectare is 100 ares, and a megacycle is 1,000,000 cycles.

MEASUREMENTS OF LENGTH

Short lengths are usually measured in centimeters (an inch is about 2½ centimeters and a foot is about 30 centimeters). Each centimeter can be divided into 10 parts, each being 1 millimeter. Millimeters are used mostly for smaller measurements, so for general use, the 10 parts of a centimeter are given their decimal equivalents of .1 cm (1/10 of a centimeter), .5 cm (5/10 or 1/2 of a centimeter), etc. The relationships and simplicity of using decimals can be shown as:

$$10 \text{ mm} = 1 \text{ cm and } 100 \text{ cm} = 1 \text{ meter}$$
$$1 \text{ mm} = .1 \text{ cm and } 1 \text{ cm} = .01 \text{ meter}$$

As in the customary system of inches and feet, addition of units must be done with *similar* units. The conversion from one unit to another in the metric system is much easier than in the customary system. Because it is a decimal system, conversion is easily done by dividing or multiplying with multiples of *10* rather than by 3's, 12's and fractions.

Multiplication or division with multiples of 10 is done simply by moving decimal points. To multiply, move the decimal point to the *right* the same number of places as there are zeros in the multiplier. For instance, to multiply by 10, move one place; to multiply by 100, move two places, and so on. In division, the decimal point is moved to the *left,* using the same procedure.

To change meters to cm, multiply by 100 (3 meters = 300 cm)
To change meters to mm, multiply by 1,000 (2.8 m = 2800 mm)
To change cm to meters, divide by 100 (35 cm = .35 m)
To change mm to meters, divide by 1,000 (48 mm = .048 m)
To change mm to cm, divide by 10 (48 mm = 4.8 cm)

When adding linear metric units, several combinations are possible by following the above unit changes.

Example:

Add 3 meters 28 centimeters and 4 meters 36 centimeters.

Solution:

For answer in centimeters:

3 m 28 cm =   328 cm (300 cm + 28 cm)
4 m 36 cm = + 436 cm (400 cm + 36 cm)
              764 cm

For answer in meters:

28 cm = .28 m, so 3 m 28 cm = 3.28 m
36 cm = .36 m, so 4 m 36 cm = <u>4.36 m</u>

7.64 meters

Or, for a combination answer:

3 m 28 cm
<u>+ 4 m 36 cm</u>

7 m 64 cm (which also equals 7.64 m, or 764 cm)

Usually, if more than 100 cm are used in a measurement, it should be changed to meters. Thus, 4 m 189 cm is converted to 5 m 89 cm (189 cm = 1 m 89 cm).

A *kilometer* is equal to 1,000 meters and is approximately 6/10 of a mile (0.6 miles), or a little more than 1/2 a mile.

To change km to meters, *multiply* by 1,000 (6 km = 6,000 m)
To change meters to km, *divide* by 1,000 (530 m = .530 km)

Kilometers can be changed to approximate miles by multiplying by 0.6. Therefore, to change 82 km to miles:

$$82 \text{ km} \times 0.6 = 49.2 \text{ miles}$$

To change miles to km, divide miles by 0.6. Thus, 30 miles equals 50 km (30/.6 = 50).

Exact conversion factors of metric units of length are included at the end of this appendix. Some of the more common approximate conversion factors that can easily be used in addition to those already discussed are:

1 inch = approximately 2½ centimeters
1 foot = approximately 30 centimeters
1 yard = approximately 0.9 meters

To change meters to yards, add 10% to the length in meters and the answer will be the approximate number of yards. To find the number of yards in 15 meters, for example, add 10% (1.5) and the answer is approximately 16.5 yards (1.5 + 15 = 16.5). Similarly, to change yards to meters, multiply yards by 0.9 and the answer will be the approximate number of meters. For example, 20 yards equals 20 $\times$ .9 = 18 meters.

MEASURES OF AREA

Area is the surface included within a geometric shape and is designated by square units of measure. The methods for finding area are the same in the metric system as in the customary system except that metric units are used instead of customary units.

The square metric units that are used are the square centimeter (cm^2), square meters (m^2), and square kilometers (km^2). The exponent after each unit means that it is a "squared" unit. Just as $3^2 = 3 \times 3$, $cm^2 = cm \times cm$, $m^2 = m \times m$, and so on.

Because area equals length times width ($A = LW$), the units that are multiplied must be *similar* units in order to obtain a "squared" unit. A square centimeter is a square that is one centimeter wide and one centimeter long. If one dimension is given in centimeters and one in meters, one of the dimensions must be changed in order to obtain the square measure or area.

Conversion to one unit or the other can be done as was shown in the preceding section on linear measurement. For ease in computation, it is best to convert all units to the larger unit before multiplying.

Example:

What is the area of a rectangular lot that measures 24 m 58 cm wide and 127 m long?

Solution:

Change to the same units:

$$24 \text{ m } 58 \text{ cm} = 24.58 \text{ m}$$

Apply the area formula, $A = LW$

$$A = 127 \text{ m} \times 24.58 \text{ m}$$
$$A = 3{,}121.66 \text{ m}^2$$

To find the number of square centimeters in one square meter, change the dimensions of 1 m $\times$ 1 m to 100 cm $\times$ 100 cm (equivalents). Multiplying, we find that 1 m^2 = 10,000 cm^2. If the answer to the above example were required in square centimeters then, we would multiply the m^2 by 10,000 and find that the area of the rectangle in square centimeters to be 31,316,600 cm^2.

The Acre, Are, and Hectare

We know that an acre is a unit of square measure having no *linear* units of measure. It contains 4,840 square yards, or 160 square rods, or 43,560 square feet. One square mile contains 640 acres.

As a unit, it will probably be in use long after other customary units have been replaced by metric units. It will be necessary then to convert metric units to acres.

The metric unit comparable to the acre is the *are*. The are is an area of 100 square meters (approximately 120 square yards). The prefix *hecto* means 100, so a *hectare* is 100 ares, or 10,000 square meters. The *hectare* and *are* are the metric units used for measuring land areas.

$$1 \text{ are} = 100 \text{ m}^2$$
$$1 \text{ hectare} = 100 \text{ ares} = 10,000 \text{ m}^2$$

One hectare contains approximately 2½ acres (2.4711 acres exactly) and for conversion purposes the simplest approach is to convert metric area to hectares and then to acres. To change hectares to acres, multiply by 2.5 (approximate).

For example:

1 hectare = 2.5 acres,
4 hectares = 4 × 2.5 = 10 acres, and
5.8 hectares = 5.8 × 2.5 = 14.5 acres.
To change acres to hectares, divide by 2.5:
8 acres = 8/2.5 = 3.2 hectares

Example:

How many acres are contained in a parcel of land measuring 1.2 kilometers by 800 meters?

Solution:

1.2 km = 1,200 meters (decimal point moved 3 places to right)
Area = 1,200 m × 800 m = 960,000 m^2

There are 10,000 square meters in 1 hectare, so

960,000 m^2/10,000 m^2 = 96 hectares
96 hectares = 96 × 2.5 = 240 acres

By changing to *larger* units first, the computation is easier:

800 meters = .80 kilometers
A = 1.2 km X .80 km = .96 km^2
1 km^2 = 100 hectares, so .96 km^2 X 100 = 96 hectares
96 hectares = 96 X 2.5 = 240 acres

The simplicity of the metric system can also be seen by the use of the square kilometer. A square kilometer (km^2) is a square that is 1 km X 1 km, or 1,000 meters X 1,000 meters. There are, therefore, 100,000 square meters in a square kilometer. A hectare is 10,000 square meters, so a square kilometer contains 100 hectares and therefore 10,000 ares.

1 square kilometer = 100,000 m^2
1 square kilometer = 100 hectares = 10,000 ares
Also, 100 hectares = 250 acres (100 X 2.5) so,
1 square kilometer = 250 acres (approx.)

One square mile is 1 mile X 1 mile, and 1 mile equals approximately 1.6 kilometers. Therefore, one square mile is *also* 1.6 km X 1.6 km, or 2.56 km^2 (1.6 X 1.6 = 2.56). So, there are approximately 2.6 square kilometers in 1 square mile.

MEASURES OF VOLUME

Volume is the amount of space that an object contains or occupies. It is a three dimensional measure and therefore involves *cubic* measure. One cubic unit has equal units of each dimension. Thus, a cubic centimeter (cm^3) has dimensions of

1 cm X 1 cm X 1 cm, and a cubic meter (m^3) has dimensions of
1 m X 1 m X 1 m.

By substitution, 1 cubic meter could also be measured as 100 cm X 100 cm X 100 cm, and a cubic meter would therefore be equal to 1,000,000 cubic centimeters. Because of the large number of cubic centimeters involved, conversions are rarely made from cubic meters to cubic centimeters.

The cubic centimeter does have a relationship however to the common metric unit of volume, usually liquid, called the *liter*.

A liter is the volume contained in a cube that measures 10 cm X 10 cm X 10 cm. Therefore, 1 liter = 1,000 cm^3. A milliliter is

1/1000 of a liter and therefore, 1 cubic centimeter equals 1 milliliter. A cubic meter, as shown above, contains 1,000,000 cubic centimeters, which is the same as 1,000 liters (1,000,000/1,000).

It is obvious then, that 1 cubic meter is *also* equal to 1,000 liters. These relationships were designed as such and emphasize the simplicity of the metric system.

$$
\begin{aligned}
1 \text{ liter} &= 1{,}000 \text{ milliliters} \\
1 \text{ liter} &= 1{,}000 \text{ cubic centimeters} \\
1 \text{ milliliter} &= 1 \text{ cubic centimeter} \\
1 \text{ cubic meter} &= 1{,}000 \text{ liters}
\end{aligned}
$$

Metric volumes are found with the same formulas used in our customary system, using the metric base unit of the meter, and, in most cases of liquid volumes, the liter.

The measures of mass, weight (gram), and temperature are shown in the tables of this appendix.

CONVERSIONS

The approximate conversions shown in the preceding sections are easy to use. Exact conversions are more difficult and can be computed from the various tables that are included in this appendix. Other tables are also available from many sources.

Once conversion to metric has been completed in the United States, there will be little need for such tables. The following pages contain tables from various government sources and publications including National Bureau of Standards (NBS) Special Publications 389 and 304A.

Additional sources of metric information are available from the U.S. Government Printing Office, Washington, D.C., the U.S. Metric Association, Boulder Colorado, 80302, and the National Council of Teachers of Mathematics, 1906 Association Drive, Reston, Virginia, 22091.

Approximate Conversions *to* Metric Measures

Symbol	When You Know	Multiply by	To Find	Symbol
		LENGTH		
in	inches	*2.5	centimeters	cm
ft	feet	30	centimeters	cm
yd	yards	0.9	meters	m
mi	miles	1.6	kilometers	km
		AREA		
in^2	square inches	6.5	square centimeters	cm^2
ft^2	square feet	0.09	square meters	m^2
yd^2	square yards	0.8	square meters	m^2
mi^2	square miles	2.6	square kilometers	km^2
	acres	0.4	hectares	ha
		MASS (weight)		
oz	ounces	28	grams	g
lb	pounds	0.45	kilograms	kg
	short tons (2000 lb)	0.9	tonnes	t
		VOLUME		
tsp	teaspoons	5	milliliters	ml
Tbsp	tablespoons	15	milliliters	ml
fl oz	fluid ounces	30	milliliters	ml
c	cups	0.24	liters	l
pt	pints	0.47	liters	l
qt	quarts	0.95	liters	l
gal	gallons	3.8	liters	l
ft^3	cubic feet	0.03	cubic meters	m^3
yd^3	cubic yards	0.76	cubic meters	m^3
		TEMPERATURE (exact)		
°F	Fahrenheit temperature	5/9 (after subtracting 32)	Celsius temperature	°C

TABLE I

Approximate Conversions *from* Metric Measures

Symbol	When You Know	Multiply by	To Find	Symbol

LENGTH

Symbol	When You Know	Multiply by	To Find	Symbol
mm	millimeters	0.04	inches	in
cm	centimeters	0.4	inches	in
m	meters	3.3	feet	ft
m	meters	1.1	yards	yd
km	kilometers	0.6	miles	mi

AREA

Symbol	When You Know	Multiply by	To Find	Symbol
cm^2	square centimeters	0.16	square inches	in^2
m^2	square meters	1.2	square yards	yd^2
km^2	square kilometers	0.4	square miles	mi^2
ha	hectares (10,000 m^2)	2.5	acres	

MASS (weight)

Symbol	When You Know	Multiply by	To Find	Symbol
g	grams	0.035	ounces	oz
kg	kilograms	2.2	pounds	lb
t	tonnes (1000 kg)	1.1	short tons	

VOLUME

Symbol	When You Know	Multiply by	To Find	Symbol
ml	milliliters	0.03	fluid ounces	fl oz
l	liters	2.1	pints	pt
l	liters	1.06	quarts	qt
l	liters	0.26	gallons	gal
m^3	cubic meters	35	cubic feet	ft^3
m^3	cubic meters	1.3	cubic yards	yd^3

TEMPERATURE (exact)

Symbol	When You Know	Multiply by	To Find	Symbol
°C	Celsius temperature	9/5 (then add 32)	Fahrenheit temperature	°F

°F
°F   32   98.6   212
-40   0   40   80   120   160   200
-40   -20   0   20   40   60   80   100
°C   37   °C

TABLE II

EXACT COMMON CONVERSIONS TO METRIC

WHEN YOU KNOW	MULTIPLY BY	TO FIND
inches	25.4	millimeters
feet	0.3048	meters
yards	0.9144	meters
miles	1.609 34	kilometers
square yards	0.836 127	square meters
acres	0.404 686	hectares
cubic yards	0.764 555	cubic meters
quarts (liquid)	0.946 353	liters
ounces (avdp)	28.349 5	grams
pounds (avdp)	0.453 592	kilograms
Fahrenheit (temp)	5/9 (after subtracting 32)	Celsius (temp)

TABLE III

EXACT COMMON CONVERSIONS FROM METRIC

WHEN YOU KNOW	MULTIPLY BY	TO FIND
millimeters	0.039 370	inches
meters	3.280 84	feet
meters	1.093 61	yards
kilometers	0.621 371	miles
square meters	1.195 99	square yards
hectares	2.471 05	acres
cubic meters	1.307 95	cubic yards
liters	1.056 69	quarts (liquid)
grams	0.035 274	ounces (avdp)
kilograms	2.20462	pounds (avdp)
Celsius (temp)	9/5 (then add 32)	Fahrenheit (temp)

TABLE IV

MULTIPLES AND PREFIXES

Multiples and Submultiples		Prefixes
1 000 000 000 000	10^{12}	tera
1 000 000 000	10^{9}	giga
1 000 000	10^{6}	*mega*
1 000	10^{3}	*kilo*
100	10^{2}	*hecto*
10	10^{1}	*deka*
BASE UNIT 1	10^{0}	
0.1	10^{-1}	*deci*
0.01	10^{-2}	*centi*
0.001	10^{-3}	*milli*
0.000 001	10^{-6}	micro
0.000 000 001	10^{-9}	nano
0.000 000 000 001	10^{-12}	pico
0.000 000 000 000 001	10^{-15}	femto
0.000 000 000 000 000 001	10^{-18}	atto

These prefixes may be applied to all metric and SI units. The most commonly used prefixes are italicized.

TABLE V

Appendix III

The Compound Interest and Annuity Tables

The most important tool in the mathematics of finance and real estate is the Compound Interest and Annuity Table. Its use and construction were detailed in Chapter 3 and, as mentioned in the chapter, this Appendix contains some of the more commonly used rate tables.

The first three columns of the tables represent FUTURE VALUES and are the COMPOUND INTEREST FUNCTIONS:

COLUMN 1, Amount of 1, is the *future worth of one dollar* with interest. It represents what a *lump sum* deposit will grow to in the future. The symbol is $S = (1 + i)^n$.

COLUMN 2, Amount of 1 *per Period*, is the *future worth of installments* or deposits of one dollar made per period. It represents what a series of deposits will grow to in the future. The symbol is $s_{\overline{n}|\,i}$.

COLUMN 3, Sinking Fund, is the *amount needed for deposit* in order to have *one dollar in the future*. Each factor in the column represents the amount of deposit that will grow to one dollar. It is the reciprocal of column 2 and its symbol is $1/s_{\overline{n}|\,i}$.

The second three columns represent PRESENT VALUES and are the ANNUITY FUNCTIONS:

COLUMN 4, Present Value (or Worth) of 1, is the *value that one dollar in the future has today.* It is the value at present for a payment in the future. It is the reciprocal of column 1 and is also called the *reversion factor.* The symbol is v^n.

COLUMN 5, Present Value of 1 per Period, is the *value that one dollar of future periodic payments has today.* It is the cumulative total of the present value of 1 (column 4). Column 5 is also used as the *Inwood Factor.* The symbol is $a_{\overline{n}|i}$.

COLUMN 6, Periodic Payment (or Partial Payment), in real estate terminology, is the mortgage *payment necessary to amortize a loan of one dollar.* It is the reciprocal of column 5 and its symbol is $1/a_{\overline{n}|i}$. It is also used to find the Constant Annual Percent.

COMPOUND INTEREST AND ANNUITY TABLES

The tables in this appendix are reproduced from FINANCIAL COMPOUND INTEREST AND ANNUITY TABLES, 5th Ed., publication #376, pages 314-315, 350-351, 638-39, 670-71, 690-91, 706-07, 714-15, 722-23, 730-31, and 733-1 to 733-4, Copyright 1970, Financial Publishing Company, Boston.

P E R I O D S	AMOUNT OF 1 How $1 left at compound interest will grow.	AMOUNT OF 1 PER PERIOD How $1 deposited periodically will grow.	SINKING FUND Periodic deposit that will grow to $1 at future date.
1	1.006 666 6667	1.000 000 0000	1.000 000 0000
2	1.013 377 7778	2.006 666 6667	.498 338 8704
3	1.020 133 6296	3.020 044 4444	.331 120 9548
4	1.026 934 5205	4.040 178 0741	.247 513 8426
5	1.033 780 7506	5.067 112 5946	.197 351 0518
6	1.040 672 6223	6.100 893 3452	.163 910 4215
7	1.047 610 4398	7.141 565 9675	.140 025 3116
8	1.054 594 5094	8.189 176 4073	.122 112 4018
9	1.061 625 1394	9.243 770 9167	.108 180 9587
10	1.068 702 6404	10.305 396 0561	.097 036 5423
11	1.075 827 3246	11.374 098 6965	.087 919 0542
12	1.082 999 5068	12.449 926 0211	.080 321 7624
13	1.090 219 5035	13.532 925 5279	.073 893 8523
14	1.097 487 6335	14.623 145 0315	.068 384 7420
15	1.104 804 2178	15.720 632 6650	.063 610 6715
16	1.112 169 5792	16.825 436 8828	.059 433 8208
17	1.119 584 0431	17.937 606 4620	.055 748 7980
18	1.127 047 9367	19.057 190 5051	.052 473 6319
19	1.134 561 5896	20.184 238 4418	.049 543 6081
20	1.142 125 3335	21.318 800 0314	.046 906 9553
21	1.149 739 5024	22.460 925 3649	.044 521 7632
22	1.157 404 4324	23.610 664 8673	.042 353 7417
23	1.165 120 4620	24.768 069 2998	.040 374 5640
24	1.172 887 9317	25.933 189 7618	.038 560 6248
25	1.180 707 1846	27.106 077 6935	.036 892 0952
26	1.188 578 5659	28.286 784 8782	.035 352 1973
27	1.196 502 4230	29.475 363 4440	.033 926 6385
28	1.204 479 1058	30.671 865 8670	.032 603 1681
29	1.212 508 9665	31.876 344 9728	.031 371 2255
30	1.220 592 3596	33.088 853 9392	.030 221 6572
31	1.228 729 6420	34.309 446 2988	.029 146 4919
32	1.236 921 1729	35.538 175 9408	.028 138 7543
33	1.245 167 3141	36.775 097 1138	.027 192 3143
34	1.253 468 4295	38.020 264 4279	.026 301 7634
35	1.261 824 8857	39.273 732 8574	.025 462 3110
36	1.270 237 0516	40.535 557 7431	.024 669 6988
37	1.278 705 2986	41.805 794 7947	.023 920 1289
38	1.287 230 0006	43.084 500 0934	.023 210 2032
39	1.295 811 5340	44.371 730 0940	.022 536 8720
40	1.304 450 2775	45.667 541 6279	.021 897 3907
41	1.313 146 6127	46.971 991 9055	.021 289 2824
42	1.321 900 9235	48.285 138 5182	.020 710 3061
43	1.330 713 5963	49.607 039 4416	.020 158 4294
44	1.339 585 0203	50.937 753 0379	.019 631 8043
45	1.348 515 5871	52.277 338 0581	.019 128 7475
46	1.357 505 6910	53.625 853 6452	.018 647 7218
47	1.366 555 7289	54.983 359 3362	.018 187 3209
48	1.375 666 1004	56.349 915 0651	.017 746 2557
49	1.384 837 2078	57.725 581 1655	.017 323 3423
50	1.394 069 4558	59.110 418 3733	.016 917 4915
51	1.403 363 2522	60.504 487 8291	.016 527 6996
52	1.412 719 0072	61.907 851 0813	.016 153 0401
53	1.422 137 1339	63.320 570 0885	.015 792 6563
54	1.431 618 0481	64.742 707 2224	.015 445 7551
55	1.441 162 1685	66.174 325 2706	.015 111 6010
56	1.450 769 9163	67.615 487 4390	.014 789 5111
57	1.460 441 7157	69.066 257 3553	.014 478 8503
58	1.470 177 9938	70.526 699 0710	.014 179 0274
59	1.479 979 1804	71.996 877 0648	.013 889 4913
60	1.489 845 7083	73.476 856 2452	.013 609 7276
n	$s=(1+i)^n$	$s_{\overline{n}|}=\dfrac{(1+i)^n-1}{i}$	$\dfrac{1}{s_{\overline{n}|}}=\dfrac{i}{(1+i)^n-1}$

.00666666
per period

ANNUALLY
If compounded
annually
nominal annual rate is

2/3%

SEMIANNUALLY
If compounded
semiannually
nominal annual rate is

1⅓%

QUARTERLY
If compounded
quarterly
nominal annual rate is

2⅔%

MONTHLY
If compounded
monthly
nominal annual rate is

8%

i = .00666666
$j_{(2)}$ = .01333333
$j_{(4)}$ = .02666666
$j_{(12)}$ = .08

302

PRESENT WORTH OF 1 — What $1 due in the future is worth today.	PRESENT WORTH OF 1 PER PERIOD — What $1 payable periodically is worth today.	PARTIAL PAYMENT — Annuity worth $1 today. Periodic payment necessary to pay off a loan of $1.	PERIODS	RATE
				2/3%
.993 377 4834	.993 377 4834	1.006 666 6667	1	
.986 798 8246	1.980 176 3081	.505 005 5371	2	
.980 263 7531	2.960 440 0411	.337 787 6215	3	.00666666
.973 771 9203	3.934 211 9614	.254 180 5093	4	per period
.967 323 0996	4.901 535 0610	.204 017 7184	5	
.960 916 9864	5.862 452 0473	.170 577 0882	6	
.954 553 2977	6.817 005 3450	.146 691 9783	7	
.948 231 7527	7.765 237 0977	.128 779 0685	8	
.941 952 0722	8.707 189 1699	.114 847 6254	9	
.935 713 9790	9.642 903 1489	.103 703 2089	10	
.929 517 1977	10.572 420 3466	.094 585 7209	11	
.923 361 4547	11.495 781 8013	.086 988 4291	12	
.917 246 4781	12.413 028 2794	.080 560 5190	13	
.911 171 9981	13.324 200 2775	.075 051 4087	14	
.905 137 7465	14.229 338 0240	.070 277 3382	15	
.899 143 4568	15.128 481 4808	.066 100 4874	16	
.893 188 8644	16.021 670 3452	.062 415 4647	17	
.887 273 7063	16.908 944 0515	.059 140 2986	18	
.881 397 7215	17.790 341 7730	.056 210 2748	19	
.875 560 6505	18.665 902 4236	.053 573 6220	20	ANNUALLY
.869 762 2356	19.535 664 6592	.051 188 4299	21	If compounded annually
.864 002 2208	20.399 666 8800	.049 020 4083	22	nominal annual rate is
.858 280 3518	21.257 947 2317	.047 041 2307	23	
.852 596 3759	22.110 543 6077	.045 227 2915	24	**2/3%**
.846 950 0423	22.957 493 6500	.043 558 7619	25	
.841 341 1017	23.798 834 7517	.042 018 8640	26	
.835 769 3063	24.634 604 0580	.040 593 3052	27	
.830 234 4102	25.464 838 4682	.039 269 8348	28	
.824 736 1691	26.289 574 6373	.038 037 8920	29	
.819 274 3402	27.108 848 9774	.036 888 3238	30	SEMIANNUALLY
.813 848 6823	27.922 697 6597	.035 813 1586	31	If compounded semiannually
.808 458 9559	28.731 156 6156	.034 805 4209	32	nominal annual rate is
.803 104 9231	29.534 261 5387	.033 858 9810	33	
.797 786 3474	30.332 047 8861	.032 968 4301	34	**1 1/3%**
.792 502 9941	31.124 550 8802	.032 128 9777	35	
.787 254 6299	31.911 805 5101	.031 336 3655	36	
.782 041 0291	32.693 846 5333	.030 586 7956	37	
.776 861 9435	33.470 708 4767	.029 876 8698	38	
.771 717 1624	34.242 425 6392	.029 203 5386	39	
.766 606 4527	35.009 032 0919	.028 564 0573	40	QUARTERLY
.761 529 5888	35.770 561 6807	.027 955 9491	41	If compounded quarterly
.756 486 5465	36.527 048 0272	.027 376 9728	42	nominal annual rate is
.751 476 5031	37.278 524 5303	.026 825 0960	43	
.746 499 8375	38.025 024 3678	.026 298 4710	44	**2 2/3%**
.741 556 1300	38.766 580 4978	.025 795 4142	45	
.736 645 1623	39.503 225 6601	.025 314 3885	46	
.731 766 7175	40.234 992 3776	.024 853 9876	47	
.726 920 5803	40.961 912 9579	.024 412 9223	48	
.722 106 5367	41.684 019 4946	.023 990 0089	49	
.717 324 3742	42.401 343 8688	.023 584 1582	50	MONTHLY
.712 573 8817	43.113 917 7505	.023 194 3663	51	If compounded monthly
.707 854 8493	43.821 772 5998	.022 819 7068	52	nominal annual rate is
.703 167 0689	44.524 939 6687	.022 459 3230	53	
.698 510 3333	45.223 450 0020	.022 112 4218	54	
.693 884 4371	45.917 334 4391	.021 778 2677	55	**8%**
.689 289 1759	46.606 623 6150	.021 456 1777	56	
.684 724 3469	47.291 347 9619	.021 145 5170	57	
.680 189 7486	47.971 537 7105	.020 845 6941	58	i = .00666666
.675 685 1807	48.647 222 8912	.020 556 1580	59	$j_{(2)}$ = .01333333
.671 210 4444	49.318 433 3356	.020 276 3943	60	$j_{(4)}$ = .02666666
				$j_{(12)}$ = .08
$v^n = \dfrac{1}{(1+i)^n}$	$a_{\overline{n}|} = \dfrac{1-v^n}{i}$	$\dfrac{1}{a_{\overline{n}|}} = \dfrac{i}{1-v^n}$	n	

303

ANNUALLY
If compounded
annually
nominal annual rate is

¾%

SEMIANNUALLY
If compounded
semiannually
nominal annual rate is

1½%

QUARTERLY
If compounded
quarterly
nominal annual rate is

3%

MONTHLY
If compounded
monthly
nominal annual rate is

9%

i   = .0075
j₍₂₎ = .015
j₍₄₎ = .03
j₍₁₂₎ = .09

P E R I O D S	AMOUNT OF 1 How $1 left at compound interest will grow.	AMOUNT OF 1 PER PERIOD How $1 deposited periodically will grow.	SINKING FUND Periodic deposit that will grow to $1 at future date.
1	1.007 500 0000	1.000 000 0000	1.000 000 0000
2	1.015 056 2500	2.007 500 0000	.498 132 0050
3	1.022 669 1719	3.022 556 2500	.330 845 7866
4	1.030 339 1907	4.045 225 4219	.247 205 0123
5	1.038 066 7346	5.075 564 6125	.197 022 4155
6	1.045 852 2351	6.113 631 3471	.163 568 9074
7	1.053 696 1269	7.159 483 5822	.139 674 8786
8	1.061 598 8478	8.213 179 7091	.121 755 5241
9	1.069 560 8392	9.274 778 5569	.107 819 2858
10	1.077 582 5455	10.344 339 3961	.096 671 2287
11	1.085 664 4146	11.421 921 9416	.087 550 9398
12	1.093 806 8977	12.507 586 3561	.079 951 4768
13	1.102 010 4494	13.601 393 2538	.073 521 8798
14	1.110 275 5278	14.703 403 7032	.068 011 4632
15	1.118 602 5942	15.813 679 2310	.063 236 3906
16	1.126 992 1137	16.932 281 8252	.059 058 7855
17	1.135 444 5545	18.059 273 9389	.055 373 2118
18	1.143 960 3887	19.194 718 4934	.052 097 6643
19	1.152 540 0916	20.338 678 8821	.049 167 4020
20	1.161 184 1423	21.491 218 9738	.046 530 6319
21	1.169 893 0234	22.652 403 1161	.044 145 4266
22	1.178 667 2210	23.822 296 1394	.041 977 4817
23	1.187 507 2252	25.000 963 3605	.039 998 4587
24	1.196 413 5294	26.188 470 5857	.038 184 7423
25	1.205 386 6309	27.384 884 1151	.036 516 4956
26	1.214 427 0306	28.590 270 7459	.034 976 9335
27	1.223 535 2333	29.804 697 7765	.033 551 7578
28	1.232 711 7476	31.028 233 0099	.032 228 7125
29	1.241 957 0857	32.260 944 7574	.030 997 2323
30	1.251 271 7638	33.502 901 8431	.029 848 1608
31	1.260 656 3021	34.754 173 6069	.028 773 5226
32	1.270 111 2243	36.014 829 9090	.027 766 3397
33	1.279 637 0585	37.284 941 1333	.026 820 4795
34	1.289 234 3364	38.564 578 1918	.025 930 5313
35	1.298 903 5940	39.853 812 5282	.025 091 7023
36	1.308 645 3709	41.152 716 1222	.024 299 7327
37	1.318 460 2112	42.461 361 4931	.023 550 8228
38	1.328 348 6628	43.779 821 7043	.022 841 5732
39	1.338 311 2778	45.108 170 3671	.022 168 9329
40	1.348 348 6123	46.446 481 6449	.021 530 1561
41	1.358 461 2269	47.794 830 2572	.020 922 7650
42	1.368 649 6861	49.153 291 4841	.020 344 5175
43	1.378 914 5588	50.521 941 1703	.019 793 3804
44	1.389 256 4180	51.900 855 7290	.019 267 5051
45	1.399 675 8411	53.290 112 1470	.018 765 2073
46	1.410 173 4099	54.689 787 9881	.018 284 9493
47	1.420 749 7105	56.099 961 3980	.017 825 3242
48	1.431 405 3333	57.520 711 1085	.017 385 0424
49	1.442 140 8733	58.952 116 4418	.016 962 9194
50	1.452 956 9299	60.394 257 3151	.016 557 8657
51	1.463 854 1068	61.847 214 2450	.016 168 8770
52	1.474 833 0126	63.311 068 3518	.015 795 0265
53	1.485 894 2602	64.785 901 3645	.015 435 4571
54	1.497 038 4672	66.271 795 6247	.015 089 3754
55	1.508 266 2557	67.768 834 0919	.014 756 0455
56	1.519 578 2526	69.277 100 3476	.014 434 7843
57	1.530 975 0895	70.796 678 6002	.014 124 9564
58	1.542 457 4027	72.327 653 6897	.013 825 9704
59	1.554 025 8332	73.870 111 0923	.013 537 2749
60	1.565 681 0269	75.424 136 9255	.013 258 3552
n	$s := (1+i)^n$	$s_{\overline{n}} = \dfrac{(1+i)^n - 1}{i}$	$\dfrac{1}{s_{\overline{n}}} = \dfrac{i}{(1+i)^n - 1}$

PRESENT WORTH OF 1 What $1 due in the future is worth today.	PRESENT WORTH OF 1 PER PERIOD What $1 payable periodically is worth today.	PARTIAL PAYMENT Annuity worth $1 today. Periodic payment necessary to pay off a loan of $1.	PERIODS	RATE 3/4%
.992 555 8313	.992 555 8313	1.007 500 0000	1	
.985 167 0782	1.977 722 9094	.505 632 0050	2	
.977 833 3282	2.955 556 2377	.338 345 7866	3	
.970 554 1719	3.926 110 4096	.254 705 0123	4	.0075
.963 329 2029	4.889 439 6125	.204 522 4155	5	per period
.956 158 0178	5.845 597 6303	.171 068 9074	6	
.949 040 2162	6.794 637 8464	.147 174 8786	7	
.941 975 4006	7.736 613 2471	.129 255 5241	8	
.934 963 1768	8.671 576 4239	.115 319 2858	9	
.928 003 1532	9.599 579 5771	.104 171 2287	10	
.921 094 9411	10.520 674 5182	.095 050 9398	11	
.914 238 1550	11.434 912 6731	.087 451 4768	12	
.907 432 4119	12.342 345 0850	.081 021 8798	13	
.900 677 3319	13.243 022 4169	.075 511 4632	14	
.893 972 5378	14.136 994 9547	.070 736 3908	15	
.887 317 6554	15.024 312 6101	.066 558 7855	16	
.880 712 3131	15.905 024 9232	.062 873 2118	17	
.874 156 1420	16.779 181 0652	.059 597 6643	18	
.867 648 7762	17.646 829 8414	.056 667 4020	19	
.861 189 8523	18.508 019 6937	.054 030 6319	20	ANNUALLY If compounded annually nominal annual rate is
.854 779 0097	19.362 798 7034	.051 645 4266	21	
.848 415 8905	20.211 214 5940	.049 477 4817	22	
.842 100 1395	21.053 314 7335	.047 498 4587	23	
.835 831 4040	21.889 146 1374	.045 684 7423	24	3/4%
.829 609 3340	22.718 755 4714	.044 016 4956	25	
.823 433 5821	23.542 189 0535	.042 476 9335	26	
.817 303 8036	24.359 492 8571	.041 051 7578	27	
.811 219 6562	25.170 712 5132	.039 728 7125	28	
.805 180 8001	25.975 893 3134	.038 497 2323	29	
.799 186 8984	26.775 080 2118	.037 348 1608	30	SEMIANNUALLY If compounded semiannually nominal annual rate is
.793 237 6163	27.568 317 8281	.036 273 5226	31	
.787 332 6216	28.355 650 4497	.035 266 3397	32	
.781 471 5847	29.137 122 0344	.034 320 4795	33	
.775 654 1784	29.912 776 2128	.033 430 5313	34	1½%
.769 880 0778	30.682 656 2907	.032 591 7023	35	
.764 148 9606	31.446 805 2513	.031 799 7327	36	
.758 460 5068	32.205 265 7581	.031 050 8228	37	
.752 814 3988	32.958 080 1569	.030 341 5732	38	
.747 210 3214	33.705 290 4783	.029 668 0329	39	
.741 647 9617	34.446 938 4400	.029 030 1561	40	QUARTERLY If compounded quarterly nominal annual rate is
.736 127 0091	35.183 065 4492	.028 422 7650	41	
.730 647 1555	35.913 712 6046	.027 844 5175	42	
.725 208 0948	36.638 920 6994	.027 293 3804	43	
.719 809 5233	37.358 730 2227	.026 767 5051	44	3%
.714 451 1398	38.073 181 3625	.026 265 2073	45	
.709 132 6449	38.782 314 0074	.025 784 9493	46	
.703 853 7419	39.486 167 7493	.025 325 3242	47	
.698 614 1359	40.184 781 8852	.024 885 0424	48	
.693 413 5344	40.878 195 4195	.024 462 9194	49	
.688 251 6470	41.566 447 0665	.024 057 8657	50	MONTHLY If compounded monthly nominal annual rate is
.683 128 1856	42.249 575 2521	.023 668 8770	51	
.678 042 8641	42.927 618 1163	.023 295 0265	52	
.672 995 3986	43.600 613 5149	.022 935 4571	53	
.667 985 5073	44.268 599 0222	.022 589 3754	54	9%
.663 012 9105	44.931 611 9327	.022 256 0455	55	
.658 077 3305	45.589 689 2633	.021 934 7843	56	
.653 178 4918	46.242 867 7551	.021 624 9564	57	i = .0075
.648 316 1209	46.891 183 8760	.021 325 9704	58	$j_{(2)}$ = .015
.643 489 9463	47.534 673 8224	.021 037 2749	59	$j_{(4)}$ = .03
.638 699 6986	48.173 373 5210	.020 758 3552	60	$j_{(12)}$ = .09
$v^n = \dfrac{1}{(1+i)^n}$	$a_{\overline{n}\rceil} = \dfrac{1-v^n}{i}$	$\dfrac{1}{a_{\overline{n}\rceil}} = \dfrac{i}{1-v^n}$	n	

305

P E R I O D S	AMOUNT OF 1 How $1 left at compound interest will grow.	AMOUNT OF 1 PER PERIOD How $1 deposited periodically will grow.	SINKING FUND Periodic deposit that will grow to $1 at future date.
1	1.040 000 0000	1.000 000 0000	1.000 000 0000
2	1.081 600 0000	2.040 000 0000	.490 196 0784
3	1.124 864 0000	3.121 600 0000	.320 348 5392
4	1.169 858 5600	4.246 464 0000	.235 490 0454
5	1.216 652 9024	5.416 322 5600	.184 627 1135
6	1.265 319 0185	6.632 975 4624	.150 761 9025
7	1.315 931 7792	7.898 294 4809	.126 609 6120
8	1.368 569 0504	9.214 226 2601	.108 527 8320
9	1.423 311 8124	10.582 795 3105	.094 492 9927
10	1.480 244 2849	12.006 107 1230	.083 290 9443
11	1.539 454 0563	13.486 351 4079	.074 149 0393
12	1.601 032 2186	15.025 805 4642	.066 552 1727
13	1.665 073 5073	16.626 837 6828	.060 143 7278
14	1.731 676 4476	18.291 911 1901	.054 668 9731
15	1.800 943 5055	20.023 587 6377	.049 941 1004
16	1.872 981 2457	21.824 531 1432	.045 819 9992
17	1.947 900 4956	23.697 512 3889	.042 198 5221
18	2.025 816 5154	25.645 412 8845	.038 993 3281
19	2.106 849 1760	27.671 229 3998	.036 138 6184
20	2.191 123 1430	29.778 078 5758	.033 581 7503
21	2.278 768 0688	31.969 201 7189	.031 280 1054
22	2.369 918 7915	34.247 969 7876	.029 198 8111
23	2.464 715 5432	36.617 888 5791	.027 309 0568
24	2.563 304 1649	39.082 604 1223	.025 586 8313
25	2.665 836 3315	41.645 908 2872	.024 011 9628
26	2.772 469 7847	44.311 744 6187	.022 567 3805
27	2.883 368 5761	47.084 214 4034	.021 238 5406
28	2.998 703 3192	49.967 582 9796	.020 012 9752
29	3.118 651 4519	52.966 286 2987	.018 879 9342
30	3.243 397 5100	56.084 937 7507	.017 830 0991
31	3.373 133 4104	59.328 335 2607	.016 855 9524
32	3.508 058 7468	62.701 468 6711	.015 948 5897
33	3.648 381 0967	66.209 527 4180	.015 103 5665
34	3.794 316 3406	69.857 908 5147	.014 314 7715
35	3.946 088 9942	73.652 224 8553	.013 577 3224
36	4.103 932 5540	77.598 313 8495	.012 886 8780
37	4.268 089 8561	81.702 246 4035	.012 239 5655
38	4.438 813 4504	85.970 336 2596	.011 631 9191
39	4.616 365 9884	90.409 149 7100	.011 060 8274
40	4.801 020 6279	95.025 515 6984	.010 523 4893
41	4.993 061 4531	99.826 536 3264	.010 017 3765
42	5.192 783 9112	104.819 597 7794	.009 540 2007
43	5.400 495 2676	110.012 381 6906	.009 089 8859
44	5.616 515 0783	115.412 876 9582	.008 664 5444
45	5.841 175 6815	121.029 392 0365	.008 262 4558
46	6.074 822 7087	126.870 567 7180	.007 882 0488
47	6.317 815 6171	132.945 390 4267	.007 521 8855
48	6.570 528 2418	139.263 206 0438	.007 180 6476
49	6.833 349 3714	145.833 734 2855	.006 857 1240
50	7.106 683 3463	152.667 083 6570	.006 550 2004
51	7.390 950 6801	159.773 767 0032	.006 258 8497
52	7.686 588 7073	167.164 717 6834	.005 982 1236
53	7.994 052 2556	174.851 306 3907	.005 719 1451
54	8.313 814 3459	182.845 358 6463	.005 469 1025
55	8.646 366 9197	191.159 172 9922	.005 231 2426
56	8.992 221 5965	199.805 539 9119	.005 004 8662
57	9.351 910 4603	208.797 761 5083	.004 789 3234
58	9.725 986 8787	218.149 671 9687	.004 584 0087
59	10.115 026 3539	227.875 658 8474	.004 388 3581
60	10.519 627 4081	237.990 685 2013	.004 201 8451
n	$s=(1+i)^n$	$s_{\overline{n}}=\dfrac{(1+i)^n-1}{i}$	$\dfrac{1}{s_{\overline{n}}}=\dfrac{i}{(1+i)^n-1}$

.04
per period

ANNUALLY
If compounded
annually
nominal annual rate is
4%

SEMIANNUALLY
If compounded
semiannually
nominal annual rate is
8%

QUARTERLY
If compounded
quarterly
nominal annual rate is
16%

MONTHLY
If compounded
monthly
nominal annual rate is
48%

i = .04
$j_{(2)}$ = .08
$j_{(4)}$ = .16
$j_{(12)}$ = .48

306

PRESENT WORTH OF 1 What $1 due in the future is worth today.	PRESENT WORTH OF 1 PER PERIOD What $1 payable periodically is worth today.	PARTIAL PAYMENT Annuity worth $1 today. Periodic payment necessary to pay off a loan of $1.	PERIODS	RATE 4%
.961 538 4615	.961 538 4615	1.040 000 0000	1	
.924 556 2130	1.886 094 6746	.530 196 0784	2	
.888 996 3587	2.775 091 0332	.360 348 5392	3	.04
.854 804 1910	3.629 895 2243	.275 490 0454	4	per period
.821 927 1068	4.451 822 3310	.224 627 1135	5	
.790 314 5257	5.242 136 8567	.190 761 9025	6	
.759 917 8132	6.002 054 6699	.166 609 6120	7	
.730 690 2050	6.732 744 8750	.148 527 8320	8	
.702 586 7356	7.435 331 6105	.134 492 9927	9	
.675 564 1688	8.110 895 7794	.123 290 9443	10	
.649 580 9316	8.760 476 7109	.114 149 0393	11	
.624 597 0496	9.385 073 7605	.106 552 1727	12	
.600 574 0861	9.985 647 8466	.100 143 7278	13	
.577 475 0828	10.563 122 9295	.094 668 9731	14	
.555 264 5027	11.118 387 4322	.089 941 1004	15	
.533 908 1757	11.652 295 6079	.085 819 9992	16	
.513 373 2459	12.165 668 8537	.082 198 5221	17	
.493 628 1210	12.659 296 9747	.078 993 3281	18	
.474 642 4240	13.133 939 3988	.076 138 6184	19	
.456 386 9462	13.590 326 3450	.073 581 7503	20	ANNUALLY If compounded annually nominal annual rate is
.438 833 6021	14.029 159 9471	.071 280 1054	21	
.421 955 3867	14.451 115 3337	.069 198 8111	22	
.405 726 3333	14.856 841 6671	.067 309 0568	23	
.390 121 4743	15.246 963 1414	.065 586 8313	24	
.375 116 8023	15.622 079 9437	.064 011 9628	25	4%
.360 689 2329	15.982 769 1766	.062 567 3805	26	
.346 816 5701	16.329 585 7467	.061 238 5406	27	
.333 477 4713	16.663 063 2180	.060 012 9752	28	
.320 651 4147	16.983 714 6327	.058 879 9342	29	
.308 318 6680	17.292 033 3007	.057 830 0991	30	SEMIANNUALLY If compounded semiannually nominal annual rate is
.296 460 2577	17.588 493 5583	.056 855 3524	31	
.285 057 9401	17.873 551 4984	.055 948 5897	32	
.274 094 1731	18.147 645 6715	.055 103 5665	33	
.263 552 0896	18.411 197 7611	.054 314 7715	34	
.253 415 4707	18.664 613 2318	.053 577 3224	35	8%
.243 668 7219	18.908 281 9537	.052 886 8780	36	
.234 296 8479	19.142 578 8016	.052 239 5655	37	
.225 285 4307	19.367 864 2323	.051 631 9191	38	
.216 620 6064	19.584 484 8388	.051 060 8274	39	
.208 289 0447	19.792 773 8834	.050 523 4893	40	QUARTERLY If compounded quarterly nominal annual rate is
.200 277 9276	19.993 051 8110	.050 017 3765	41	
.192 574 9303	20.185 626 7413	.049 540 2007	42	
.185 168 2023	20.370 794 9436	.049 089 8859	43	
.178 046 3483	20.548 841 2919	.048 664 5444	44	
.171 198 4118	20.720 039 7038	.048 262 4558	45	16%
.164 613 8575	20.884 653 5613	.047 882 0488	46	
.158 282 5553	21.042 936 1166	.047 521 8855	47	
.152 194 7647	21.195 130 8814	.047 180 6476	48	
.146 341 1199	21.341 472 0013	.046 857 1240	49	
.140 712 6153	21.482 184 6167	.046 550 2004	50	MONTHLY If compounded monthly nominal annual rate is
.135 300 5917	21.617 485 2083	.046 258 8497	51	
.130 096 7228	21.747 581 9311	.045 982 1236	52	
.125 093 0027	21.872 674 9337	.045 719 1451	53	
.120 281 7333	21.992 956 6671	.045 469 1025	54	
.115 655 5128	22.108 612 1799	.045 231 2426	55	48%
.111 207 2239	22.219 819 4037	.045 004 8662	56	
.106 930 0229	22.326 749 4267	.044 789 3234	57	
.102 817 3297	22.429 566 7564	.044 584 0087	58	i = .04
.098 862 8171	22.528 429 5735	.044 388 3581	59	$j_{(2)}$ = .08
.095 060 4010	22.623 489 9745	.044 201 8451	60	$j_{(4)}$ = .16

$j_{(12)}$ = .48

$$v^n = \frac{1}{(1+i)^n} \qquad a_{\overline{n}|} = \frac{1-v^n}{i} \qquad \frac{1}{a_{\overline{n}|}} = \frac{i}{1-v^n} \qquad n$$

307

P E R I O D S	AMOUNT OF 1 How $1 left at compound interest will grow.	AMOUNT OF 1 PER PERIOD How $1 deposited periodically will grow.	SINKING FUND Periodic deposit that will grow to $1 at future date.
1	1.050 000 0000	1.000 000 0000	1.000 000 0000
2	1.102 500 0000	2.050 000 0000	.487 804 8780
3	1.157 625 0000	3.152 500 0000	.317 208 5646
4	1.215 506 2500	4.310 125 0000	.232 011 8326
5	1.276 281 5625	5.525 631 2500	.180 974 7981
6	1.340 095 6406	6.801 912 8125	.147 017 4681
7	1.407 100 4227	8.142 008 4531	.122 819 8184
8	1.477 455 4438	9.549 108 8758	.104 721 8136
9	1.551 328 2160	11.026 564 3196	.090 690 0800
10	1.628 894 6268	12.577 892 5355	.079 504 5750
11	1.710 339 3581	14.206 787 1623	.070 388 8915
12	1.795 856 3260	15.917 126 5204	.062 825 4100
13	1.885 649 1423	17.712 982 8465	.056 455 7652
14	1.979 931 5994	19.598 631 9888	.051 023 9695
15	2.078 928 1794	21.578 563 5882	.046 342 2876
16	2.182 874 5884	23.657 491 7676	.042 269 9080
17	2.292 018 3178	25.840 366 3560	.038 699 1417
18	2.406 619 2337	28.132 384 6738	.035 546 2223
19	2.526 950 1954	30.539 003 9075	.032 745 0104
20	2.653 297 7051	33.065 954 1029	.030 242 5872
21	2.785 962 5904	35.719 251 8080	.027 996 1071
22	2.925 260 7199	38.505 214 3984	.025 970 5086
23	3.071 523 7559	41.430 475 1184	.024 136 8219
24	3.225 099 9437	44.501 998 8743	.022 470 9008
25	3.386 354 9409	47.727 098 8180	.020 952 4573
26	3.555 672 6879	51.113 453 7589	.019 564 3207
27	3.733 456 3223	54.669 126 4468	.018 291 8599
28	3.920 129 1385	58.402 582 7692	.017 122 5304
29	4.116 135 5954	62.322 711 9076	.016 045 5149
30	4.321 942 3752	66.438 847 5030	.015 051 4351
31	4.538 039 4939	70.760 789 8782	.014 132 1204
32	4.764 941 4686	75.298 829 3721	.013 280 4189
33	5.003 188 5420	80.063 770 8407	.012 490 0437
34	5.253 347 9691	85.066 959 3827	.011 755 4454
35	5.516 015 3676	90.320 307 3518	.011 071 7072
36	5.791 816 1360	95.836 322 7194	.010 434 4571
37	6.081 406 9428	101.628 138 8554	.009 839 7945
38	6.385 477 2899	107.709 545 7982	.009 284 2282
39	6.704 751 1544	114.095 023 0881	.008 764 6242
40	7.039 988 7121	120.799 774 2425	.008 278 1612
41	7.391 988 1477	127.839 762 9546	.007 822 2924
42	7.761 587 5551	135.231 751 1023	.007 394 7131
43	8.149 666 9329	142.993 338 6575	.006 993 3328
44	8.557 150 2795	151.143 005 5903	.006 616 2506
45	8.985 007 7935	159.700 155 8699	.006 261 7347
46	9.434 258 1832	168.685 163 6633	.005 928 2036
47	9.905 971 0923	178.119 421 8465	.005 614 2109
48	10.401 269 6469	188.025 392 9388	.005 318 4306
49	10.921 333 1293	198.426 662 5858	.005 039 6453
50	11.467 399 7858	209.347 995 7151	.004 776 7355
51	12.040 769 7750	220.815 395 5008	.004 528 6697
52	12.642 808 2638	232.856 165 2759	.004 294 4966
53	13.274 948 6770	245.498 973 5397	.004 073 3368
54	13.938 696 1108	258.773 922 2166	.003 864 3770
55	14.635 630 9164	272.712 618 3275	.003 666 8637
56	15.367 412 4622	287.348 249 2439	.003 480 0978
57	16.135 783 0853	302.715 661 7060	.003 303 4300
58	16.942 572 2396	318.851 444 7913	.003 136 2568
59	17.789 700 8515	335.794 017 0309	.002 978 0161
60	18.679 185 8941	353.583 717 8825	.002 828 1845
n	$s=(1+i)^n$	$s_{\overline{n}} = \dfrac{(1+i)^n-1}{i}$	$\dfrac{1}{s_{\overline{n}}} = \dfrac{i}{(1+i)^n-1}$

.05
per period

ANNUALLY
If compounded
annually
nominal annual rate is

5%

SEMIANNUALLY
If compounded
semiannually
nominal annual rate is

10%

QUARTERLY
If compounded
quarterly
nominal annual rate is

20%

MONTHLY
If compounded
monthly
nominal annual rate is

60%

i = .05
$j_{(2)}$ = .1
$j_{(4)}$ = .2
$j_{(12)}$ = .6

308

PRESENT WORTH OF 1 What $1 due in the future is worth today.	PRESENT WORTH OF 1 PER PERIOD What $1 payable periodically is worth today.	PARTIAL PAYMENT Annuity worth $1 today. Periodic payment necessary to pay off a loan of $1.	P E R I O D S	RATE 5%
.952 380 9524	.952 380 9524	1.050 000 0000	1	
.907 029 4785	1.859 410 4308	.537 804 8780	2	
.863 837 5985	2.723 248 0294	.367 208 5646	3	.05
.822 702 4748	3.545 950 5042	.282 011 8326	4	per period
.783 526 1665	4.329 476 6706	.230 974 7981	5	
.746 215 3966	5.075 692 0673	.197 017 4681	6	
.710 681 3301	5.786 373 3974	.172 819 8184	7	
.676 839 3620	6.463 212 7594	.154 721 8136	8	
.644 608 9162	7.107 821 6756	.140 690 0800	9	
.613 913 2535	7.721 734 9292	.129 504 5750	10	
.584 679 2891	8.306 414 2183	.120 388 8915	11	
.556 837 4182	8.863 251 6364	.112 825 4100	12	
.530 321 3506	9.393 572 9871	.106 455 7652	13	
.505 067 9530	9.898 640 9401	.101 023 9695	14	
.481 017 0981	10.379 658 0382	.096 342 2876	15	
.458 111 5220	10.837 769 5602	.092 269 9080	16	
.436 296 6876	11.274 066 2478	.088 699 1417	17	
.415 520 6549	11.689 586 9027	.085 546 2223	18	
.395 733 9570	12.085 320 8597	.082 745 0104	19	
.376 889 4829	12.462 210 3425	.080 242 5872	20	ANNUALLY If compounded annually nominal annual rate is
.358 942 3646	12.821 152 7072	.077 996 1071	21	
.341 849 8711	13.163 002 5783	.075 970 5086	22	
.325 571 3058	13.488 573 8841	.074 136 8219	23	
.310 067 9103	13.798 641 7943	.072 470 9008	24	
.295 302 7717	14.093 944 5660	.070 952 4573	25	5%
.281 240 7350	14.375 185 3010	.069 564 3207	26	
.267 848 3190	14.643 033 6200	.068 291 8599	27	
.255 093 6371	14.898 127 2571	.067 122 5304	28	
.242 946 3211	15.141 073 5782	.066 045 5149	29	
.231 377 4487	15.372 451 0269	.065 051 4351	30	SEMIANNUALLY If compounded semiannually nominal annual rate is
.220 359 4749	15.592 810 5018	.064 132 1204	31	
.209 866 1666	15.802 676 6684	.063 280 4189	32	
.199 872 5396	16.002 549 2080	.062 490 0437	33	
.190 354 7996	16.192 904 0076	.061 755 4454	34	
.181 290 2854	16.374 194 2929	.061 071 7072	35	10%
.172 657 4146	16.546 851 7076	.060 434 4571	36	
.164 435 6330	16.711 287 3405	.059 839 7945	37	
.156 605 3647	16.867 892 7053	.059 284 2282	38	
.149 147 9664	17.017 040 6717	.058 764 6242	39	
.142 045 6823	17.159 086 3540	.058 278 1612	40	QUARTERLY If compounded quarterly nominal annual rate is
.135 281 6022	17.294 367 9562	.057 822 2924	41	
.128 839 6211	17.423 207 5773	.057 394 7131	42	
.122 704 4011	17.545 911 9784	.056 993 3328	43	
.116 861 3344	17.662 773 3128	.056 616 2506	44	
.111 296 5089	17.774 069 8217	.056 261 7347	45	20%
.105 996 6752	17.880 066 4968	.055 928 2036	46	
.100 949 2144	17.981 015 7113	.055 614 2109	47	
.096 142 1090	18.077 157 8203	.055 318 4306	48	
.091 563 9133	18.168 721 7336	.055 039 6453	49	
.087 203 7270	18.255 925 4606	.054 776 7355	50	MONTHLY If compounded monthly nominal annual rate is
.083 051 1685	18.338 976 6291	.054 528 6697	51	
.079 096 3510	18.418 072 9801	.054 294 4966	52	
.075 329 8581	18.493 402 8382	.054 073 3368	53	
.071 742 7220	18.565 145 5602	.053 864 3770	54	
.068 326 4019	18.633 471 9621	.053 666 8637	55	60%
.065 072 7637	18.698 544 7258	.053 480 0978	56	
.061 974 0607	18.760 518 7865	.053 303 4300	57	i = .05
.059 022 9149	18.819 541 7014	.053 136 2568	58	$j_{(2)}$ = .1
.056 212 2999	18.875 754 0013	.052 978 0161	59	$j_{(4)}$ = .2
.053 535 5237	18.929 289 5251	.052 828 1845	60	$j_{(12)}$ = .6
$v^n = \dfrac{1}{(1+i)^n}$	$a_{\overline{n}} = \dfrac{1-v^n}{i}$	$\dfrac{1}{a_{\overline{n}}} = \dfrac{i}{1-v^n}$	n	

309

P E R I O D S	AMOUNT OF 1 How \$1 left at compound interest will grow.	AMOUNT OF 1 PER PERIOD How \$1 deposited periodically will grow.	SINKING FUND Periodic deposit that will grow to \$1 at future date.
1	1.060 000 0000	1.000 000 0000	1.000 000 0000
2	1.123 600 0000	2.060 000 0000	.485 436 8932
3	1.191 016 0000	3.183 600 0000	.314 109 8128
4	1.262 476 9600	4.374 616 0000	.228 591 4924
5	1.338 225 5776	5.637 092 9600	.177 396 4004
6	1.418 519 1123	6.975 318 5376	.143 362 6285
7	1.503 630 2590	8.393 837 6499	.119 135 0181
8	1.593 848 0745	9.897 467 9088	.101 035 9426
9	1.689 478 9590	11.491 315 9834	.087 022 2350
10	1.790 847 6965	13.180 794 9424	.075 867 9582
11	1.898 298 5583	14.971 642 6389	.066 792 9381
12	2.012 196 4718	16.869 941 1973	.059 277 0294
13	2.132 928 2601	18.882 137 6691	.052 960 1053
14	2.260 903 9558	21.015 065 9292	.047 584 9090
15	2.396 558 1931	23.275 969 8850	.042 962 7640
16	2.540 351 6847	25.672 528 0781	.038 952 1436
17	2.692 772 7858	28.212 879 7628	.035 444 8042
18	2.854 339 1529	30.905 652 5485	.032 356 5406
19	3.025 599 5021	33.759 991 7015	.029 620 8604
20	3.207 135 4722	36.785 591 2035	.027 184 5570
21	3.399 563 6005	39.992 726 6758	.025 004 5467
22	3.603 537 4166	43.392 290 2763	.023 045 5685
23	3.819 749 6616	46.995 827 6929	.021 278 4847
24	4.048 934 6413	50.815 577 3545	.019 679 0050
25	4.291 870 7197	54.864 511 9957	.018 226 7182
26	4.549 382 9629	59.156 382 7155	.016 904 3467
27	4.822 345 9407	63.705 765 6784	.015 697 1663
28	5.111 686 6971	68.528 111 6191	.014 592 5515
29	5.418 387 8990	73.639 798 3162	.013 579 6135
30	5.743 491 1729	79.058 186 2152	.012 648 9115
31	6.088 100 6433	84.801 677 3881	.011 792 2196
32	6.453 386 6819	90.889 778 0314	.011 002 3314
33	6.840 589 8828	97.343 164 7133	.010 272 9350
34	7.251 025 2758	104.183 754 5961	.009 598 4254
35	7.686 086 7923	111.434 779 8719	.008 973 8590
36	8.147 251 9999	119.120 866 6642	.008 394 8348
37	8.636 087 1198	127.268 118 6640	.007 857 4274
38	9.154 252 3470	135.904 205 7839	.007 358 1240
39	9.703 507 4879	145.058 458 1309	.006 893 7724
40	10.285 717 9371	154.761 965 6188	.006 461 5359
41	10.902 861 0134	165.047 683 5559	.006 058 8551
42	11.557 032 6742	175.950 544 5692	.005 683 4152
43	12.250 454 6346	187.507 577 2434	.005 333 1178
44	12.985 481 9127	199.758 031 8780	.005 006 0565
45	13.764 610 8274	212.743 513 7907	.004 700 4958
46	14.590 487 4771	226.508 124 6181	.004 414 8527
47	15.465 916 7257	241.098 612 0952	.004 147 6805
48	16.393 871 7293	256.564 528 8209	.003 897 6549
49	17.377 504 0330	272.958 400 5502	.003 663 5619
50	18.420 154 2750	290.335 904 5832	.003 444 2864
51	19.525 363 5315	308.756 058 8582	.003 238 8028
52	20.696 885 3434	328.281 422 3897	.003 046 1669
53	21.938 698 4640	348.978 307 7331	.002 865 5076
54	23.255 020 3718	370.917 006 1970	.002 696 0209
55	24.650 321 5941	394.172 026 5689	.002 536 9634
56	26.129 340 8898	418.822 348 1630	.002 387 6472
57	27.697 101 3432	444.951 689 0528	.002 247 4350
58	29.358 927 4238	472.648 790 3959	.002 115 7359
59	31.120 463 0692	502.007 717 8197	.001 992 0012
60	32.987 690 8533	533.128 180 8889	.001 875 7215
n	$s = (1+i)^n$	$s_{\overline{n}} = \dfrac{(1+i)^n - 1}{i}$	$\dfrac{1}{s_{\overline{n}}} = \dfrac{i}{(1+i)^n - 1}$

.06
per period

ANNUALLY
If compounded
annually
nominal annual rate is

6%

SEMIANNUALLY
If compounded
semiannually
nominal annual rate is

12%

QUARTERLY
If compounded
quarterly
nominal annual rate is

24%

MONTHLY
If compounded
monthly
nominal annual rate is

72%

$i = .06$
$j_{(2)} = .12$
$j_{(4)} = .24$
$j_{(12)} = .72$

PRESENT WORTH OF 1 What $1 due in the future is worth today.	PRESENT WORTH OF 1 PER PERIOD What $1 payable periodically is worth today.	PARTIAL PAYMENT Annuity worth $1 today. Periodic payment necessary to pay off a loan of $1.	P E R I O D S	RATE **6%**
.943 396 2264	.943 396 2264	1.060 000 0000	1	
.889 996 4400	1.833 392 6664	.545 436 8932	2	
.839 619 2830	2.673 011 9495	.374 109 8128	3	.06
.792 093 6632	3.465 105 6127	.288 591 4924	4	per period
.747 258 1729	4.212 363 7856	.237 396 4004	5	
.704 960 5404	4.917 324 3260	.203 362 6285	6	
.665 057 1136	5.582 381 4396	.179 135 0181	7	
.627 412 3713	6.209 793 8110	.161 035 9426	8	
.591 898 4635	6.801 692 2745	.147 022 2350	9	
.558 394 7769	7.360 087 0514	.135 867 9582	10	
.526 787 5254	7.886 874 5768	.126 792 9381	11	
.496 969 3636	8.383 843 9404	.119 277 0294	12	
.468 839 0222	8.852 682 9626	.112 960 1053	13	
.442 300 9644	9.294 983 9270	.107 584 9090	14	
.417 265 0607	9.712 248 9877	.102 962 7640	15	
.393 646 2837	10.105 895 2715	.098 952 1436	16	
.371 364 4186	10.477 259 6901	.095 444 8042	17	
.350 343 7911	10.827 603 4812	.092 356 5406	18	
.330 513 0105	11.158 116 4917	.089 620 8604	19	
.311 804 7269	11.469 921 2186	.087 184 5570	20	ANNUALLY If compounded annually nominal annual rate is
.294 155 4027	11.764 076 6213	.085 004 5467	21	
.277 505 0969	12.041 581 7182	.083 045 5685	22	
.261 797 2612	12.303 378 9794	.081 278 4847	23	
.246 978 5483	12.550 357 5278	.079 679 0050	24	
.232 998 6305	12.783 356 1583	.078 226 7182	25	**6%**
.219 810 0288	13.003 166 1870	.076 904 3467	26	
.207 367 9517	13.210 534 1387	.075 697 1663	27	
.195 630 1431	13.406 164 2818	.074 592 5515	28	
.184 556 7388	13.590 721 0206	.073 579 6135	29	
.174 110 1309	13.764 831 1515	.072 648 9115	30	SEMIANNUALLY If compounded semiannually nominal annual rate is
.164 254 8405	13.929 085 9920	.071 792 2196	31	
.154 957 3967	14.084 043 3887	.071 002 3374	32	
.146 186 2233	14.230 229 6119	.070 272 9350	33	
.137 911 5314	14.368 141 1433	.069 598 4254	34	
.130 105 2183	14.498 246 3616	.068 973 8590	35	**12%**
.122 740 7720	14.620 987 1336	.068 394 8348	36	
.115 793 1811	14.736 780 3147	.067 857 4274	37	
.109 238 8501	14.846 019 1648	.067 358 1240	38	
.103 055 5190	14.949 074 6838	.066 893 7724	39	
.097 222 1877	15.046 296 8715	.066 461 5359	40	QUARTERLY If compounded quarterly nominal annual rate is
.091 719 0450	15.138 015 9165	.066 058 8551	41	
.086 527 4010	15.224 543 3175	.065 683 4152	42	
.081 629 6235	15.306 172 9410	.065 333 1178	43	
.077 009 0788	15.383 182 0198	.065 006 0565	44	
.072 650 0743	15.455 832 0942	.064 700 4958	45	**24%**
.068 537 8060	15.524 369 9002	.064 414 8527	46	
.064 658 3075	15.589 028 2077	.064 147 6805	47	
.060 998 4033	15.650 026 6110	.063 897 6549	48	
.057 545 6635	15.707 572 2746	.063 663 5619	49	
.054 288 3618	15.761 860 6364	.063 444 2864	50	MONTHLY If compounded monthly nominal annual rate is
.051 215 4357	15.813 076 0721	.063 238 8028	51	
.048 316 4488	15.861 392 5208	.063 046 1669	52	
.045 581 5554	15.906 974 0762	.062 865 5076	53	
.043 001 4674	15.949 975 5436	.062 696 0209	54	
.040 567 4221	15.990 542 9657	.062 536 9634	55	**72%**
.038 271 1529	16.028 814 1186	.062 387 6472	56	
.036 104 8612	16.064 918 9798	.062 247 4350	57	
.034 061 1898	16.098 980 1696	.062 115 7359	58	i = .06
.032 133 1979	16.131 113 3676	.061 992 0012	59	$j_{(2)}$ = .12
.030 314 3377	16.161 427 7052	.061 875 7215	60	$j_{(4)}$ = .24 $j_{(12)}$ = .72
$v^n = \dfrac{1}{(1+i)^n}$	$a_{\overline{n}\|} = \dfrac{1-v^n}{i}$	$\dfrac{1}{a_{\overline{n}\|}} = \dfrac{i}{1-v^n}$	n	

311

P E R I O D S	AMOUNT OF 1 How $1 left at compound interest will grow.	AMOUNT OF 1 PER PERIOD How $1 deposited periodically will grow.	SINKING FUND Periodic deposit that will grow to $1 at future date.
1	1.070 000 0000	1.000 000 0000	1.000 000 0000
2	1.144 900 0000	2.070 000 0000	.483 091 7874
3	1.225 043 0000	3.214 900 0000	.311 051 6657
4	1.310 796 0100	4.439 943 0000	.225 228 1167
5	1.402 551 7307	5.750 739 0100	.173 890 6944
6	1.500 730 3518	7.153 290 7407	.139 795 7998
7	1.605 781 4765	8.654 021 0925	.115 553 2196
8	1.718 186 1798	10.259 802 5690	.097 467 7625
9	1.838 459 2124	11.977 988 7489	.083 486 4701
10	1.967 151 3573	13.816 447 9613	.072 377 5027
11	2.104 851 9523	15.783 599 3186	.063 356 9048
12	2.252 191 5890	17.888 451 2709	.055 901 9887
13	2.409 845 0002	20.140 642 8598	.049 650 8481
14	2.578 534 1502	22.550 487 8600	.044 344 9386
15	2.759 031 5407	25.129 022 0102	.039 794 6247
16	2.952 163 7486	27.888 053 5509	.035 857 6477
17	3.158 815 2110	30.840 217 2995	.032 425 1931
18	3.379 932 2757	33.999 032 5105	.029 412 6017
19	3.616 527 5350	37.378 964 7862	.026 753 0148
20	3.869 684 4625	40.995 492 3212	.024 392 9257
21	4.140 562 3749	44.865 176 7837	.022 289 0017
22	4.430 401 7411	49.005 739 1586	.020 405 7732
23	4.740 529 8630	53.436 140 8997	.018 713 9263
24	5.072 366 9534	58.176 670 7627	.017 189 0207
25	5.427 432 6401	63.249 037 7160	.015 810 5172
26	5.807 352 9249	68.676 470 3562	.014 561 0279
27	6.213 867 6297	74.483 823 2811	.013 425 7340
28	6.648 838 3638	80.697 690 9108	.012 391 9283
29	7.114 257 0492	87.346 529 2745	.011 448 6518
30	7.612 255 0427	94.460 786 3237	.010 586 4035
31	8.145 112 8956	102.073 041 3664	.009 796 9061
32	8.715 270 7983	110.218 154 2621	.009 072 9155
33	9.325 339 7542	118.933 425 0604	.008 408 0653
34	9.978 113 5370	128.258 764 8146	.007 796 7381
35	10.676 581 4846	138.236 878 3516	.007 233 9596
36	11.423 942 1885	148.913 459 8363	.006 715 3097
37	12.223 618 1417	160.337 402 0248	.006 236 8480
38	13.079 271 4117	172.561 020 1665	.005 795 0515
39	13.994 820 4105	185.640 291 5782	.005 386 7616
40	14.974 457 8392	199.635 111 9887	.005 009 1389
41	16.022 669 8880	214.609 569 8279	.004 659 6245
42	17.144 256 7801	230.632 239 7158	.004 335 9072
43	18.344 354 7547	247.776 496 4959	.004 035 8953
44	19.628 459 5875	266.120 851 2507	.003 757 6913
45	21.002 451 7587	285.749 310 8382	.003 499 571U
46	22.472 623 3818	306.751 762 5969	.003 259 9650
47	24.045 707 0185	329.224 385 9787	.003 037 4421
48	25.728 906 5098	353.270 092 9972	.002 830 6953
49	27.529 929 9655	378.998 999 5070	.002 638 5294
50	29.457 025 0631	406.528 929 4724	.002 459 8495
51	31.519 016 8175	435.985 954 5355	.002 293 6519
52	33.725 347 9947	467.504 971 3530	.002 139 0147
53	36.086 122 3543	501.230 319 3477	.001 995 0908
54	38.612 150 9191	537.316 441 7021	.001 861 1007
55	41.315 001 4835	575.928 592 6212	.001 736 3264
56	44.207 051 5873	617.243 594 1047	.001 620 1059
57	47.301 545 1984	661.450 645 6920	.001 511 8286
58	50.612 653 3623	708.752 190 8905	.001 410 93u4
59	54.155 539 0977	759.364 844 2528	.001 316 8900
60	57.946 426 8345	813.520 383 3505	.001 229 2255
n	$s=(1+i)^n$	$s_{\overline{n}} = \dfrac{(1+i)^n-1}{i}$	$\dfrac{1}{s_{\overline{n}}} = \dfrac{i}{(1+i)^n-1}$

.07
per period

ANNUALLY
If compounded
annually
nominal annual rate is

7%

SEMIANNUALLY
If compounded
semiannually
nominal annual rate is

14%

QUARTERLY
If compounded
quarterly
nominal annual rate is

28%

MONTHLY
If compounded
monthly
nominal annual rate is

84%

i = .07
j$_{(2)}$ = .14
j$_{(4)}$ = .28
j$_{(12)}$ = .84

PRESENT WORTH OF 1 What \$1 due in the future is worth today.	PRESENT WORTH OF 1 PER PERIOD What \$1 payable periodically is worth today.	PARTIAL PAYMENT Annuity worth \$1 today. Periodic payment necessary to pay off a loan of \$1.	PERIODS	RATE **7%**
.934 579 4393	.934 579 4393	1.070 000 0000	1	
.873 438 7283	1.808 018 1675	.553 091 7874	2	
.816 297 8769	2.624 316 0444	.381 051 6657	3	.07
.762 895 2120	3.387 211 2565	.295 228 1167	4	per period
.712 986 1795	4.100 197 4359	.243 890 6944	5	
.666 342 2238	4.766 539 6598	.209 795 7998	6	
.622 749 7419	5.389 289 4016	.185 553 2196	7	
.582 009 1046	5.971 298 5062	.167 467 7625	8	
.543 933 7426	6.515 232 2488	.153 486 4701	9	
.508 349 2921	7.023 581 5409	.142 377 5027	10	
.475 092 7964	7.498 674 3373	.133 356 9048	11	
.444 011 9592	7.942 686 2966	.125 901 9887	12	
.414 964 4479	8.357 650 7444	.119 650 8481	13	
.387 817 2410	8.745 467 9855	.114 344 9386	14	
.362 446 0196	9.107 914 0051	.109 794 6247	15	
.338 734 5978	9.446 648 6029	.105 857 6477	16	
.316 574 3905	9.763 222 9934	.102 425 1931	17	
.295 863 9163	10.059 086 9097	.099 412 6017	18	
.276 508 3330	10.335 595 2427	.096 753 0148	19	
.258 419 0028	10.594 014 2455	.094 392 9257	20	ANNUALLY If compounded annually nominal annual rate is
.241 513 0867	10.835 527 3323	.092 289 0017	21	
.225 713 1652	11.061 240 4974	.090 405 7732	22	
.210 946 8833	11.272 187 3808	.088 713 9263	23	
.197 146 6199	11.469 334 0007	.087 189 0207	24	
.184 249 1775	11.653 583 1783	.085 810 5172	25	**7%**
.172 195 4930	11.825 778 6713	.084 561 0279	26	
.160 930 3673	11.986 709 0386	.083 425 7340	27	
.150 402 2124	12.137 111 2510	.082 391 9283	28	
.140 562 8154	12.277 674 0664	.081 448 6518	29	
.131 367 1172	12.409 041 1835	.080 586 4035	30	SEMIANNUALLY If compounded semiannually nominal annual rate is
.122 773 0067	12.531 814 1902	.079 796 9061	31	
.114 741 1277	12.646 555 3179	.079 072 9155	32	
.107 234 6988	12.753 790 0168	.078 408 0653	33	
.100 219 3447	12.854 009 3615	.077 796 7381	34	
.093 662 9390	12.947 672 3004	.077 233 9596	35	**14%**
.087 535 4570	13.035 207 7574	.076 715 3097	36	
.081 808 8383	13.117 016 5957	.076 236 8480	37	
.076 456 8582	13.193 473 4539	.075 795 0515	38	
.071 455 0077	13.264 928 4616	.075 386 7616	39	
.066 780 3810	13.331 708 8426	.075 009 1389	40	QUARTERLY If compounded quarterly nominal annual rate is
.062 411 5710	13.394 120 4137	.074 659 6245	41	
.058 328 5711	13.452 448 9847	.074 335 9072	42	
.054 512 6832	13.506 961 6680	.074 035 8953	43	
.050 946 4329	13.557 908 1009	.073 757 6913	44	
.047 613 4887	13.605 521 5896	.073 499 5710	45	**28%**
.044 498 5876	13.650 020 1772	.073 259 9650	46	
.041 587 4650	13.691 607 6423	.073 037 4421	47	
.038 866 7898	13.730 474 4320	.072 830 6953	48	
.036 324 1026	13.766 798 5346	.072 638 5294	49	
.033 947 7594	13.800 746 2940	.072 459 8495	50	MONTHLY If compounded monthly nominal annual rate is
.031 726 8780	13.832 473 1720	.072 293 6519	51	
.029 651 2878	13.862 124 4598	.072 139 0147	52	
.027 711 4839	13.889 835 9437	.071 995 0908	53	
.025 898 5831	13.915 734 5269	.071 861 1007	54	
.024 204 2833	13.939 938 8102	.071 736 3264	55	**84%**
.022 620 8255	13.962 559 6357	.071 620 1059	56	
.021 140 9584	13.983 700 5941	.071 511 8286	57	
.019 757 9051	14.003 458 4991	.071 410 9304	58	i = .07
.018 465 3318	14.021 923 8310	.071 316 8900	59	$j_{(2)}$ = .14
.017 257 3195	14.039 181 1504	.071 229 2255	60	$j_{(4)}$ = .28

$$v^n = \frac{1}{(1+i)^n} \qquad a_{\overline{n}|} = \frac{1-v^n}{i} \qquad \frac{1}{a_{\overline{n}|}} = \frac{i}{1-v^n} \qquad n$$

$j_{(12)}$ = .84

P E R I O D S	AMOUNT OF 1 How $1 left at compound interest will grow.	AMOUNT OF 1 PER PERIOD How $1 deposited periodically will grow.	SINKING FUND Periodic deposit that will grow to $1 at future date.
1	1.080 000 0000	1.000 000 0000	1.000 000 0000
2	1.166 400 0000	2.080 000 0000	.480 769 2308
3	1.259 712 0000	3.246 400 0000	.308 033 5140
4	1.360 488 9600	4.506 112 0000	.221 920 8045
5	1.469 328 0768	5.866 600 9600	.170 456 4546
6	1.586 874 3229	7.335 929 0368	.136 315 3862
7	1.713 824 2688	8.922 803 3597	.112 072 4014
8	1.850 930 2103	10.636 627 6285	.094 014 7606
9	1.999 004 6271	12.487 557 8388	.080 079 7092
10	2.158 924 9973	14.486 562 4659	.069 029 4887
11	2.331 638 9971	16.645 487 4632	.060 076 3421
12	2.518 170 1168	18.977 126 4602	.052 695 0169
13	2.719 623 7262	21.495 296 5771	.046 521 8052
14	2.937 193 6243	24.214 920 3032	.041 296 8528
15	3.172 169 1142	27.152 113 9275	.036 829 5449
16	3.425 942 6433	30.324 283 0417	.032 976 8720
17	3.700 018 0548	33.750 225 6850	.029 629 4315
18	3.996 019 4992	37.450 243 7398	.026 702 0959
19	4.315 701 0591	41.446 263 2390	.024 127 6275
20	4.660 957 1438	45.761 964 2981	.021 852 2088
21	5.033 833 7154	50.422 921 4420	.019 832 2503
22	5.436 540 4126	55.456 755 1573	.018 032 0684
23	5.871 463 6456	60.893 295 5699	.016 422 1692
24	6.341 180 7372	66.764 759 2155	.014 977 9616
25	6.848 475 1962	73.105 939 9527	.013 678 7791
26	7.396 353 2119	79.954 415 1490	.012 507 1267
27	7.988 061 4689	87.350 768 3609	.011 448 0962
28	8.627 106 3864	95.338 829 8297	.010 488 9057
29	9.317 274 8973	103.965 936 2161	.009 618 5350
30	10.062 656 8891	113.283 211 1134	.008 827 4334
31	10.867 669 4402	123.345 868 0025	.008 107 2841
32	11.737 082 9954	134.213 537 4427	.007 450 8132
33	12.676 049 6350	145.950 620 4381	.006 851 6324
34	13.690 133 6059	158.626 670 0732	.006 304 1101
35	14.785 344 2943	172.316 803 6790	.005 803 2646
36	15.968 171 8379	187.102 147 9733	.005 344 6741
37	17.245 625 5849	203.070 319 8112	.004 924 4025
38	18.625 275 6317	220.315 945 3961	.004 538 9361
39	20.115 297 6822	238.941 221 0278	.004 185 1297
40	21.724 521 4968	259.056 518 7100	.003 860 1615
41	23.462 483 2165	280.781 040 2068	.003 561 4940
42	25.339 481 8739	304.243 523 4233	.003 286 8407
43	27.366 640 4238	329.583 005 2972	.003 034 1370
44	29.555 971 6577	356.949 645 7210	.002 801 5156
45	31.920 449 3903	386.505 617 3787	.002 587 2845
46	34.474 085 3415	418.426 066 7690	.002 389 9085
47	37.232 012 1688	452.900 152 1105	.002 207 9922
48	40.210 573 1423	490.132 164 2793	.002 040 2660
49	43.427 418 9937	530.342 737 4217	.001 885 5731
50	46.901 612 5132	573.770 156 4154	.001 742 8582
51	50.653 741 5143	620.671 768 9286	.001 611 1575
52	54.706 040 8354	671.325 510 4429	.001 489 5903
53	59.082 524 1023	726.031 551 2783	.001 377 3506
54	63.809 126 0304	785.114 075 3806	.001 273 7003
55	68.913 856 1129	848.923 201 4111	.001 177 9629
56	74.426 964 6019	917.837 057 5239	.001 089 5180
57	80.381 121 7701	992.264 022 1259	.001 007 7963
58	86.811 611 5117	1072.645 143 8959	.000 932 2748
59	93.756 540 4326	1159.456 755 4076	.000 862 4729
60	101.257 063 6672	1253.213 295 8402	.000 797 9488
n	$s=(1+i)^n$	$s_{\overline{n}}=\dfrac{(1+i)^n-1}{i}$	$\dfrac{1}{s_{\overline{n}}}=\dfrac{i}{(1+i)^n-1}$

.08
per period

ANNUALLY
If compounded
annually
nominal annual rate is

8%

SEMIANNUALLY
If compounded
semiannually
nominal annual rate is

16%

QUARTERLY
If compounded
quarterly
nominal annual rate is

32%

MONTHLY
If compounded
monthly
nominal annual rate is

96%

$i = .08$
$j_{(2)} = .16$
$j_{(4)} = .32$
$j_{(12)} = .96$

314

PRESENT WORTH OF 1 What $1 due in the future is worth today.	PRESENT WORTH OF 1 PER PERIOD What $1 payable periodically is worth today.	PARTIAL PAYMENT Annuity worth $1 today. Periodic payment necessary to pay off a loan of $1.	PERIODS	RATE 8%
.925 925 9259	.925 925 9259	1.080 000 0000	1	
.857 338 8203	1.783 264 7462	.560 769 2308	2	
.793 832 2410	2.577 096 9872	.388 033 5140	3	.08
.735 029 8528	3.312 126 8400	.301 920 8045	4	per period
.680 583 1970	3.992 710 0371	.250 456 4546	5	
.630 169 6269	4.622 879 6640	.216 315 3862	6	
.583 490 3953	5.206 370 0592	.192 072 4014	7	
.540 268 8845	5.746 638 9437	.174 014 7606	8	
.500 248 9671	6.246 887 9109	.160 079 7092	9	
.463 193 4881	6.710 081 3989	.149 029 4887	10	
.428 882 8593	7.138 964 2583	.140 076 3421	11	
.397 113 7586	7.536 078 0169	.132 695 0169	12	
.367 697 9247	7.903 775 9416	.126 521 8052	13	
.340 461 0414	8.244 236 9830	.121 296 8528	14	
.315 241 7050	8.559 478 6879	.116 829 5449	15	
.291 890 4676	8.851 369 1555	.112 976 8720	16	
.270 268 9514	9.121 638 1069	.109 629 4315	17	
.250 249 0291	9.371 887 1360	.106 702 0959	18	
.231 712 0640	9.603 599 2000	.104 127 6275	19	
.214 548 2074	9.818 147 4074	.101 852 2088	20	ANNUALLY If compounded annually nominal annual rate is
.198 655 7476	10.016 803 1550	.099 832 2503	21	
.183 940 5070	10.200 743 6621	.098 032 0684	22	
.170 315 2843	10.371 058 9464	.096 422 1692	23	
.157 699 3373	10.528 758 2837	.094 977 9616	24	
.146 017 9049	10.674 776 1886	.093 678 7791	25	8%
.135 201 7638	10.809 977 9524	.092 507 1267	26	
.125 186 8183	10.935 164 7707	.091 448 0962	27	
.115 913 7207	11.051 078 4914	.090 488 9057	28	
.107 327 5192	11.158 406 0106	.089 618 5350	29	
.099 377 3325	11.257 783 3431	.088 827 4334	30	SEMIANNUALLY If compounded semiannually nominal annual rate is
.092 016 0487	11.349 799 3918	.088 107 2841	31	
.085 200 0451	11.434 999 4368	.087 450 8132	32	
.078 888 9306	11.513 888 3674	.086 851 6324	33	
.073 045 3061	11.586 933 6736	.086 304 1101	34	
.067 634 5427	11.654 568 2163	.085 803 2646	35	16%
.062 624 5766	11.717 192 7928	.085 344 6741	36	
.057 985 7190	11.775 178 5119	.084 924 4025	37	
.053 690 4806	11.828 868 9925	.084 538 9361	38	
.049 713 4080	11.878 582 4004	.084 185 1297	39	
.046 030 9333	11.924 613 3337	.083 860 1615	40	QUARTERLY If compounded quarterly nominal annual rate is
.042 621 2345	11.967 234 5683	.083 561 4940	41	
.039 464 1061	12.006 698 6743	.083 286 8407	42	
.036 540 8389	12.043 239 5133	.083 034 1370	43	
.033 834 1101	12.077 073 6234	.082 801 5156	44	
.031 327 8797	12.108 401 5032	.082 587 2845	45	32%
.029 007 2961	12.137 408 7992	.082 389 9085	46	
.026 858 6075	12.164 267 4067	.082 207 9922	47	
.024 869 0810	12.189 136 4877	.082 040 2660	48	
.023 026 9268	12.212 163 4145	.081 885 5731	49	
.021 321 2286	12.233 484 6431	.081 742 8582	50	MONTHLY If compounded monthly nominal annual rate is
.019 741 8783	12.253 226 5214	.081 611 1575	51	
.018 279 5169	12.271 506 0383	.081 489 5903	52	
.016 925 4786	12.288 431 5169	.081 377 3506	53	
.015 671 7395	12.304 103 2564	.081 273 7003	54	
.014 510 8699	12.318 614 1263	.081 177 9629	55	96%
.013 435 9906	12.332 050 1170	.081 089 5180	56	
.012 440 7321	12.344 490 8490	.081 007 7963	57	
.011 519 1964	12.356 010 0454	.080 932 2748	58	i = .08
.010 665 9226	12.366 675 9680	.080 862 4729	59	$j_{(2)}$ = .16
.009 875 8542	12.376 551 8222	.080 797 9488	60	$j_{(4)}$ = .32
$v^n = \dfrac{1}{(1+i)^n}$	$a_{\overline{n}\rvert} = \dfrac{1-v^n}{i}$	$\dfrac{1}{a_{\overline{n}\rvert}} = \dfrac{i}{1-v^n}$	n	$j_{(12)}$ = .96

315

.09
per period

ANNUALLY
If compounded
annually
nominal annual rate is

9%

SEMIANNUALLY
If compounded
semiannually
nominal annual rate is

18%

QUARTERLY
If compounded
quarterly
nominal annual rate is

36%

MONTHLY
If compounded
monthly
nominal annual rate is

108%

i   = .09
$j_{(2)}$ = .18
$j_{(4)}$ = .36
$j_{(12)}$ = 1.08

PERIODS	AMOUNT OF 1 How $1 left at compound interest will grow.	AMOUNT OF 1 PER PERIOD How $1 deposited periodically will grow.	SINKING FUND Periodic deposit that will grow to $1 at future date.
1	1.090 000 0000	1.000 000 0000	1.000 000 0000
2	1.188 100 0000	2.090 000 0000	.478 468 8995
3	1.295 029 0000	3.278 100 0000	.305 054 7573
4	1.411 581 6100	4.573 129 0000	.218 668 6621
5	1.538 623 9549	5.984 710 6100	.167 092 4570
6	1.677 100 1108	7.523 334 5649	.132 919 7833
7	1.828 039 1208	9.200 434 6757	.108 690 5168
8	1.992 562 6417	11.028 473 7966	.090 674 3778
9	2.171 893 2794	13.021 036 4382	.076 798 8021
10	2.367 363 6746	15.192 929 7177	.065 820 0899
11	2.580 426 4053	17.560 293 3923	.056 946 6567
12	2.812 664 7818	20.140 719 7976	.049 650 6585
13	3.065 804 6121	22.953 384 5794	.043 566 5597
14	3.341 727 0272	26.019 189 1915	.038 433 1730
15	3.642 482 4597	29.360 916 2188	.034 058 8627
16	3.970 305 8811	33.003 398 6784	.030 299 9097
17	4.327 633 4104	36.973 704 5595	.027 046 2485
18	4.717 120 4173	41.301 337 9699	.024 212 2907
19	5.141 661 2548	46.018 458 3871	.021 730 4107
20	5.604 410 7678	51.160 119 6420	.019 546 4750
21	6.108 807 7369	56.764 530 4098	.017 616 6348
22	6.658 600 4332	62.873 338 1466	.015 904 9930
23	7.257 874 4722	69.531 938 5798	.014 381 8800
24	7.911 083 1747	76.789 813 0520	.013 022 5607
25	8.623 080 6604	84.700 896 2267	.011 806 2505
26	9.399 157 9198	93.323 976 8871	.010 715 3599
27	10.245 082 1326	102.723 134 8069	.009 734 9054
28	11.167 139 5246	112.968 216 9396	.008 852 0473
29	12.172 182 0818	124.135 356 4641	.008 055 7226
30	13.267 678 4691	136.307 538 5459	.007 336 3514
31	14.461 769 5314	149.575 217 0150	.006 685 5995
32	15.763 328 7892	164.036 986 5464	.006 096 1861
33	17.182 028 3802	179.800 315 3356	.005 561 7255
34	18.728 410 9344	196.982 343 7158	.005 076 5971
35	20.413 967 9185	215.710 754 6502	.004 635 8375
36	22.251 225 0312	236.124 722 5687	.004 235 0500
37	24.253 835 2840	258.375 947 5999	.003 870 3293
38	26.436 680 4595	282.629 782 8839	.003 538 1975
39	28.815 981 7009	309.066 463 3434	.003 235 5500
40	31.409 420 0540	337.882 445 0443	.002 959 6092
41	34.236 267 8588	369.291 865 0983	.002 707 8853
42	37.317 531 9661	403.528 132 9572	.002 478 1420
43	40.676 109 8431	440.845 664 9233	.002 268 3675
44	44.336 959 7290	481.521 774 7664	.002 076 7493
45	48.327 286 1046	525.858 734 4954	.001 901 6514
46	52.676 741 8540	574.186 020 6000	.001 741 5959
47	57.417 648 6209	626.862 762 4540	.001 595 2455
48	62.585 236 9967	684.280 411 0748	.001 461 3892
49	68.217 908 3264	746.865 648 0716	.001 338 9289
50	74.357 520 0758	815.083 556 3980	.001 226 8681
51	81.049 696 8826	889.441 076 4738	.001 124 3016
52	88.344 169 6021	970.490 773 3565	.001 030 4065
53	96.295 144 8663	1058.834 942 9585	.000 944 4343
54	104.961 707 9042	1155.130 087 8248	.000 865 7034
55	114.408 261 6156	1260.091 795 7290	.000 793 5930
56	124.705 005 1610	1374.500 057 3447	.000 727 5373
57	135.928 455 6255	1499.205 062 5057	.000 667 0202
58	148.162 016 6318	1635.133 518 1312	.000 611 5709
59	161.496 598 1287	1783.295 534 7630	.000 560 7595
60	176.031 291 9602	1944.792 132 8917	.000 514 1938
n	$s = (1+i)^n$	$s_{\overline{n}|} = \dfrac{(1+i)^n - 1}{i}$	$\dfrac{1}{s_{\overline{n}|}} = \dfrac{i}{(1+i)^n - 1}$

PRESENT WORTH OF 1 What $1 due in the future is worth today.	PRESENT WORTH OF 1 PER PERIOD What $1 payable periodically is worth today.	PARTIAL PAYMENT Annuity worth $1 today. Periodic payment necessary to pay off a loan of $1.	PERIODS	RATE 9%
.917 431 1927	.917 431 1927	1.090 000 0000	1	
.841 679 9933	1.759 111 1859	.568 468 8995	2	
.772 183 4801	2.531 294 6660	.395 054 7573	3	.09
.708 425 2111	3.239 719 8771	.308 668 6621	4	per period
.649 931 3863	3.889 651 2634	.257 092 4570	5	
.596 267 3269	4.485 918 5902	.222 919 7833	6	
.547 034 2448	5.032 952 8351	.198 690 5168	7	
.501 866 2797	5.534 819 1147	.180 674 3778	8	
.460 427 7795	5.995 246 8943	.166 798 8021	9	
.422 410 8069	6.417 657 7012	.155 820 0899	10	
.387 532 8504	6.805 190 5515	.146 946 6567	11	
.355 534 7251	7.160 725 2766	.139 650 6585	12	
.326 178 6469	7.486 903 9235	.133 566 5597	13	
.299 246 4650	7.786 150 3885	.128 433 1730	14	
.274 538 0413	8.060 688 4299	.124 058 8827	15	
.251 869 7627	8.312 558 1925	.120 299 9097	16	
.231 073 1768	8.543 631 3693	.117 046 2485	17	
.211 993 7402	8.755 625 1094	.114 212 2907	18	
.194 489 6699	8.950 114 7793	.111 730 4107	19	
.178 430 8898	9.128 545 6691	.109 546 4750	20	ANNUALLY If compounded annually nominal annual rate is
.163 698 0640	9.292 243 7331	.107 616 6348	21	
.150 181 7101	9.442 425 4432	.105 904 9930	22	
.137 781 3854	9.580 206 8286	.104 381 8800	23	
.126 404 9408	9.706 611 7694	.103 022 5607	24	
.115 967 8356	9.822 579 6049	.101 806 2505	25	9%
.106 392 5097	9.928 972 1146	.100 715 3599	26	
.097 607 8070	10.026 579 9217	.099 734 9054	27	
.089 548 4468	10.116 128 3685	.098 852 0473	28	
.082 154 5384	10.198 282 9069	.098 055 7226	29	
.075 371 1361	10.273 654 0430	.097 336 3514	30	SEMIANNUALLY If compounded semiannually nominal annual rate is
.069 147 8313	10.342 801 8743	.096 685 5995	31	
.063 438 3773	10.406 240 2517	.096 096 1861	32	
.058 200 3462	10.464 440 5979	.095 561 7255	33	
.053 394 8130	10.517 835 4109	.095 076 5971	34	
.048 986 0670	10.566 821 4779	.094 635 8375	35	18%
.044 941 3459	10.611 762 8237	.094 235 0500	36	
.041 230 5925	10.652 993 4163	.093 870 3293	37	
.037 826 2317	10.690 819 6480	.093 538 1975	38	
.034 702 9648	10.725 522 6128	.093 235 5500	39	
.031 837 5824	10.757 360 1952	.092 959 6092	40	QUARTERLY If compounded quarterly nominal annual rate is
.029 208 7912	10.786 568 9865	.092 707 8853	41	
.026 797 0562	10.813 366 0426	.092 478 1420	42	
.024 584 4552	10.837 950 4978	.092 268 3675	43	
.022 554 5461	10.860 505 0439	.092 076 7493	44	
.020 692 2441	10.881 197 2880	.091 901 6514	45	36%
.018 983 7102	10.900 180 9981	.091 741 5959	46	
.017 416 2479	10.917 597 2460	.091 595 2455	47	
.015 978 2090	10.933 575 4550	.091 461 3892	48	
.014 658 9074	10.948 234 3624	.091 338 9289	49	
.013 448 5389	10.961 682 9013	.091 226 8681	50	MONTHLY If compounded monthly nominal annual rate is
.012 338 1091	10.974 021 0104	.091 124 3016	51	
.011 319 3661	10.985 340 3765	.091 030 4065	52	
.010 384 7396	10.995 725 1160	.090 944 4343	53	
.009 527 2840	11.005 252 4000	.090 865 7034	54	
.008 740 6275	11.013 993 0276	.090 793 5930	55	108%
.008 018 9243	11.022 011 9519	.090 727 5373	56	
.007 356 8113	11.029 368 7632	.090 667 0202	57	
.006 749 3682	11.036 118 1314	.090 611 5709	58	i = .09
.006 192 0809	11.042 310 2123	.090 560 7595	59	$j_{(2)}$ = .18
.005 680 8082	11.047 991 0204	.090 514 1938	60	$j_{(4)}$ = .36 $j_{(12)}$ = 1.08
$$v^n = \frac{1}{(1+i)^n}$$	$$a_{\overline{n}|} = \frac{1-v^n}{i}$$	$$\frac{1}{a_{\overline{n}|}} = \frac{i}{1-v^n}$$	n	

317

10%

P E R I O D S	AMOUNT OF 1 How $1 left at compound interest will grow.	AMOUNT OF 1 PER PERIOD How $1 deposited periodically will grow.	SINKING FUND Periodic deposit that will grow to $1 at future date.
1	1.100 000 0000	1.000 000 0000	1.000 000 0000
2	1.210 000 0000	2.100 000 0000	.476 190 4762
3	1.331 000 0000	3.310 000 0000	.302 114 8036
4	1.464 100 0000	4.641 000 0000	.215 470 8037
5	1.610 510 0000	6.105 100 0000	.163 797 4808
6	1.771 561 0000	7.715 610 0000	.129 607 3804
7	1.948 717 1000	9.487 171 0000	.105 405 4997
8	2.143 588 8100	11.435 888 1000	.087 444 0176
9	2.357 947 6910	13.579 476 9100	.073 640 5391
10	2.593 742 4601	15.937 424 6010	.062 745 3949
11	2.853 116 7061	18.531 167 0611	.053 963 1420
12	3.138 428 3767	21.384 283 7672	.046 763 3151
13	3.452 271 2144	24.522 712 1439	.040 778 5238
14	3.797 498 3358	27.974 983 3583	.035 746 2232
15	4.177 248 1694	31.772 481 6942	.031 473 7769
16	4.594 972 9864	35.949 729 8636	.027 816 6207
17	5.054 470 2850	40.544 702 8499	.024 664 1344
18	5.559 917 3135	45.599 173 1349	.021 930 2222
19	6.115 909 0448	51.159 090 4484	.019 546 8682
20	6.727 499 9493	57.274 999 4933	.017 459 6248
21	7.400 249 9443	64.002 499 4426	.015 624 3898
22	8.140 274 9387	71.402 749 3868	.014 005 0630
23	8.954 302 4326	79.543 024 3255	.012 571 8127
24	9.849 732 6758	88.497 326 7581	.011 299 7764
25	10.834 705 9434	98.347 059 4339	.010 168 0722
26	11.918 176 5377	109.181 765 3773	.009 159 0386
27	13.109 994 1915	121.099 941 9150	.008 257 6423
28	14.420 993 6106	134.209 936 1065	.007 451 0132
29	15.863 092 9717	148.630 929 7171	.006 728 0747
30	17.449 402 2689	164.494 022 6889	.006 079 2483
31	19.194 342 4958	181.943 424 9578	.005 496 2140
32	21.113 776 7454	201.137 767 4535	.004 971 7167
33	23.225 154 4199	222.251 544 1989	.004 499 4063
34	25.547 669 8619	245.476 698 6188	.004 073 7064
35	28.102 436 8481	271.024 368 4806	.003 689 7051
36	30.912 680 5329	299.126 805 3287	.003 343 0638
37	34.003 948 5862	330.039 485 8616	.003 029 9405
38	37.404 343 4448	364.043 434 4477	.002 746 9250
39	41.144 777 7893	401.447 777 8925	.002 490 9840
40	45.259 255 5682	442.592 555 6818	.002 259 4144
41	49.785 181 1250	487.851 811 2499	.002 049 8028
42	54.763 699 2375	537.636 992 3749	.001 859 9911
43	60.240 069 1612	592.400 691 6124	.001 688 0466
44	66.264 076 0774	652.640 760 7737	.001 532 2365
45	72.890 483 6851	718.904 836 8510	.001 391 0047
46	80.179 532 0536	791.795 320 5361	.001 262 9527
47	88.197 485 2590	871.974 852 5897	.001 146 8221
48	97.017 233 7849	960.172 337 8487	.001 041 4797
49	106.718 957 1634	1057.189 571 6336	.000 945 9041
50	117.390 852 8797	1163.908 528 7970	.000 859 1740
51	129.129 938 1677	1281.299 381 6766	.000 780 4577
52	142.042 931 9844	1410.429 319 8443	.000 709 0040
53	156.247 225 1829	1552.472 251 8287	.000 644 1339
54	171.871 947 7012	1708.719 477 0116	.000 585 2336
55	189.059 142 4713	1860.591 424 7128	.000 531 7476
56	207.965 056 7184	2069.650 567 1841	.000 483 1734
57	228.761 562 3902	2277.615 623 9025	.000 439 0556
58	251.637 718 6293	2506.377 186 2927	.000 398 9822
59	276.801 490 4922	2758.014 904 9220	.000 362 5796
60	304.481 639 5414	3034.816 395 4142	.000 329 5092
n	$s = (1+i)^n$	$s_{\overline{n}|} = \dfrac{(1+i)^n - 1}{i}$	$\dfrac{1}{s_{\overline{n}|}} = \dfrac{i}{(1+i)^n - 1}$

.1
per period

ANNUALLY
If compounded
annually
nominal annual rate is

10%

SEMIANNUALLY
If compounded
semiannually
nominal annual rate is

20%

QUARTERLY
If compounded
quarterly
nominal annual rate is

40%

MONTHLY
If compounded
monthly
nominal annual rate is

120%

$i = .1$
$j_{(2)} = .2$
$j_{(4)} = .4$
$j_{(12)} = 1.2$

318

PRESENT WORTH OF 1 What $1 due in the future is worth today.	PRESENT WORTH OF 1 PER PERIOD What $1 payable periodically is worth today.	PARTIAL PAYMENT Annuity worth $1 today. Periodic payment necessary to pay off a loan of $1.	PERIODS	RATE 10%
.909 090 9091	.909 090 9091	1.100 000 0000	1	
.826 446 2810	1.735 537 1901	.576 190 4762	2	
.751 314 8009	2.486 851 9910	.402 114 8036	3	.1
.683 013 4554	3.169 865 4463	.315 470 8037	4	per period
.620 921 3231	3.790 786 7694	.263 797 4808	5	
.564 473 9301	4.355 260 6995	.229 607 3804	6	
.513 158 1182	4.868 418 8177	.205 405 4997	7	
.466 507 3802	5.334 926 1979	.187 444 0176	8	
.424 097 6184	5.759 023 8163	.173 640 5391	9	
.385 543 2894	6.144 567 1057	.162 745 3949	10	
.350 493 8995	6.495 061 0052	.153 963 1420	11	
.318 630 8177	6.813 691 8229	.146 763 3151	12	
.289 664 3797	7.103 356 2026	.140 778 5238	13	
.263 331 2543	7.366 687 4569	.135 746 2232	14	
.239 392 0494	7.606 079 5063	.131 473 7769	15	
.217 629 1358	7.823 708 6421	.127 816 6207	16	
.197 844 6689	8.021 553 3110	.124 664 1344	17	
.179 858 7899	8.201 412 1009	.121 930 2222	18	
.163 507 9908	8.364 920 0917	.119 546 8682	19	
.148 643 6280	8.513 563 7198	.117 459 6248	20	ANNUALLY If compounded annually nominal annual rate is
.135 130 5709	8.648 694 2907	.115 624 3898	21	
.122 845 9736	8.771 540 2643	.114 005 0630	22	
.111 678 1578	8.883 218 4221	.112 571 8127	23	
.101 525 5980	8.984 744 0201	.111 299 7764	24	
.092 295 9982	9.077 040 0182	.110 168 0722	25	10%
.083 905 4529	9.160 945 4711	.109 159 0386	26	
.076 277 6844	9.237 223 1556	.108 257 6423	27	
.069 343 3495	9.306 566 5051	.107 451 0132	28	
.063 039 4086	9.369 605 9137	.106 728 0747	29	
.057 308 5533	9.426 914 4670	.106 079 2483	30	SEMIANNUALLY If compounded semiannually nominal annual rate is
.052 098 6848	9.479 013 1518	.105 496 2140	31	
.047 362 4407	9.526 375 5926	.104 971 7167	32	
.043 056 7643	9.569 432 3569	.104 499 4063	33	
.039 142 5130	9.608 574 8699	.104 073 7064	34	
.035 584 1027	9.644 158 9726	.103 689 7051	35	20%
.032 349 1843	9.676 508 1569	.103 343 0638	36	
.029 408 3494	9.705 916 5063	.103 029 9405	37	
.026 734 8631	9.732 651 3694	.102 746 9250	38	
.024 304 4210	9.756 955 7903	.102 490 9840	39	
.022 094 9282	9.779 050 7185	.102 259 4144	40	QUARTERLY If compounded quarterly nominal annual rate is
.020 086 2983	9.799 137 0168	.102 049 8028	41	
.018 260 2712	9.817 397 2880	.101 859 9911	42	
.016 600 2465	9.833 997 5345	.101 688 0466	43	
.015 091 1332	9.849 088 6678	.101 532 2365	44	
.013 719 2120	9.862 807 8798	.101 391 0047	45	40%
.012 472 0109	9.875 279 8907	.101 262 9527	46	
.011 338 1918	9.886 618 0825	.101 146 8221	47	
.010 307 4470	9.896 925 5295	.101 041 4797	48	
.009 370 4064	9.906 295 9359	.100 945 9041	49	
.008 518 5513	9.914 814 4872	.100 859 1740	50	MONTHLY If compounded monthly nominal annual rate is
.007 744 1375	9.922 558 6247	.100 780 4577	51	
.007 040 1250	9.929 598 7498	.100 709 0040	52	
.006 400 1137	9.935 998 8634	.100 644 1339	53	
.005 818 2851	9.941 817 1486	.100 585 2336	54	
.005 289 3501	9.947 106 4987	.100 531 7476	55	120%
.004 808 5001	9.951 914 9988	.100 483 1734	56	
.004 371 3637	9.956 286 3626	.100 439 0556	57	
.003 973 9670	9.960 260 3296	.100 398 9822	58	i = .1
.003 612 6973	9.963 873 0269	.100 362 5796	59	$j_{(2)}$ = .2
.003 284 2703	9.967 157 2972	.100 329 5092	60	$j_{(4)}$ = .4 $j_{(12)}$ = 1.2
$v^n = \dfrac{1}{(1+i)^n}$	$a_{\overline{n}\rvert} = \dfrac{1-v^n}{i}$	$\dfrac{1}{a_{\overline{n}\rvert}} = \dfrac{i}{1-v^n}$	n	

319

Appendix IV

Tables

CONSTANT ANNUAL PERCENT

MONTHLY PAYMENT IN ARREARS

Description: This table shows the percent of the principal amount of a loan needed each year to pay off the loan when the actual payments are monthly and paid in arrears. Divide the percent by 12 to get the level monthly payment per $100 that includes both interest and principal.

Example: The Constant Annual Percent needed to pay off a 6%, 30-year loan if payments are made monthly in arrears is 7.20%. Divide by 12 to get the actual monthly payment. The Constant Annual Payment for a $50,000 loan is $3,600.00, the monthly payment is $300.00.

INTEREST RATE	5 yr	6 yr	7 yr	8 yr	9 yr	10 yr	11 yr	12 yr	13 yr	14 yr	15 yr	16 yr	17 yr	18 yr	19 yr	20 yr
4.00	22.10	18.78	16.41	14.63	13.25	12.15	11.26	10.51	9.88	9.35	8.88	8.48	8.12	7.81	7.53	7.28
4.125	22.17	18.85	16.48	14.70	13.32	12.23	11.33	10.58	9.96	9.42	8.96	8.55	8.20	7.89	7.61	7.36
4.25	22.24	18.92	16.55	14.77	13.40	12.30	11.40	10.66	10.03	9.49	9.03	8.63	8.28	7.96	7.68	7.44
4.375	22.31	18.98	16.62	14.84	13.47	12.37	11.47	10.73	10.10	9.57	9.11	8.71	8.35	8.04	7.76	7.52
4.50	22.38	19.05	16.69	14.91	13.54	12.44	11.55	10.81	10.18	9.65	9.18	8.78	8.43	8.12	7.84	7.60
4.625	22.44	19.12	16.76	14.98	13.61	12.51	11.62	10.88	10.25	9.72	9.26	8.86	8.51	8.20	7.92	7.68
4.75	22.51	19.19	16.83	15.05	13.68	12.59	11.69	10.95	10.33	9.80	9.34	8.94	8.59	8.28	8.01	7.76
4.875	22.58	19.26	16.90	15.13	13.75	12.66	11.77	11.03	10.41	9.87	9.42	9.02	8.67	8.36	8.09	7.84
5.00	22.65	19.33	16.97	15.20	13.83	12.73	11.84	11.10	10.48	9.95	9.49	9.10	8.75	8.44	8.17	7.92
5.125	22.72	19.40	17.04	15.27	13.90	12.81	11.92	11.18	10.56	10.03	9.57	9.18	8.83	8.52	8.25	8.01
5.25	22.79	19.47	17.11	15.34	13.97	12.88	11.99	11.25	10.63	10.11	9.65	9.26	8.91	8.60	8.33	8.09
5.375	22.86	19.54	17.18	15.41	14.04	12.95	12.07	11.33	10.71	10.18	9.73	9.34	8.99	8.69	8.42	8.18
5.50	22.93	19.61	17.25	15.48	14.12	13.03	12.14	11.41	10.79	10.26	9.81	9.42	9.07	8.77	8.50	8.26
5.625	23.00	19.68	17.32	15.56	14.19	13.10	12.22	11.48	10.87	10.34	9.89	9.50	9.15	8.85	8.58	8.34
5.75	23.07	19.75	17.39	15.63	14.26	13.18	12.29	11.56	10.94	10.42	9.97	9.58	9.24	8.94	8.67	8.43
5.875	23.13	19.82	17.46	15.70	14.34	13.25	12.37	11.64	11.02	10.50	10.05	9.66	9.32	9.02	8.75	8.52
6.00	23.20	19.89	17.54	15.77	14.41	13.33	12.45	11.72	11.10	10.58	10.13	9.74	9.40	9.10	8.84	8.60
6.125	23.27	19.96	17.61	15.85	14.49	13.40	12.52	11.79	11.18	10.66	10.21	9.82	9.49	9.19	8.92	8.69
6.25	23.34	20.03	17.68	15.92	14.56	13.48	12.60	11.87	11.26	10.74	10.29	9.91	9.57	9.27	9.01	8.78
6.375	23.41	20.11	17.75	15.99	14.64	13.55	12.68	11.95	11.34	10.82	10.38	9.99	9.65	9.36	9.10	8.86
6.50	23.48	20.18	17.82	16.07	14.71	13.63	12.75	12.03	11.42	10.90	10.46	10.07	9.74	9.44	9.18	8.95
6.625	23.55	20.25	17.90	16.14	14.79	13.71	12.83	12.11	11.50	10.98	10.54	10.16	9.82	9.53	9.27	9.04
6.75	23.63	20.32	17.97	16.22	14.86	13.78	12.91	12.19	11.58	11.07	10.62	10.24	9.91	9.62	9.36	9.13
6.875	23.70	20.39	18.04	16.29	14.94	13.86	12.99	12.27	11.66	11.15	10.71	10.33	9.99	9.70	9.45	9.22
7.00	23.77	20.46	18.12	16.37	15.01	13.94	13.07	12.35	11.74	11.23	10.79	10.41	10.08	9.79	9.54	9.31
7.125	23.84	20.54	18.19	16.44	15.09	14.02	13.14	12.43	11.82	11.31	10.87	10.50	10.17	9.88	9.62	9.40
7.25	23.91	20.61	18.26	16.52	15.16	14.09	13.22	12.51	11.91	11.40	10.96	10.58	10.25	9.97	9.71	9.49
7.375	23.98	20.68	18.34	16.59	15.24	14.17	13.30	12.59	11.99	11.48	11.04	10.67	10.34	10.06	9.80	9.58
7.50	24.05	20.75	18.41	16.67	15.32	14.25	13.38	12.67	12.07	11.56	11.13	10.75	10.43	10.14	9.89	9.67
7.625	24.12	20.83	18.49	16.74	15.40	14.33	13.46	12.75	12.15	11.65	11.21	10.84	10.52	10.23	9.98	9.76
7.75	24.19	20.90	18.56	16.82	15.47	14.41	13.54	12.83	12.24	11.73	11.30	10.93	10.61	10.32	10.08	9.86
7.875	24.26	20.97	18.63	16.89	15.55	14.49	13.62	12.91	12.32	11.82	11.39	11.02	10.69	10.41	10.17	9.95
8.00	24.34	21.04	18.71	16.97	15.63	14.56	13.70	12.99	12.40	11.90	11.47	11.10	10.78	10.50	10.26	10.04
8.125	24.41	21.12	18.78	17.05	15.71	14.64	13.78	13.08	12.49	11.99	11.56	11.19	10.87	10.60	10.35	10.14
8.25	24.48	21.19	18.86	17.12	15.78	14.72	13.87	13.16	12.57	12.07	11.65	11.28	10.96	10.69	10.44	10.23
8.375	24.55	21.27	18.93	17.20	15.86	14.80	13.95	13.24	12.65	12.16	11.73	11.37	11.05	10.78	10.54	10.32
8.50	24.62	21.34	19.01	17.28	15.94	14.88	14.03	13.33	12.74	12.24	11.82	11.46	11.14	10.87	10.63	10.42
8.625	24.70	21.41	19.08	17.35	16.02	14.96	14.11	13.41	12.82	12.33	11.91	11.55	11.24	10.96	10.72	10.51
8.75	24.77	21.49	19.16	17.43	16.10	15.04	14.19	13.49	12.91	12.42	12.00	11.64	11.33	11.06	10.82	10.61
8.875	24.84	21.56	19.24	17.51	16.18	15.13	14.28	13.58	13.00	12.50	12.09	11.73	11.42	11.15	10.91	10.71
9.00	24.92	21.64	19.31	17.59	16.26	15.21	14.36	13.66	13.08	12.59	12.18	11.82	11.51	11.24	11.01	10.80
9.125	24.99	21.71	19.39	17.66	16.34	15.29	14.44	13.75	13.17	12.68	12.27	11.91	11.60	11.34	11.10	10.90
9.25	25.06	21.78	19.46	17.74	16.42	15.37	14.52	13.83	13.25	12.77	12.36	12.00	11.70	11.43	11.20	11.00
9.375	25.13	21.86	19.54	17.82	16.50	15.45	14.61	13.92	13.34	12.86	12.45	12.09	11.79	11.53	11.29	11.09
9.50	25.21	21.93	19.62	17.90	16.58	15.53	14.69	14.00	13.43	12.95	12.54	12.18	11.88	11.62	11.39	11.19
9.625	25.28	22.01	19.69	17.98	16.66	15.61	14.78	14.09	13.52	13.03	12.63	12.28	11.98	11.72	11.49	11.29
9.75	25.35	22.09	19.77	18.06	16.74	15.70	14.86	14.17	13.60	13.12	12.72	12.37	12.07	11.81	11.58	11.39
9.875	25.43	22.16	19.85	18.13	16.82	15.78	14.94	14.26	13.69	13.21	12.81	12.46	12.16	11.91	11.68	11.49
10.00	25.50	22.24	19.93	18.21	16.90	15.86	15.03	14.35	13.78	13.30	12.90	12.56	12.26	12.00	11.78	11.59
10.125	25.58	22.31	20.00	18.29	16.98	15.95	15.11	14.43	13.87	13.39	12.99	12.65	12.35	12.10	11.88	11.68
10.25	25.65	22.39	20.08	18.37	17.06	16.03	15.20	14.52	13.96	13.48	13.08	12.74	12.45	12.20	11.98	11.78
10.375	25.72	22.46	20.16	18.45	17.14	16.11	15.28	14.61	14.05	13.58	13.18	12.84	12.55	12.29	12.08	11.88
10.50	25.80	22.54	20.24	18.53	17.23	16.20	15.37	14.69	14.14	13.67	13.27	12.93	12.64	12.39	12.17	11.99
10.625	25.87	22.62	20.32	18.61	17.31	16.28	15.46	14.78	14.22	13.76	13.36	13.03	12.74	12.49	12.27	12.09
10.75	25.95	22.69	20.39	18.69	17.39	16.37	15.54	14.87	14.31	13.85	13.46	13.12	12.84	12.59	12.37	12.19
10.875	26.02	22.77	20.47	18.77	17.47	16.45	15.63	14.96	14.40	13.94	13.55	13.22	12.93	12.69	12.47	12.29
11.00	26.10	22.85	20.55	18.86	17.56	16.54	15.72	15.05	14.50	14.03	13.64	13.31	13.03	12.79	12.57	12.39
11.125	26.17	22.92	20.63	18.94	17.64	16.62	15.80	15.14	14.59	14.13	13.74	13.41	13.13	12.88	12.68	12.49
11.25	26.25	23.00	20.71	19.02	17.72	16.71	15.89	15.23	14.68	14.22	13.83	13.51	13.23	12.98	12.78	12.60
11.375	26.32	23.08	20.79	19.10	17.81	16.79	15.98	15.32	14.77	14.31	13.93	13.60	13.32	13.08	12.88	12.70
11.50	26.40	23.15	20.87	19.18	17.89	16.88	16.07	15.40	14.86	14.41	14.02	13.70	13.42	13.18	12.98	12.80
11.625	26.47	23.23	20.95	19.27	17.97	16.96	16.15	15.49	14.95	14.50	14.12	13.80	13.52	13.29	13.08	12.91
11.75	26.55	23.31	21.03	19.34	18.06	17.05	16.24	15.58	15.04	14.59	14.21	13.89	13.62	13.39	13.18	13.01
11.875	26.62	23.39	21.11	19.43	18.14	17.13	16.33	15.68	15.14	14.69	14.31	13.99	13.72	13.49	13.29	13.11

CONSTANT ANNUAL PERCENT*

MONTHLY PAYMENT IN ARREARS

Description: This table shows the percent of the principal amount of a loan needed each year to pay off the loan when the actual payments are monthly and paid in arrears. Divide the percent by 12 to get the level monthly payment per $100 that includes both interest and principal.

Example: The Constant Annual Percent needed to pay off a 6%, 30-year loan if payments are made monthly in arrears is 7.20%. Divide by 12 to get the actual monthly payment. The Constant Annual Payment for a $50,000 loan is $3,600.00, the monthly payment is $300.00.

INTEREST RATE	21 yr	22 yr	23 yr	24 yr	25 yr	26 yr	27 yr	28 yr	29 yr	30 yr	31 yr	32 yr	33 yr	34 yr	35 yr	40 yr
4.00	7.05	6.85	6.66	6.49	6.34	6.20	6.07	5.95	5.84	5.73	5.64	5.55	5.47	5.39	5.32	5.02
4.125	7.13	6.93	6.74	6.58	6.42	6.28	6.15	6.03	5.92	5.82	5.73	5.64	5.56	5.48	5.41	5.11
4.25	7.21	7.01	6.83	6.66	6.51	6.37	6.24	6.12	6.01	5.91	5.81	5.73	5.65	5.57	5.50	5.21
4.375	7.29	7.09	6.91	6.74	6.59	6.45	6.32	6.21	6.10	6.00	5.90	5.82	5.74	5.66	5.59	5.30
4.50	7.37	7.17	6.99	6.83	6.67	6.54	6.41	6.29	6.18	6.09	5.99	5.91	5.83	5.75	5.68	5.40
4.625	7.46	7.26	7.08	6.91	6.76	6.62	6.50	6.38	6.27	6.17	6.08	6.00	5.92	5.85	5.78	5.50
4.75	7.54	7.34	7.16	7.00	6.85	6.71	6.58	6.47	6.36	6.26	6.17	6.09	6.01	5.94	5.87	5.59
4.875	7.62	7.42	7.24	7.08	6.93	6.80	6.67	6.56	6.45	6.36	6.27	6.18	6.10	6.03	5.97	5.69
5.00	7.71	7.51	7.33	7.17	7.02	6.89	6.76	6.65	6.54	6.45	6.36	6.28	6.20	6.13	6.06	5.79
5.125	7.79	7.59	7.42	7.25	7.11	6.97	6.85	6.74	6.63	6.54	6.45	6.37	6.29	6.22	6.16	5.89
5.25	7.87	7.68	7.50	7.34	7.20	7.06	6.94	6.83	6.73	6.63	6.54	6.46	6.39	6.32	6.25	5.99
5.375	7.96	7.76	7.59	7.43	7.28	7.15	7.03	6.92	6.82	6.72	6.64	6.56	6.48	6.42	6.35	6.09
5.50	8.04	7.85	7.68	7.52	7.37	7.24	7.12	7.01	6.91	6.82	6.73	6.65	6.58	6.51	6.45	6.19
5.625	8.13	7.94	7.76	7.61	7.46	7.33	7.21	7.11	7.01	6.91	6.83	6.75	6.68	6.61	6.55	6.30
5.75	8.22	8.03	7.85	7.70	7.55	7.42	7.31	7.20	7.10	7.01	6.92	6.85	6.77	6.71	6.65	6.40
5.875	8.30	8.11	7.94	7.79	7.65	7.52	7.40	7.29	7.19	7.10	7.02	6.94	6.87	6.81	6.75	6.50
6.00	8.39	8.20	8.03	7.88	7.74	7.61	7.49	7.39	7.29	7.20	7.12	7.04	6.97	6.91	6.85	6.61
6.125	8.48	8.29	8.12	7.97	7.83	7.70	7.59	7.48	7.38	7.30	7.21	7.14	7.07	7.01	6.95	6.71
6.25	8.57	8.38	8.21	8.06	7.92	7.80	7.68	7.58	7.48	7.39	7.31	7.24	7.17	7.11	7.05	6.82
6.375	8.66	8.47	8.30	8.15	8.01	7.89	7.78	7.67	7.58	7.49	7.41	7.34	7.27	7.21	7.15	6.92
6.50	8.75	8.56	8.39	8.24	8.11	7.98	7.87	7.77	7.68	7.59	7.51	7.44	7.37	7.31	7.25	7.03
6.625	8.84	8.65	8.49	8.34	8.20	8.08	7.97	7.87	7.77	7.69	7.61	7.54	7.47	7.41	7.36	7.14
6.75	8.93	8.74	8.58	8.43	8.30	8.17	8.06	7.96	7.87	7.79	7.71	7.64	7.58	7.52	7.46	7.25
6.875	9.02	8.83	8.67	8.52	8.39	8.27	8.16	8.06	7.97	7.89	7.81	7.74	7.68	7.62	7.57	7.35
7.00	9.11	8.93	8.76	8.62	8.49	8.37	8.26	8.16	8.07	7.99	7.91	7.85	7.78	7.72	7.67	7.46
7.125	9.20	9.02	8.86	8.71	8.58	8.46	8.36	8.26	8.17	8.09	8.02	7.95	7.89	7.83	7.78	7.57
7.25	9.29	9.11	8.95	8.81	8.68	8.56	8.46	8.36	8.27	8.19	8.12	8.05	7.99	7.93	7.88	7.68
7.375	9.38	9.21	9.05	8.90	8.78	8.66	8.55	8.46	8.37	8.29	8.22	8.16	8.09	8.04	7.99	7.79
7.50	9.47	9.30	9.14	9.00	8.87	8.76	8.65	8.56	8.47	8.40	8.32	8.26	8.20	8.15	8.10	7.90
7.625	9.57	9.39	9.24	9.10	8.97	8.86	8.75	8.66	8.58	8.50	8.43	8.36	8.31	8.25	8.20	8.01
7.75	9.66	9.49	9.33	9.19	9.07	8.96	8.85	8.76	8.68	8.60	8.53	8.47	8.41	8.36	8.31	8.12
7.875	9.76	9.58	9.43	9.29	9.17	9.06	8.96	8.86	8.78	8.71	8.64	8.58	8.52	8.47	8.42	8.24
8.00	9.85	9.68	9.53	9.39	9.27	9.16	9.06	8.97	8.88	8.81	8.74	8.68	8.63	8.57	8.53	8.35
8.125	9.94	9.78	9.62	9.49	9.37	9.26	9.16	9.16	9.07	8.99	8.91	8.85	8.79	8.73	8.68	8.46
8.25	10.04	9.87	9.72	9.59	9.47	9.36	9.26	9.17	9.09	9.02	8.95	8.90	8.84	8.79	8.75	8.57
8.375	10.14	9.97	9.82	9.69	9.57	9.46	9.36	9.28	9.20	9.13	9.06	9.00	8.95	8.90	8.86	8.69
8.50	10.23	10.07	9.92	9.79	9.67	9.56	9.47	9.38	9.30	9.23	9.17	9.11	9.06	9.01	8.97	8.80
8.625	10.33	10.16	10.02	9.89	9.77	9.66	9.57	9.48	9.41	9.34	9.28	9.22	9.17	9.12	9.08	8.92
8.75	10.43	10.26	10.12	9.99	9.87	9.77	9.67	9.59	9.51	9.45	9.38	9.33	9.28	9.23	9.19	9.03
8.875	10.52	10.36	10.22	10.09	9.97	9.87	9.78	9.69	9.62	9.55	9.49	9.44	9.39	9.34	9.30	9.15
9.00	10.62	10.46	10.32	10.19	10.08	9.97	9.88	9.80	9.73	9.66	9.60	9.55	9.50	9.45	9.41	9.26
9.125	10.72	10.56	10.42	10.29	10.18	10.08	9.99	9.91	9.83	9.77	9.71	9.66	9.61	9.56	9.53	9.38
9.25	10.82	10.66	10.52	10.39	10.28	10.18	10.09	10.01	9.94	9.88	9.82	9.77	9.72	9.68	9.64	9.49
9.375	10.92	10.76	10.62	10.50	10.39	10.29	10.20	10.12	10.05	9.99	9.93	9.88	9.83	9.79	9.75	9.61
9.50	11.01	10.86	10.72	10.60	10.49	10.39	10.31	10.23	10.16	10.10	10.04	9.99	9.94	9.90	9.86	9.73
9.625	11.11	10.96	10.82	10.70	10.59	10.50	10.41	10.34	10.27	10.20	10.15	10.10	10.05	10.01	9.98	9.84
9.75	11.21	11.06	10.93	10.81	10.70	10.60	10.52	10.44	10.38	10.31	10.26	10.21	10.17	10.13	10.09	9.96
9.875	11.31	11.16	11.03	10.91	10.80	10.71	10.63	10.55	10.48	10.43	10.37	10.32	10.28	10.24	10.21	10.08
10.00	11.41	11.26	11.13	11.01	10.91	10.82	10.73	10.66	10.59	10.54	10.48	10.44	10.39	10.36	10.32	10.19
10.125	11.52	11.37	11.23	11.12	11.02	10.92	10.84	10.77	10.70	10.65	10.60	10.55	10.51	10.47	10.44	10.31
10.25	11.62	11.47	11.34	11.22	11.12	11.03	10.95	10.88	10.82	10.76	10.71	10.66	10.62	10.58	10.55	10.43
10.375	11.72	11.57	11.44	11.33	11.23	11.14	11.06	10.99	10.93	10.87	10.82	10.77	10.73	10.70	10.67	10.55
10.50	11.82	11.68	11.55	11.43	11.34	11.25	11.17	11.10	11.04	10.98	10.93	10.89	10.85	10.81	10.78	10.67
10.625	11.92	11.78	11.65	11.54	11.44	11.36	11.28	11.21	11.15	11.09	11.05	11.00	10.96	10.93	10.90	10.79
10.75	12.03	11.88	11.76	11.65	11.55	11.46	11.39	11.32	11.26	11.21	11.16	11.12	11.08	11.05	11.02	10.91
10.875	12.13	11.99	11.86	11.75	11.66	11.57	11.50	11.43	11.37	11.32	11.27	11.23	11.19	11.16	11.13	11.03
11.00	12.23	12.09	11.97	11.86	11.77	11.68	11.61	11.54	11.48	11.43	11.39	11.35	11.31	11.28	11.25	11.14
11.125	12.34	12.20	12.08	11.97	11.87	11.79	11.72	11.65	11.60	11.55	11.50	11.46	11.43	11.39	11.37	11.26
11.25	12.44	12.30	12.18	12.08	11.98	11.90	11.83	11.77	11.71	11.66	11.62	11.58	11.54	11.51	11.48	11.38
11.375	12.54	12.41	12.29	12.18	12.09	12.01	11.94	11.88	11.82	11.77	11.73	11.69	11.66	11.63	11.60	11.50
11.50	12.65	12.51	12.40	12.29	12.20	12.12	12.05	11.99	11.94	11.89	11.85	11.81	11.77	11.74	11.72	11.62
11.625	12.75	12.62	12.50	12.40	12.31	12.23	12.16	12.10	12.05	12.00	11.96	11.92	11.89	11.86	11.84	11.74
11.75	12.86	12.73	12.61	12.51	12.42	12.35	12.28	12.22	12.16	12.12	12.08	12.04	12.01	11.98	11.95	11.87
11.875	12.96	12.83	12.72	12.62	12.53	12.46	12.39	12.33	12.28	12.23	12.19	12.16	12.13	12.10	12.07	11.99

*Reprinted from *The Thorndike Encyclopedia of Banking and Financial Tables* by David Thorndike with permission of the publisher, Warren, Gorham, & Lamont, Inc., 210 South Street, Boston, Massachusetts, 02111.

CONSTANT ANNUAL PERCENT *

ANNUAL PAYMENTS

Interest Rate (%)	Loan Term In Years				
	5	10	15	20	25
6	23.74	13.59	10.30	8.72	7.83
6.5	24.07	13.92	10.64	9.08	8.20
7	24.39	14.24	10.98	9.44	8.59
7.5	24.72	14.57	11.33	9.81	8.98
7.75	24.89	14.74	11.51	10.00	9.17
8	25.05	14.91	11.69	10.19	9.37
8.25	25.22	15.08	11.87	10.38	9.57
8.50	25.38	15.25	12.05	10.57	9.78
8.75	25.55	15.42	12.23	10.77	9.98
9	25.71	15.59	12.41	10.96	10.19
9.25	25.88	15.76	12.59	11.16	10.39
9.50	26.05	15.93	12.78	11.35	10.60
9.75	26.22	16.11	12.97	11.55	10.81
10	26.38	16.28	13.15	11.75	11.02
11	27.06	16.99	13.91	12.56	11.88

*Reprinted from *The Thorndike Encyclopedia of Banking and Financial Tables* by David Thorndike with permission of the publisher, Warren, Gorham, & Lamont, Inc., 210 South Street, Boston, Massachusetts, 02111.

PERCENTAGE OF PRINCIPAL UNPAID
AT END OF 5-10-15 YEARS
BY INTEREST RATE

Loan Term	6%	6½%	7%	5 YEARS 7½%	8%	9%	10%
10 years	57	58	59	59	60	61	62
15 years	76	77	77	78	79	80	81
20 years	85	86	86	87	88	89	90
25 years	90	91	91	92	92	93	94
30 years	93	94	94	95	95	96	97

Loan Term	6%	6½%	7%	10 YEARS 7½%	8%	9%	10%
15 years	44	44	45	46	47	49	50
20 years	64	66	67	68	69	71	73
25 years	76	77	79	80	81	83	84
30 years	84	85	86	87	88	89	91

Loan Term	6%	6½%	7%	15 YEARS 7½%	8%	9%	10%
20 years	37	38	39	40	41	43	45
25 years	58	59	61	62	64	66	69
30 years	71	72	74	75	77	79	81

RECIPROCALS FOR

CONVERSION OF MEASURES

Dividing by a number is the same as multiplying by its reciprocal. This table lists the *reciprocals* that can be used for multiplying (instead of dividing) to obtain certain conversions of measures.

TO CHANGE	TO	MULTIPLY BY
Lineal feet	miles	.00019
Lineal yards	miles	.0006
Square inches	square feet	.007
Square feet	square yards	.111
Square feet	acres	.000023
Square yards	acres	.0002067
Acres	square yards	.4840
Cubic inches	cubic feet	.00058
Cubic feet	cubic yards	.03704
Links	yards	.22
Links	feet	.66
Feet	links	1.5

UNITED STATES TABLES OF MEASUREMENTS

LINEAR MEASURE

12 inches	=	1 foot
3 feet	=	1 yard
5½ yards	=	1 rod
16½ feet	=	1 rod
320 rods	=	1 mile
1,760 yards	=	1 mile
5,280 feet	=	1 mile

SQUARE MEASURE

144 square inches	=	1 square foot
9 square feet	=	1 square yard
30¼ square yards	=	1 square rod
272¼ square feet	=	1 square rod
160 square rods	=	1 acre
640 acres	=	1 square mile

CUBIC MEASURE

1,728 cubic inches	=	1 cubic foot
27 cubic feet	=	1 cubic yard
128 cubic feet	=	1 cord (of wood)

LIQUID MEASURE

4 gills	=	1 pint
2 pints	=	1 quart
4 quarts	=	1 gallon

DRY MEASURE

2 pints	=	1 quart
8 quarts	=	1 peck
4 pecks	=	1 bushel

WEIGHT (AVOIRDUPOIS)

16 ounces	=	1 pound
100 pounds	=	1 hundredweight
20 hundredweight	=	1 ton
2,000 pounds	=	1 ton
2,240 pounds	=	1 long ton

TABLE OF LAND AND GEOGRAPHIC MEASURE

7.94 inches	=	1 link
25 links	=	1 rod
16.50 feet	=	1 rod
4 rods	=	1 chain
10 chains	=	1 furlong
8 furlongs	=	1 mile
320 rods	=	1 mile
5,280 feet	=	1 mile
10 square chains	=	1 acre
160 square rods	=	1 acre
640 acres	=	1 square mile
43,560 square feet	=	1 acre
1 square acre	=	208.7 feet on each side
60 miles	=	1 degree
Gunter's chain	=	100 links
100 links	=	22 yards
1 Section	=	640 acres (or 1 square mile)
1 Township	=	36 sections
1 knot (nautical)	=	6,086 feet
1 fathom (nautical)	=	6 feet

AREAS OF PLANE FIGURES

Area of a square = the square of the two sides, or
$A = s^2$

Area of a rectangle = multiply length times width, or
$A = L \times W$

Area of a triangle = one half the product of the base times the height when the height is known, or
$A = \frac{1}{2}bh$

If the height is unknown but the length of the three sides is known, find s with the formula $s = \frac{a + b + c}{2}$, and use the value for s in the formula

$A = \sqrt{s(s-a)(s-b)(s-c)}.$

Area of a parallelogram = base times height, or
$A = bh$

Area of a trapezoid = the height times one half the sum of the parallel sides, or
$A = h(\frac{b + b'}{2})$

Area of a circle = the product of the radius squared times π (3.1416), or
$A = (\pi)r^2$

328

INDEX

U

unit costs, 248
unit-in-place cost method of estimating,
    244, 253–254
units
  labor hours per, 244
  of work, 243
United States Rule, The, 46–47
useful life, 191–193

V

VA, 186
valuation
  depth, 211
  front foot, 210
  property, 227–228
  also see appraising
Vara, 121
vertex, 127, 135
volume, 163–174
  of cone, 168
  of cylinder, 166
  of pyramid, 168
  of rectangular solids, 164–166
  of sphere, 168
  of triangular prism, 167

W

wages
  hourly, 242–243
  prevailing, 243
  scale, 242–243
waste,
  accounting for, 249–250
  estimating, 249
work, average rate of, 245

Y

yield, 187–188, 258, 264–265
  anticipated, 265
  current or equity, 214, 264, 268–271
  deferred, 266–267
  discount, 33
  equity, 265
  expected, 187, 188
  how to determine, 264
  investment, 267
  mortgage, 186
  rate, 186, 265, 268–270
  true, 265, 266